HOW TO GET A JOB IN THE NEW YORK METROPOLITAN AREA

THOMAS M. CAMDEN
JOAN MARK

THE INSIDER'S GUIDE SERIES

Surrey Books
CHICAGO

HOW TO GET A JOB IN THE NEW YORK METROPOLITAN AREA

Published by Surrey Books, Inc., 230 E. Ohio St., Suite 120. Chicago, IL 60611. Telephone: (312) 751-7330.

This book is manufactured in the United States of America.
4th Edition. 1 2 3 4 5

Library of Congress Cataloging-in-Publication data:
Camden, Thomas M., 1938-
      How to get a job in the New York Metropolitan Area / Thomas M.
      Camden. — 4th ed.
      445p.   cm.
      Includes bibliographical references and index.
      ISBN 0-940625-64-4
      1. Job hunting—New York Metropolitan Area. 2. Job vacancies—New York Metropolitan Area. 3. Vocational guidance—Information services—New York Metropolitan Area. 4. New York Metropolitan Area—Industries—Directories. I. Title.
HF5382.75.U62N53 1994   93-33155
650.14'09747'1—dc20   CIP

AVAILABLE TITLES IN THIS SERIES — all $15.95
(Pacific Rim and Europe $17.95)

How To Get a Job in Atlanta by Thomas M. Camden, Diane C. Thomas, and Bill Osher, Ph.D.

How To Get a Job in Greater Boston by Thomas M. Camden and Paul Tanklefsky.

How To Get a Job in Chicago by Thomas M. Camden and Susan Schwartz.

How To Get a Job in Dallas/Fort Worth by Thomas M. Camden and Richard S. Citrin, Ph.D.

How To Get a Job in Europe by Robert Sanborn, Ed.D.

How To Get a Job in Houston by Thomas M. Camden and Robert Sanborn, Ed.D.

How To Get a Job in The New York Metropolitan Area by Thomas M. Camden and Joan Mark.

How To Get a Job in the Pacific Rim by Robert Sanborn, Ed.D., and Anderson Brandao.

How To Get a Job in The San Francisco Bay Area by Thomas M. Camden and Don Casella, Ph.D.

How To Get a Job in Seattle/Portland by Thomas M. Camden and Robert W. Thirsk, Ed.D.

How To Get a Job in Southern California by Thomas M. Camden and Jonathan Palmer.

How To Get a Job in Washington, DC, by Thomas M. Camden and Kathy Strawser.

Single copies may be ordered directly from the publisher. Send check or money order for book price plus $3.50 for first book and $1.50 for each additional book to cover insurance, shipping, and handling to Surrey Books at the above address. For quantity discounts, please contact the publisher.

Editorial production by Bookcrafters, Inc., Chicago.
Cover design by Hughes Design, Chicago.
Typesetting by On Track Graphics, Chicago.
"How To Get a Job Series" is distributed to the trade by Publishers Group West.

Acknowledgments

The authors would like to acknowledge the contributions of Cozata Solloway, research assistant, Fran LeFevre, Suzanne Rognalsen, and Anthony Smith for their assistance in updating this edition.

Thanks also go to Publisher Susan Schwartz, Managing Editor Gene DeRoin, Art Director Sally Hughes, and all of those who worked so hard on this book.

Note to Our Readers

We, the authors and editors, have made every effort to supply you with the most useful, up-to-date information available to help you find the job you want. Each name, address, and phone number has been verified by our staff of fact checkers. But offices move and people change jobs, so we urge you to call before you write or visit. And if you think we should include information on companies, organizations, or people that we've missed, please let us know.

The publisher, authors, and editors make no guarantee that the employers listed in this book have jobs available.

CONTENTS

3 Writing a Resume That Works

The resume—what it is, what it can and cannot do for you. The basics of a good resume. How-to books for further reference. Pros and cons of hiring someone else to write your resume. Firms that prepare resumes—where they are, what they cost, how to evaluate them. What NOT to do with a resume. Cover letters. Choosing a resume format. Sample resumes and cover letters.

4 Researching the New York Job Market

The importance of doing your homework. The local libraries' job information centers and university career resource centers. The Big Four directories and how they can help you. Dozens of other directories that might very well come in handy. New York newspapers and how to use them. Pros and cons of answering want ads. Trade magazines—what they are, where to find them, how to use them. Listing of trade magazines that focus on the New York area. Local feature magazines and newspapers.

5 Developing a Strategy: The ABCs of Networking

The importance of having a strategy. How long will it take to find a job? Tried and true advice about nurturing your ego. Establishing a job-hunting schedule. Networking—the key to a successful job search. The exploratory interview. Developing professional contacts. How to keep yourself organized. How to identify and contact hiring authorities. Tips for landing an interview. Selected books on job-hunting strategy. A unique list of hundreds of selected New York area networks, professional organizations, clubs, and societies, with descriptions, people to contact, and phone numbers.

6 Using Professional Employment Services

Employment agencies—what they can and cannot do for you. Listing of selected New York area employment agencies. Executive search firms—how they operate, pros and cons. Selected list of area firms. Career consultants—some words to the wise and questions to ask before retaining a career consultant. Social service agencies. Government employment services.

7 How To Succeed In an Interview
Page 114

The interview objective and how to prepare. Mastering the five-minute resume. The interview as a sales presentation. Steps to a successful interview. What interviewers look for. Handling the interview, anticipating tough questions, and making sure you get your own questions answered. What to do following the interview. Format for the "thank-you" letter. Books on interviewing. How to use your references.

8 What To Do If Money Gets Tight
Page 125

Reviewing your assets and liabilities. Pros and cons of part-time and temporary work. Helpful hints on finding stop-gap jobs, including a list of selected sources for part-time work. Books on part-time employment. If you need further help—federal, state, and local government and private charitable assistance programs.

9 Where To Turn If Your Confidence Wilts
Page 135

Tips for dealing with rejection. Recognizing danger signals. Guidelines for seeking professional counseling or therapy. How to check on a therapist's reputation. Selected counseling centers and institutions that offer therapy and support—what programs they offer. What to do if you get fired. Beating the job-hunt blues.

10 Selecting the Right Job for You
Page 144

You don't have to jump at the first offer. What you should know about any job offer. Finding the right employment culture. Salary strategy. Books on negotiating salary. Factors to consider when comparing job offers—sample checklist. What to do after you accept a job.

11 Employers in the New York Metropolitan Area *Page 150*

Names, addresses, phone numbers of the area's top 1,500 employers arranged by industry, with descriptions and contacts, where possible. Useful professional organizations, professional publications, and directories. Candid interviews and helpful hints.

How To Get the Most from This Book

So you want to get a job in the New York metropolitan area? Well, you've picked up the right book. Whether you're a recent graduate, new in town, or an old hand at the great New York Job Search; whether or not you're currently employed; even if you're not fully convinced that you are employable—this book is crammed with helpful information.

It contains the combined wisdom of two top professionals: Tom Camden, a personnel professional and nationally known career consultant; and Joan Mark, a career development professional and consultant and Executive Director of Pace University's Career Services and Cooperative Education.

Tom contributes expert advice on both basic and advanced job-search techniques, from how to write a resume to suggestions for racking up extra points in an employment interview.

Joan combines her knowledge of the New York working world with an impressive network of contacts in a wide variety of fields. She provides you with an insider's look at New York, as well as accessible areas of Connecticut and New Jersey and parts of Long

1

Island and Westchester. Whether you're looking for a job in the city or the suburbs, her extensive listings will save you hours of research time.

Dozens of other New York insiders have contributed tips, warnings, jokes, and observations in candid, behind-the-scenes interviews. All of which is to say that we have done our level best to pack more useful information between these covers than you'll find anywhere else.

We would love to guarantee that this book is the only resource you will need to find the job of your dreams, but we are not miracle workers. This is a handbook, not a Bible. There's just no getting around the fact that finding work takes work. You are the only person who can land the job you want.

What we can do—and, we certainly hope, have done—is to make the work of job hunting in New York and environs easier and more enjoyable for you. We have racked our brains, and those of many others, to provide you with the most extensive collection of local resources in print.

To get the most from this book, first browse through the Table of Contents. Acquaint yourself with each chapter's major features, see what appeals to you, and turn to the sections that interest you the most.

It may not be necessary or useful for you to read this book from cover to cover. If you're currently employed, for example, you can probably skip Chapter 8—What To Do If Money Gets Tight. If you have no interest in using a professional employment service, you'll only need to browse through Chapter 6.

There are certain parts of this book, however, that no one should overlook. One of them is Chapter 4—Researching the New York Job Market. Unless you're a professional librarian, we'd bet money that you won't be able to read this chapter without discovering at least a few resources that you never knew existed. We've tried to make it as easy as possible for you to get the inside information that can put you over the top in an employment interview.

Chapter 5 is another Don't Miss—especially our unique listing of organizations that you should know about to develop your network of professional contacts. We strongly suggest that you read Chapter 7, even if you think you already know all about how to handle an interview. And then, of course, there's Chapter 11—listings of the New York area's top 1,500 employers of white-collar workers.

There's another thing you should know about in order to get the most from this book. Every chapter, even the ones you don't think you need to read, contains at least one helpful hint or insider interview that is set off from the main text. Take some time to browse through them. They contain valuable nuggets of information and important tips.

Keep in mind that no one book can do it all for you. While we've touched on the basic tasks of any job search—self-analysis, developing a resume, researching the job market, figuring out a strategy, generating leads, interviewing, and selecting the right job—we don't have space to go into great detail on each and every topic. What we have done is to supply suggestions for further reading. Smart users of this book will turn to those books when they need to know more about a particular subject.

New York in the '90s

What can you expect to find if you're looking for a job in the New York metropolitan area in the mid 1990s? You've heard the dismal news from the economic forecasters. The Port Authority of New York and New Jersey stated that there would be a loss of 67,000 more jobs in 1993 in the New York region—the fourth straight year of job losses. Corporate restructuring and resultant layoffs have impacted on the tri-state area. However, although there appears to be further losses for manufacturers, construction companies, and some government agencies, there are also clear signs of recovery.

In New York City, Wall Street, retail sales, tourism, health and social services are healthier, according to Samuel Ehrenhalt, Regional Commissioner of the Bureau of Labor Statistics. The health care industry has grown rapidly, making it the City's largest employer. This sector has added 30,000 jobs since 1989 and has eclipsed banks, real estate concerns, corporate headquarters, publishing houses, and other traditionally large employers. After health care, business services, wholesale trade, banking, and social services are the City's largest employers.

Ehrenhalt highlights growth areas for the metropolitan New York area, which reflect "hot" trends nationally: knowledge and information processing industries; and training and retraining workers to prepare them for higher-skilled jobs crucial to industrial development. This was reiterated in a recent poll among 300 top corporate executives, where it was found that requirements for entry-level jobs are becoming far more rigorous across a spectrum of industries.

Many jobs are found in small business today. Small businesses account for 97 percent of the companies in New York and 46 percent of the jobs. In Westchester County small and mid-sized companies specializing in technology and health care services tend to be faring well despite the economy, according to Noreen L. Preston, an economist with the Westchester County Office of Economic Development.

Economists are cautiously optimistic about New York's future, but the Chief Economist for the Port Authority of New York and New Jersey says that the recovery will not translate into job growth for the region until 1994. But when job growth does begin, New York is prepared for recovery not only through its growing small businesses but also as headquarters for more Fortune 500 service companies than any other area in the country.

What does this all mean for you? It means that finding a job will take more work and you should be examining a variety of opportunities in small organizations as well as large companies and emerging growth areas. There are jobs out there, and this book will be one of your tools for finding the right job for you.

Alair Townsend, Publisher of *Crain's* magazine, speaking at a recent New York college graduation said: "The sluggish economy means fewer job choices. Getting the first job may take longer than you hoped, and getting the right job even longer. Worse still, you may feel you don't know what the right job is...the most important thing I have learned is that careers last a long time...[and] you may be certain about what field you want to work in....Nevertheless, opportunities will emerge and disappear. There will be choices to be made and forks in the road to be taken—if you're lucky and prepared. Shifts allow you to explore new areas in new settings with new people. Change broadens your experience and sharpens your focus on where your interests truly lie."

So for those of you starting out and for those of you who are career changers or job changers—GOOD LUCK!

New in town?

Have you just moved to the New York City area? Or are you considering a move? In addition to this book, you could probably use some personalized assistance. New York City's **Convention and Visitor's Bureau** (212) 397-8222 can provide you with maps and information on hotels, shopping, and restaurants. Area bookstores have as many as 50 different guides covering the entire city, or a specific interest or geographic area. Detailed maps can also be obtained at local bookstores.

You can reach the New York City **Chamber of Commerce** offices at:

Manhattan: (212) 493-7400
Queens: (718) 784-7700
Brooklyn: (718) 875-1000
Bronx: (718) 829-4111
Staten Island: (718) 727-1900

In Nassau and Westchester counties, the **Divisions of Commerce** located in the county seat offices can give you the names and numbers of local chambers of commerce. In **Westchester**, call (914) 948-2110 for the county Chamber of Commerce; in **Nassau**, call (516) 571-4160. Local chambers work individually with welcome organizations.

Some Chambers of Commerce publish helpful directories of local businesses. An example is Westchester County's *The Golden Apple Guide 1993.* ■

Need Help Finding Your Way Around New York?

If you need information about transportation around the New York area, the following data should be useful.

New York City consists of five boroughs: Manhattan, Brooklyn, Queens, Staten Island, and the Bronx. The two major suburban commuter areas are Westchester and Long Island. Combined, these metropolitan and suburban communities contain one of the most extensive transportation systems in the country. The following information will make getting to your job interviews a little easier. We've included some helpful hints, along with useful phone numbers and other information.

For **bus and subway information,** you can call the New York City Transit Authority Information Bureau at (212) 330-1234. For up-to-the-minute information on emergency bulletins or weather conditions, dial (212) 976-2323. Maps of the transit system are available by writing MAPS, New York City Transit Authority, 370 Jay Street, Brooklyn, New York 11201. Be sure to include a stamped, self-addressed envelope and to specify the boroughs for which you need maps.

The major intersections for most subway lines in Manhattan are Penn Station at 33rd Street and Seventh Avenue, and Grand Central Station at 42nd Street and Lexington Avenue. All lines are marked "Local" or "Express." Be sure to take careful note of the time of day you're traveling; some lines change from local to express during rush hours. You should always allow extra time for unexpected delays. You will find subway and train information booths in both Penn Station and Grand Central Station. If you're not sure where you're going, it's a good idea to check with the people at the booths. It's always a good idea to travel with a map. Even experienced riders find a map helpful when they have to improvise.

The Port Authority Bus Terminal at 42nd Street and Eighth Avenue dispatches the majority of buses running in Manhattan. You can, of course, grab a bus anywhere in the city. Signs are posted on every street, but maps are still your best bet. City buses run interboro, but there are also a number of independent bus lines servicing these areas. Many of these companies run express service to and from Manhattan on a daily basis. The companies listed below offer such a service. Give them a call for information about schedules and routes.

Queens:	Triborough Bus Lines (718) 335-1000
	Queens Bus Lines (718) 995-4700
Brooklyn:	Command Buses (718) 272-0900
Bronx:	Liberty Bus Lines (212) 652-8400
	New York Bus Company (718) 994-5500
Staten Island:	Academy Bus (718) 442-8666

If you can afford it, you may prefer to take **taxicabs** to and from your interviews. Unlike most other cities around the country, you can hire a taxi in New York simply by standing on any street corner and hailing a passing cab.

Taxi stands are found at most major hotels in the city as well as at area airports. Although most cab drivers will travel to any borough, many are reluctant to travel to Staten Island. You may find the **Staten Island Ferry** a better bet. For information on ferry schedules, call the Bureau of Ferry and General Aviation Operations-Manhattan Terminals at (212) 806-6940. To obtain a written schedule, you can visit the dock office in lower Manhattan next to Battery Park.

Now for information about **inter-urban travel.** If you are traveling to Manhattan from Westchester, you can ride the Metro North Commuter Rail. The Long Island Railroad travels between Long Island and Manhattan. Metro North trains arrive in Manhattan at Grand Central Terminal while Long Island Railroad trains arrive at Penn Station. Metro North also services sections of the Bronx. For fare and schedule information, call 1-800-METRO-INFO.

The Long Island Railroad also provides service to Queens and Brooklyn. Fare and schedule information is available at (516) 822-5477.

The PATH trains of New Jersey Transit connect to Penn Station in New York. For information on New Jersey Transit call 800-772-2222 (in NJ) or (201) 491-7000 (elsewhere).

The Metropolitan Suburban Bus Authority provides service in and out of Nassau County. For information call (516) 222-1000. The Bee-Line system serves Westchester County through the Department of Transportation, (914) 682-2020.

Airport information

The three major airports serving the New York City area are John F. Kennedy International, La Guardia, and Newark. For information, call **Port Authority Airport Information** at (718) 656-4520. Information about the JFK Express, a special bus and subway service from JFK to Manhattan, is available at (718) 330-1234. ■

Establishing an Objective: How To Discover What You Want To Do

One of the most common mistakes job seekers make is not establishing an objective before beginning the job search. Practically everyone wants a job that provides personal satisfaction, growth, good salary and benefits, prestige, and a desirable location. But unless you have a more specific idea of the kind of work you want, you probably won't find it. It is important to know what you want to do, and what you are capable of doing.

Many of our readers already have a clear objective in mind. You may want a job as a systems analyst, paralegal, production assistant, sales manager, or any one of the thousands of other occupations at which New Yorkers work. That's important—in fact, establishing an objective is a necessary first step in any successful job search.

But anyone who's looking for work, or thinking about changing jobs or careers, can benefit from a thorough self-appraisal. What follows is a list of highly personal questions designed to provide you with insights you may never have considered and to help you answer the Big Question, "What do I want to do?"

To get the most from this exercise, write out your answers. This will take some time, but it will help to ensure that you give each question careful thought. The more effort you put into this exercise, the better prepared you'll be to answer the tough questions that are bound to come up in any job interview. The exercise also will serve as the foundation for constructing a decent resume—a subject we'll discuss in more detail in the next chapter.

When you've completed the exercise, consider sharing your answers with a trusted friend or relative. Self-analysis is a difficult task. Although we think we know ourselves, we seldom have the objectivity to see ourselves clearly, to outline our personal and professional strengths and weaknesses, to evaluate our needs, and to set realistic objectives. Someone who knows you well can help.

Questions About Me

1. Taking as much time as necessary—and understanding the purpose of this appraisal—honestly describe the kind of person you are. Here are some questions to get you started. Are you outgoing or are you more of a loner? How well-disciplined are you? Are you quick-tempered? Easygoing? Are you a leader or a follower? Do you tend to take a conventional, practical approach to problems? Or are you more imaginative and experimental? How sensitive are you to others?
2. Describe the kind of person others think you are.
3. What do you want to accomplish with your life?
4. What role does your job play in that goal?
5. What impact do you have on other people?
6. What are your accomplishments to date? Are you satisfied with them?
7. What role does money play in your standard of values?
8. Is your career the center of your life or just a part of it? Which should it be?
9. What are your main interests?
10. What do you enjoy most?
11. What displeases you most?

Questions About My Job

1. Beginning with your most recent employment and then working back toward school graduation, describe in detail each job you had. Include in this summary your title, company, responsibilities, salary, achievements and successes, failures, and reason for leaving.
2. How would you change anything in your job history if you could?
3. In your career thus far, what responsibilities have you enjoyed most? Why?
4. What kind of job do you think would be a perfect match for your talents and interests?
5. What responsibilities do you want to avoid?
6. How hard are you really prepared to work?

7. If you want the top job in your field, are you prepared to pay the price?
8. What have your subordinates thought about you as a boss? As a person?
9. What have your superiors thought about you as an employee? As a person?
10. Can your work make you happier? Should it?
11. If you have been fired from any job, what was the reason?
12. How long do you want to work before retirement?

Your answers to these highly personal questions should help you to see more clearly who you are, what you want, what your gifts are, and what you realistically have to offer. They should also reveal what you don't want and what you can't do. It's important to evaluate any objective you're considering in the light of your answers to these questions.

A banker's story

One of our friends is a vice president at Citibank. We asked her for her job-hunting philosophy. "Use the occasion of a job change to do some real self-searching about your beliefs and goals," she suggests. "I went to a 'career shrink,' a person trained in the techniques that Richard Bolles outlines in *What Color Is Your Parachute?* That's a book, by the way, that I can't recommend too highly. Anyway, my career shrink assigned me to write an autobiography. It took me a month to finish, and it was 80 pages long. But it made me take a good, hard look at myself.

"I would advise every job hunter to do the same thing. Read over what you've written, figure out what you've said and what it means. Based on that thoughtful process, be willing to take a risk. That's what I did, and it certainly was a good investment. Women tend to take fewer risks than they ought to for their own self-interest." ■

People who are entering the job market for the first time, those who have been working for one company for many years, and those who are considering a career change need more help in determining their objectives. Vocational analysis, also known as career planning or life planning, is much too broad a subject to try to cover here. But we can refer you to some excellent books.

CAREER STRATEGY BOOKS

Beatty, Richard H. *Get the Right Job in 60 Days or Less*. New York: John Wiley & Sons, 1991.

Bolles, Richard N. *The Three Boxes of Life and How to Get Out of Them.* Berkeley, CA: Ten Speed Press, 1983.

Bolles, Richard N. *What Color Is Your Parachute?* Berkeley, CA: Ten Speed Press, 1993. The Bible for job hunters and career changers, this book is revised every year and is widely regarded as the most useful and creative manual available. Try it! We think you'll like it.

Borchard, David C. *Your Career: Choices, Chances, Changes.* Dubuque, IA: Kendall-Hunt, 1988.

Breidenbach, Monica E. *Career Development: Taking Charge of Your Career.* Englewood Cliffs, NJ: Prentice-Hall, 1988.

Camden, Thomas M. *The Job Hunter's Final Exam.* Chicago: Surrey Books, 1990.

Charland, William A., Jr. *Life Work: Meaningful Employment in a World of Change.* New York: Continuum, 1986.

Clawson, James G., et al. *Self Assessment and Career Development.* Englewood Cliffs, NJ: Prentice-Hall, 1985.

Davidson, Jeffrey P. *Blow Your Own Horn: How to Market Yourself and Your Career.* New York: Simon and Schuster, 1988.

Dyer, Sonya, and Jacqueline McMakin. *Working From the Heart.* San Diego, CA: LuraMedia, 1989.

Figler, Howard. *The Complete Job-Search Handbook.* New York: H. Holt & Co., 1988.

Green, Gordon W., Jr. *Getting Ahead At Work.* Washington, DC: Carol Publishing Group, 1988.

Haldane, Bernard. *Career Satisfaction and Success: A Guide to Job Freedom.* New York: AMACOM, 1982.

Jackson, Tom. *Guerrilla Tactics in the New Job Market.* New York: Bantam Books, 1991.

Kennedy, Joyce Lain. *Joyce Lain Kennedy's Career Book.* Lincolnwood, IL: VGM Career Horizons, 1988.

Krannich, Ronald L. *Careering and Re-Careering for the 1990s: The Complete Guide to Planning Your Future.* Manassas, VA: Impact Publications, 1989.

Lewis, Adele. *Fast Track Careers for the 90's.* New York: Scott Foresman, 1990.

Michelozzi, Betty. *Coming Alive from Nine to Five: The Career Search Handbook.* Mountain View, CA: Mayfield Publishing Co., 1988.

Mitchell, Joyce Slayton. *The College Board Guide to Jobs and Career Planning.* College Entrance Examination Board of New York, 1990.

Munschauer, John L. *Jobs for English Majors and Other Smart People.* Princeton, NJ: Peterson's Guides, 1991.

Petras, Ross and Kathryn. *Jobs '93.* New York: Simon & Schuster, 1993.

Powell, C. Randall. *Career Planning Today.* New York: Kendall-Hunt, 1990.

Shapiro, Michele. *Your Personal Career Consultant: A Step-by-Step Guide.* Englewood Cliffs, NJ: Prentice-Hall, 1988.

Sinetar, Marsha. *Do What You Love, The Money Will Follow.* Mahwah, NJ: Paulist Press, 1987.

Wendleton, Kate. *Through the Brick Wall: How to Job Hunt in a Tight Market.* New York: Vellard Books, 1992.

If you're still in **college or have recently graduated**, the following books will be of particular interest:

Basta, Nicholas. *Major Options: The Student's Guide to Linking College Majors, Career Opportunities During and After College.* New York: Stonesong Press, 1991.

Baumgardner, Steve. *College and Job: Conversations with Recent Graduates.* New York: Hunt Science Press, 1988.

Bloch, Deborah P. *How to Get and Get Ahead on Your First Job*. New York: National Textbook, 1988.

Bloom, Bruce J. *Fast Track to the Best Job*. Manassas, VA: Impact, 1991.

Bouchard, Jerry. *Graduating to the 9-5 World*. Manassas, VA: Impact, 1991.

Carter, Carol. *Majoring in the Rest of Your Life*. New York: The Noonday Press, 1990.

Figler, Howard. *Liberal Education and Careers Today*. Manassas, VA: Impact, 1989.

Fox, Marcia R. *Put Your Degree to Work: The New Professional's Guide to Career Planning*. New York: Norton, 1988.

Holton, Ed. *The New Professional*. Princeton, NJ: Peterson's Guides, 1991.

Kalt, Neil C. *Flight Path: How to Get the Job That Launches Your Career After College*. New York: Simon & Schuster, 1989.

King, James B. *Negotiating the Briar Patch: Resume and Job Search Strategies for the College Graduate*. New York: Kendall-Hunt, 1986.

La Fevre, John L. *How You Really Get Hired: The Inside Story from a College Recruiter*, 2nd ed. New York: Prentice-Hall, 1989.

Malnig, L.R., and S.L. Morrow. *What Can I Do With a Major In....?* Ridgefield, NJ: Abbott Press, 1984.

Osher, Bill, and Sioux Henley Campbell. *The Blue Chip Graduate: A Four Year College Plan For Career Success*. Atlanta: Peachtree Publishers, 1987.

Shingleton, John D. *Career Planning for the 1990's: A Guide for Today's Graduates*. Garrett Park, MD: Garrett Park Press, 1991.

Steele, John E., and Marilyn S. Morgan. *Career Planning and Development for College Students and Recent Graduates*. Illinois: VGM Career Horizons, 1991.

For those of you involved in a **mid-life career change**, here are some books that might prove helpful:

Allen, Jeffrey G. *Finding the Right Job at Midlife*. New York: Simon and Schuster, 1985.

Anthony, Rebecca, and Gerald Roe. *Over 40 and Looking for Work? A Guide for Unemployed,Underemployed and Unhappily Employed*. Holbrook, MA: Bob Adams, 1991.

Bardwick, Judith M. *The Plateauing Trap*. New York: AMACOM, 1987.

Bicker, C.E. *Executive Reemployment, Out Not Down....A Positive Approach*. Hawthorne, NJ: Career Press, 1989.

Bird, Caroline. *Second Careers: New Ways to Work After 50*. 1992.

Birsner, E. Patricia. *The Forty-Plus Job Hunting Guide: Official Handbook of the 40-Plus Club*. New York: Facts on File, 1990.

Falvey, Jack. *What's Next? Career Strategies After 35*. Charlottesville, VT: Williamson Publishing Co., 1987.

Gerberg, Robert J. *Robert Gerberg's Job Changing System*. Kansas City, MO: Andrews-McMeel, 1986.

Goldstein, Dr. Ross, and Diana Landau. *Fortysomething*. Manassas, VA: Impact, 1991.

Hecklinger, Fred J., and Bernadette M. Black. *Training for Life: A Practical Guide to Career and Life Planning*. Dubuque, IA: Kendall-Hunt, 1991.

Hyatt, Carole. *Shifting Gears: How to Master Career Change and Find the Work That's Right for You*. New York: Simon & Schuster, 1990.

Montana, Patrick J. *Stepping Out, Starting Over*. New York: National Center for Career Life Planning, 1988.

Moreau, Daniel. *Take Charge of Your Career: How to Survive and Profit from a Mid-Career Change*. Washington, DC: Kiplinger Books, 1990.

Riehle, Kathleen A. *What Smart People Do When Losing Their Jobs*. New
    York: John Wiley & Sons, 1991.
Simon, Dr. Sidney B. *Getting Unstuck*. Manassas, VA, 1988.

For workers who are nearing **retirement age** or have already
reached it, here are some books that might be useful:

Hardy, Karen. *Fifty and Starting Over: Career Strategies for Success*. N.
    Hollywood, CA: Newcastle Pub. Co., 1991.
Myers, Albert, and Christopher P. Anderson. *Success Over Sixty*. New York:
    Summit Books, 1984.
Schultz, James H. *The Economics of Aging*. Belmont, CA: Wadsworth, 1988.
    In-depth study of the economic status of older persons, with emphasis on
    various sources of retirement income, including work, pensions, and
    social security.
Strasser, Stephen, and John Sena. *Transitions: Successful Strategies from
    Mid-Career to Retirement*. Hawthorne, NJ: Career Press, 1990.

And for **handicapped** job seekers, these titles could prove
helpful:

Bolles, Richard N. *The 1993 What Color is Your Parachute?* Berkeley, CA:
    Ten Speed Press, 1993.
Hoffa, Helynn, and Gary Morgan. *Yes You Can*. Manassas, VA: Impact,
    1990.
Lobodinski, Jeanine, McFadden, Deborah, and Arlene Markowicz. *Market-
    ing Your Abilities: A Guide for the Disabled Job-Seeker*. San Diego, CA:
    Mainstream, 1984.
Marks, Edith, and Adele Lewis. *Job Hunting for the Disabled*. Woodbury,
    NY: Barrons, 1987.
Rabbi, Rami, and Diane Croft. *Take Charge: A Strategic Guide for Blind Job
    Seekers*. Boston, MA: National Braille Press, 1989.

For **women** in the work force, these titles will be of interest:

Berryman, Sue E. *Routes into the Mainstream: Career Choices of Women and
    Minorities*. New York: National Center for Research in Vocational Edu-
    cation, 1988.
Betz, Nancy E. *The Career Psychology of Women*. Orlando: Academic Press,
    1987.
Fox, Mary F., and Sharlene Hesse-Biber. *Women at Work*. Mayfield Publi-
    cations, 1984.
Gutek, Barbara, and Laurie Larwood, eds. *Women's Career Development*.
    Newbury Park, CA: Sage, 1986.
Jaffe, Betsy. *Altered Ambitions*. New York: Donald A. Fine, 1991.
Josefowitz, Natasha. *Paths to Power: A Working Woman's Guide from First
    Job to Top Executive*. Reading, MA.: Addison-Wesley, 1980.
Lunnenborg, Patricia. *Women Changing Work*. New York: Bergin & Garvey,
    1990.
Morrow, Jodie B., and Myrna Lebov. *Not Just a Secretary: Using the Job to
    Get Ahead*. New York: Wiley Press, 1984.
Nivens, Beatrice. *The Black Woman's Career Guide*. New York: Anchor
    Books, 1987.
Scollard, Jeanette. *Risk to Win: A Woman's Guide to Success*. New York:
    MacMillan, 1989.
Thomas, Marian. *Balancing Career and Family*. Manassas, VA: Impact,
    1991.

Thompson, Charlotte E. *Single Solutions—An Essential Guide for the Single Career Woman*. Brookline, MA: Branden, 1990.

Wyse, Lois. *The Six-Figure Woman (and How to Be One)*. New York: Linden Press, 1984. How to break into top corporate management.

Zeitz, Baila, Ph.D., and Lorraine Dusky. *The Best Companies for Women*. New York: Simon & Schuster, 1989.

Also for mid-life women, a magazine called *Vintage '45* covers money management, careers, health, travel, and creative writing. P.O. Box 266, Orinda, CA 94563.

Professional Vocational Analysis

It would be great if there were some psychological test that would confirm without a doubt who you are and precisely what job, career, or field best suits you. Unfortunately, there isn't. Professionals in vocational planning have literally dozens of tests at their disposal designed to assess personality and aptitude for particular careers.

The test probably used most commonly is the Strong-Campbell Interest Inventory(SCII). This multiple-choice test takes about an hour to administer and is scored by machine. The SCII has been around since 1933. The most recent revision, in 1981, made a serious and generally successful attempt to eliminate sex bias.

The SCII offers information about an individual's interests on three different levels. First, the test provides a general statement about the test-taker's interest patterns. These patterns suggest not only promising occupations but also characteristics of the most compatible work environments and personality traits affecting work.

Second, the test reports how interested a person is in a specific work activity compared with other men and women. Finally, the occupational scales compare the test-taker with satisfied workers in some 90 different occupations. If you think you'd enjoy being a librarian, for example, you can compare yourself with other librarians and see how similar your likes and dislikes are. The occupational scales indicate the degree of probability, confirmed by extensive research, that you'll be satisfied with the choice of a particular occupation.

Personality/vocational tests come in a variety of formats. Many are multiple choice; some require you to finish incomplete sentences; others are autobiographical questionnaires. No single test should ever be used as an absolute. Personality tests are more important for generating discussion and for providing data that can be used in making judgments.

In the New York area, vocational guidance and testing are available from a variety of career consultants. A list of selected sources follows. One word of caution: career consultants are generally in business to direct an entire employment campaign. Vocational testing is only one of the services they provide. Because career consulting firms are private, for-profit businesses with high overhead costs, they usually charge more for testing than local community colleges (listed below) or social service agencies. A fuller discussion of services offered by career consultants is provided in Chapter 6. Also in Chapter 6 is a list of social service agencies, some of which offer vocational testing.

What To Expect from a Career Counselor

For one thing, counselors offer an objective viewpoint, says one licensed professional career counselor we know. "You may not be able to discuss everything with family, friends, and especially coworkers if you happen still to be working. A trained professional can serve as a sounding board and offer strategies and information that you can't get elsewhere. We can essentially help a person become more resourceful."

This particular career counselor usually spends four sessions with individuals who want to establish a sense of direction for their careers. Here's what sessions cover:

- Exploring problems that have blocked progress and considering solutions.
- Establishing career objectives and determining strengths and areas to work on.
- Writing a career plan with a strategy to achieve goals.

"A counselor should help people develop methods and a framework from which to base continual exploration about what they want from a career, even after they are employed," our counselor friend says.

All too often people look for "quick fixes" in order to get back to work, she says. "In haste, they may not take time to reflect on where their career is going, to make sure they look for a job that will be challenging and satisfying."

Who's good?
Who's not?

A listing in this book does not constitute an endorsement of any consulting firm or vocational testing service. Before embarking on a lengthy or expensive series of tests, try to get the opinion of one or more people who have already used the service you're considering. Reputable firms will provide references. You can also contact:

Better Business Bureau of Long Island
(516) 420-0500

Better Business Bureau of Metropolitan New York (212) 533-6200

Better Business Bureau of Westchester
(914) 428-1230

Nassau County Department of Consumer Affairs
(516) 535-2600

New York City Department of Consumer Affairs
(212) 487-4398

Westchester County Office of Consumer Complaints (914) 285-2155 ■

CAREER COUNSELORS AND CONSULTANTS

Also see the listings of Social Service and Government career and employment services in Chapter 6.

Bennett-Rones Associates
701 Westchester Ave., #308w
White Plains, NY 10604
(914) 681-0116
Barbara Bennett-Rones, Pres.

Career and Educational Consultants
1501 Broadway
New York, NY 10036
(212) 308-2455
Aptitude testing, career counseling. First interview $85, other interviews $70-$75.

Career Planning Institute
342 Madison Ave.
New York, NY 10017
(212) 599-0032
Offers career planning, vocational testing, and resume writing. Fees: $135 for one-hour counseling session; $205 for one-page resume writing session—100 copies plus cover letter.

Crystal-Barkley Corporation
152 Madison Ave., 23rd Floor
New York, NY 10016
(212) 889-8500
Services include seminars, a 40-hour group course, one-on-one sessions for $150/hour, and computer software instruction for $99.95.

Federation Employment and Guidance Service
510 Sixth Ave.
New York, NY 10011-8059
(212) 366-8400
Career development services, including vocational testing. Fees: $50 for initial conference to determine need; $250 for testing; $50 per session for individual counseling.

Johnson O'Connor Research Foundation
11 E. 62nd St.
New York, NY 10021
(212) 838-0550
Services offered for aptitude testing and career direction. Comprehensive testing including 19 aptitude tests and an evaluation in 3 sessions. Fee $480. Offices in 11 cities around the country.

Lifework Associates
310 Madison Ave., Suite 2108

New York, NY 10022
(212) 370-3580
Career counseling and vocational testing. Offers package programs designed to suit clients' needs for additional counseling or testing. Specializes in career transition counseling.

The Personnel Laboratory
733 Summer St.
Stamford, CT 06901
(800) 535-5603
Offers package that includes initial evaluation, vocational testing program, interpretation of test results, and written report. Fee: $350.

Personnel Sciences Center
276 5th Ave., Suite 704
New York, NY 10001
(212) 683- 3008
Contact: Dr. Jeffrey A. Goldberg
Testing takes a total of 15 hours. Tests are evaluated by a trained psychologist. Fee $420.

Shapiro, Ruth, Associates
200 E. 30th St.
New York, NY
(212) 889-4284
Consulting on all career issues including job search strategies, resumes and cover letters, and self-assessment. Fees are on a sliding scale from $75. Book: *How to Write Job Search Letters That Lead to Interviews*.

COLLEGES OFFERING TESTING AND VOCATIONAL GUIDANCE TO THE PUBLIC

Columbia University Teacher's College
Center for Psychological Services
525 W. 120th St.
New York, NY
(212) 678-3262
A low-cost sliding fee scale from $2-$30 is offered by this training program for students.

Hofstra University Counseling Center
1000 Fulton Ave.
Hempstead, NY 11550
(516) 463-6788
Offers career counseling and vocational testing. Includes initial evaluation meeting, testing sessions, and two review sessions with counselor. Open to public. Fee: $360.

New York University
Career & Life Planning
50 W. 4th St., Room 327
New York, NY 10012-1165
(212) 998-7060
Cost of services varies; approx. $60-$375.

Note: Other colleges and universities in the metropolitan area
offer these services to alumni and students at minimal or no cost
(see list of colleges and universities in Chapter 11, under "Education").

Thinking of Starting Your Own Small Business?

Free information available at the U.S. Small Business Administration offices will answer many of your basic questions about starting
a small business. Information packets deal with income tax preparation, loan programs for small businesses, assistance in obtaining
government contracts, and solving management and technical problems. To find out more, attend one of the SBA workshops. Or for
personal assistance, call or drop by one of the SBA offices.

Questions are answered by staff members and volunteers in the
SCORE (Service Corps of Retired Executives) program. These
retired executives draw upon years of experience in helping people
start their own business or better manage the one they have. They,
in turn, receive a great deal of support and advice from members of
ACE (Active Corps of Executives), a group of professionals who
volunteer their services.

You can find useful information on the ins and outs of becoming
an independent contractor, too. Management training programs co-
sponsored by the SBA are held all over the area, often at local
community colleges.

You'll find the SBA offices at:

26 Federal Plaza
New York, NY 10278
(212) 264-4354
and
35 Pinelawn Road
Melville, NY 11747
(516) 454-0750

The Washington Hot Line number is: **(212) 653-7557**.

SCORE counselors will meet with you by appointment at your
business location or at SCORE counseling centers. In an emergency,
they will counsel you on the telephone. SCORE's main offices are
located at :

26 Federal Plaza
New York, NY 10278
(212) 264-4507 and

17

400 County Seat Drive South
Mineola, NY 11501
(516) 571-3303

For a more intense approach, the U.S. Small Business Administration supports the **Small Business Development Centers** (SBDCs). Staffed by full-time professional consultants, the SBDCs specialize in free one-on-one counseling, and focus on business plan development. Their services include marketing assistance, financial planning and analysis, and financing strategies. They also offer seminars and workshops that may command a nominal fee.

There are 19 SBDCs in New York State, and all are campus-based. In New York City the SBDCs are located at:

Manhattan   Pace University
One Pace Plaza
Room W 480
New York, NY 10038
(212) 346-1899

Brooklyn   Kingsborough Community College
2001 Oriental Blvd.
Bldg. T4, Room 4204
Manhattan Beach
Brooklyn, NY 11235
(718) 368-4619

Bronx   School of Business
Manhattan College
Farrell Hall
Bronx, NY 10471
(718) 884-1880

Queens   York College, CUNY
Science Building 107
Jamaica, NY 11451
(718) 262-2880

Pace University also operates an **Outreach Center** in Harlem located at:

Adam Clayton Powell, Jr.
New York State Office Bldg.
163 W. 125th St., Room 1307
New York, NY 10027
(212) 865-4299

Writing a Resume That Works

Volumes have been written about how to write a resume. That's because, in our opinion, generations of job seekers have attached great importance to the creation and perfection of their resumes. Keep in mind that no one ever secured a job offer on the basis of a resume alone. The way to land a good position is to succeed in the employment interview. You have to convince a potential employer that you're the best person for the job. No piece of paper will do that for you.

The resume also goes by the name of *curriculum vitae* ("the course of one's life"), or *vitae* ("life") for short. These terms are a little misleading, however. A resume cannot possibly tell the story of your life, especially since, as a rule, it shouldn't be more than two pages long. The French word *résumé* means "a summing up." In the American job market, a resume is a concise, written summary of your work experience, education, accomplishments, and personal background—the essentials an employer needs to evaluate your qualifications.

A resume is nothing more or less than a simple marketing tool, a print ad for yourself. It is sometimes useful in generating interviews. But it is most effective when kept in reserve until after you've met an employer in person. Sending a follow-up letter after the interview, along with your resume, reminds the interviewer of that wonderful person he or she met last Thursday.

The Basics of a Good Resume

The resume is nothing for you to agonize over. But since almost every employer will ask you for one at some point in the hiring process, make sure that yours is a good one.

1. Current and comprehensive. What do we mean by a good resume? First, be sure it's up to date and comprehensive. At a minimum it should include your name, address, and phone number; a complete summary of your work experience; and an education profile. (College grads need not include their high school backgrounds.)

In general, your work experience should include the name, location, and dates of employment of every job you've held since leaving school, plus a summary of your responsibilities and, most important, your accomplishments on each job. If you're a recent graduate, or have held several jobs, you can present your experience chronologically. Begin with your present position and work backward to your first job. If you haven't had that many jobs, organize your resume to emphasize the skills you've acquired through experience.

2. Concise. A second rule of resume-writing is to keep the resume concise. Most employers don't want to read more than two pages, and one page is preferable. In most cases your resume will be scanned, not read in detail. Describe your experience in short, pithy phrases. Avoid large blocks of copy. Your resume should read more like a chart than a short story.

There are no hard and fast rules on what to include in your resume besides work experience and education. A statement of your objective is optional. A personal section containing date of birth, marital status, and so on, is rarely used and an employer can get this information from you or from an application. If you have served in the military, you ought to mention that in your resume. Your salary history and references, however, should not be included in your resume; these should be discussed in person during the interview.

Keep in mind that a resume is a sales tool. Make sure that it illustrates your unique strengths in a style and format you can be comfortable with. Indicate any unusual responsibilities you've been given or examples of how you've saved the company money or helped it grow. Include any special recognition of your ability. For example, if your salary increased substanially within a year or two, you might state the increase in terms of a percentage.

3. Honest. Third, keep your resume honest. Never lie, exaggerate, embellish, or deceive. Tell the truth about your education, accomplishments, and work history. You needn't account for every single work day that elapsed between jobs, however. If you left one position on November 15 and began the next on February 1, you can minimize such gaps by simply listing years worked instead of months.

4. Professional. Fourth, your resume should have a professional look. A good-quality word processor or personal computer is accessible to most people these days, either at home, at a photocopying center, or on most college campuses.

Another advantage of using a word processor or computer is that your resume can be stored on a disk so that you can update it easily, or even tailor your resume to a specific company.

No matter what method you use to prepare your resume, be sure to proofread it before making the final copies. A misspelled word or typing error reflects badly on you, even if it's not your fault. Read every word out loud, letter for letter and comma for comma. Get a friend to help you.

Do not make copies of your resume on a photocopy machine. Have it printed professionally by a good "quick" printer or use a laser printer. The resume you leave behind after an interview or send ahead to obtain an interview may be photocopied several times, and copies of copies can be very hard to read. You should also avoid such gimmicks as using colored paper (unless it's very light cream or light gray) or using a paper size other than 8 1/2 x 11".

Our purpose here is not to tell you how to write the ideal resume (there is no such thing) but rather to provide some general guidelines. The following books are full of all the how-to information you'll need to prepare an effective resume and are available from bookstores or your local library. (See Chapter 4 for a list of New York area libraries.)

BOOKS ON RESUME WRITING

Asher, Donald. *From College to Career: Entry Level Resumes For Any Major.* Berkeley, CA: Ten Speed Press, 1992.

Beatty, Richard. *The Perfect Cover Letter.* New York: John Wiley and Sons, 1989.

Bostwick, Burdette. *Resume Writing.* New York: John Wiley and Sons, 1990.

Corwin, Leonard. *Your Resume: Key to a Better Job.* New York: Arco, 1988.

Coxford, Lola M. *Resume Writing Made Easy.* New York: Gorsuch, 1992.

Foxman, Loretta D., and Walter L. Polsky. *Resumes That Work: How to Sell Yourself on Paper.* New York: John Wiley and Sons, 1988.

Jackson, Tom. *The Perfect Resume.* New York: Anchor/Doubleday, 1990.

Krannich, Ronald L., and Caryl R. *Dynamite Resumes.* Manassas, VA: Impact, 1992.

Krannich, Ronald L., and William J. Banis. *High Impact Resumes and Letters.* Career Management Concepts, 1992.

Lewis, Adele. *How to Write a Better Resume.* Woodbury, NY: Barron's Educational Series, 1989.

Nadler, Burton Jay. *Liberal Arts Power. What It Is and How to Sell It on Your Resume.* Princeton, NJ: Peterson's Guides, 1989.

Parker, Yana. *Damn Good Resume Guidelines.* Berkeley, CA: Ten Speed Press, 1989.

Smith, Michael Holley. *The Resume Writer's Handbook,* 2nd ed. New York: Harper and Row, 1987.

Yates, Martin J. *Cover Letters That Knock 'Em Dead.* Holbrook, MA: Bob Adams, 1992.

21

Should You Hire Someone Else To Write Your Resume?

In general, if you have reasonable writing skills, it's better to prepare your own resume than to ask someone else to do it. If you write your own job history, you'll be better prepared to talk about it in the interview. "Boiler plate" resumes also tend to look alike.

On the other hand, a professional resume writer can be objective about your background and serve as a sounding board on what you should and shouldn't include. You might also consider a professional if you have trouble writing in the condensed style that a good resume calls for.

Here is a list of New York area firms that will assist you in preparing your resume. Remember that a listing in this book does not constitute an endorsement. Before engaging a professional writer, ask for a recommendation from someone whose judgment you trust—a personnel director, college placement officer, or knowledgeable friend. Check with the Better Business Bureau and other consumer advocates listed in Chapter 2 to see if there have been any complaints made about the resume service you are considering.

PROFESSIONAL RESUME PREPARERS

Manhattan

Career Blazers—Resume Service Division
590 5th Ave., 7th Floor
New York, NY 10036
(800) 925-7373
Offers free consultations. A division of the employment agency Career Blazers.

Career Marketing Group
450 7th Ave.
New York, NY 10123
(212) 665-6950
Fees vary. Resume writing and interviewing skills.

Compu-Craft Business Services
124 E. 40th St., Suite 403
New York, NY 10016
(212) 697-4005
Fees vary on the length and type of interview. The basic resume for an entry-level applicant is $85-$100, including 50 resume copies typeset and printed.

National Professional Writers Group
450 7th Ave.
New York, NY 10123
(212) 695-6950
Fees vary. Write profiles, essays, and resumes.

Network Resumes
60 E. 42nd St.
New York, NY 10165
(212) 687-2411
Fees are moderate depending on service. Complete job search
services, including resume preparation and writing, training in
networking, interviewing, researching, and salary negotiation.

Professional Resume and Writing Service
420 Madison Ave., Suite 401
New York, NY 10017
(212) 223-2560
Fees: based on amount of time spent interviewing and counseling
client as well as actually preparing resume. Multiple copies
provided; cover letters written. Entry- and executive-level resumes prepared.

Resume Exchange
87 Nassau St., Suite 507
New York, NY 10038
(212) 962-0378
Fees: vary depending on amount of time spent preparing resume.

Queens

Career Resumes
108-10 Queens Blvd.
Forest Hills, NY 11375
(800) 729-6569
Fees vary. Resumes and other correspondence.

Mendez Litho
70-01 Queens Blvd.
Woodside, NY 11377
(718) 639-7500
Fee: $100 per page to write resumes, excluding printing. $25 for
typesetting, $.40 per copy for printing. Cover letters and 24-hour
service available.

Resumes USA
80-02 Kew Gardens Road
Kew Gardens, NY 11415
(718) 894-0200
Fee: $25 and up. Change of career corporate writing, cover letters,
and resume writing.

Brooklyn

A Mimeograph and Letter Service
105 Court St.
Brooklyn, NY 11201

(718) 625-3393
Fee: $59 for resume writing and $39 for resume printing.

Lewis, Arthur, E., Assoc.
32 Court St.
Brooklyn, NY 11201
(718) 625-1230
Interview client, write resume, and write cover letter. Appointments only. One-day service. Fee of $150 includes writing, 50 copies, and cover letters.

How to choose a professional

Before engaging a professional to help you write your resume, run through the following checklist of questions.
• **What will it cost?** Some firms charge a set fee. Others charge by the hour. Though many firms will not quote an exact price until they know the details, you should obtain minimum and maximum costs before you go ahead.
• **What does the price include?** Does the fee cover only writing? Or does it include typesetting? Most firms will charge extra for printing.
• **What happens if you're not satisfied?** Will the writer make changes you request? Will changes or corrections cost extra?
• **How do this writer's fees and experience stack up against others?** It's wise to shop around before you buy writing services, just as you would when purchasing any other service. ■

Nassau County

Printing Mart of Long Island
154 Mineola Blvd.
Mineola, NY 11501
(516) 746-3640
Fee: $41.95-46.95 to type and print 50 copies of one-page resume. Offers resume-writing service; fee: $130.

Word Dynamics
734 Walt Whitman Road
Melville, NY
(516) 549-9880
Fee: $25.50 - $30.90 to type and print 50 copies of one-page resume; $180.00 to write resume.

Westchester County

Career Resumes
Routes 22 & 35
Katonah, NY 10536

(914) 232-1412
Office in White Plains/Tarrytown 800-800-1220.
Resume writing and printing $75 and up.

Career Strategies International
50 Main St.
White Plains, NY 10601
(914) 682-2080
Offices in Mt. Kisco, NY, and Greenwich, CT, offering career
development and job search services, including resume writing.

Catalyst Professional Resumes
25 3rd St.
Tarrytown, NY
(914) 332-1196
Offices also in Stamford, CT (203) 348-6186; Fairfield, CT (203)
259-8227; Paramus, NJ (201) 843-4455; and several locations in
Westchester County (800)-732-4448.
Services such as resume and cover letter writing and printing and
referrals to search firms. Costs are approximately $75+ for
writing, and $25 for typesetting. Printing costs more and varies
with number of copies.

The following **quick printers** have locations in many areas.
They offer fast copying services as well as resume printing and word
processors.

Kinkos Copies
24 E. 12th St.
(212) 924-0802
New York, NY
2872 Broadway
(212) 316-3390

Minuteman Press
141 E. 44th St.
New York, NY
(212) 661-1717

Pip Printing
69 W. 55th St.
New York, NY
(212) 245-3654
1010 Avenue of the Americas
(212) 391-2858
30 E. 23rd St.
(212) 255-8238

Sir Speedy Business Printers
260 W. 36th St.
New York, NY
(800) 564-9775

What NOT To Do with Your Resume Once You Have It Printed

Do not change your resume except to correct an obvious error. Everyone to whom you show the resume will have some suggestion for improving it: "Why didn't you tell 'em that you had a scholarship?" or "Wouldn't this look better in italics?" The time to consider those kinds of questions is before you go to the typesetter. Afterward, the only thing to keep in mind is that there is no such thing as a perfect resume, except typographically.

The power of verbs

Gary J. has been an engineer in New York for 20 years. During those years, he has changed jobs 7 times, enhancing his career with each move. Gary realized early that using powerful, active verbs to describe his accomplishments made his resume stand out. Here are some sample verbs that job seekers in various career areas might use to help build a more effective resume.

Management
Supervised
Administered
Planned
Implemented

Methods and Controls
Restructured
Cataloged
Verified
Analyzed
Investigated
Systematized

Public Relations/ Human Relations
Monitored
Handled
Sponsored
Integrated
Creative
Devised
Effected
Evaluated
Invented
Originated
Conceived

Advertising/ Promotion
Convinced
Generated
Promoted
Recruited
Tailored
Sparked

Communications
Facilitated
Edited
Consulted
Disseminated
Interpreted

Resourcefulness
Rectified
Pioneered
Achieved
Arranged
Initiated

Negotiations
Engineered
Mediated
Proposed
Negotiated
Reviewed ■

A second point to remember: do NOT send out a mass mailing. If you send letters to 700 company presidents, you can expect a response of from 1 to 2 percent—and 95 percent of the responses will be negative. The shotgun approach is expensive; it takes time and costs money for postage and printing. You'll get much better results if you are selective about where you send your resume. We'll discuss this at greater length in Chapter 5. The important thing is to concentrate on known hiring authorities in whom you are interested.

Always Include a Cover Letter

This brings us to a third important "don't": Do NOT send your resume without a cover letter. Whether you are answering a want ad or following up an inquiry call or interview, you should always include a letter with your resume. If at all possible, the letter should be addressed to a specific person—the one who's doing the hiring— and not "To Whom It May Concern."

A good cover letter, like a good resume, is brief—usually not more than three or four paragraphs. No paragraph should be longer than three or four sentences. If you've already spoken to the contact person by phone, remind him or her of your conversation in the first paragraph. If you and the person to whom you are writing know someone in common, the first paragraph is the place to mention it. You should also include a hard-hitting sentence about why you're well qualified for the job in question.

In the next paragraph or two, specify what you could contribute to the company in terms that indicate you've done your homework on the firm and the industry.

Finally, either request an interview or tell the reader that you will follow up with a phone call within a week to arrange a mutually convenient meeting.

Remember that the focus of your job search is to sell yourself as a match to fit an employer's needs. You should emphasize that you match the company's needs throughout all of your communication— your resume, phone calls, cover letter, and follow-up letters.

Choosing a Resume Format

There are a number of different methods for composing a quality resume. Every career counselor and resume compiler has his or her own favorite method and style. As the person being represented by the resume, you must choose the style and format that best suits and sells you. Many resume books will use different terms for the various styles. We will highlight the three most popular types.

1. The chronological resume is the traditional style, most often used in the workplace and job search; that does not mean it is the most effective. Positive aspects of the chronological resume include the traditionalist approach that employers may expect. It also can highlight past positions that you may wish your potential employer to notice. This resume is also very adaptable, with only the reverse chronological work history as the essential ingredient.

2. The functional resume is most common among career changers, people reentering the job market after a lengthy absence, and those wishing to highlight aspects of their experience not related directly to employment. This resume ideally focuses on the many skills one has used at his or her employment and the accomplishments one has achieved. It shows a potential employer that you can do and have done a good job. What it doesn't highlight is where you have done it.

3. The combination resume combines the best features of a functional resume and a chronological resume. This allows job seekers to highlight skills and accomplishments while still maintaining the somewhat traditional format of reverse chronological order of positions held and organizations worked for.

Here are some sample resumes and cover letters to help you with your own. The books listed earlier in this chapter will supply many more examples than we have room for here.

SAMPLE CHRONOLOGICAL RESUME

Stuart Lindman
555 Maple Avenue
Tarrytown, NY 10591
(914) 555-9431

EXPERIENCE:

June 1993-Present

CAHILL PRODUCTS INC., New York, NY
Marketing Assistant
• Developed and implemented plan introducing promotional items to retailers
• Maintained client database
• Assisted managers with sales calls to new accounts

Sept. 1992-
June 1993

HARRIS UTILITIES, Bronx, NY
Corporate Communications Assistant
• Edited and published internal newsletter on desktop publishing
• Wrote press releases for media
• Updated and maintained media database

Summer 1992

CEREBRAL PALSY ASSOCIATION, New York, NY
Walk-A-Thon Coordinator
• Planned recruitment campaign for high school volunteers

1990-1992

SAMS RESTAURANT, Hudson, NY
Headwaiter
• Supervised dining room on weekends

EDUCATION:

Pace University, New York, New York
BBA, Marketing, 1993

HONORS:

Dean's List
Trustee Scholarship

**COMPUTER
SKILLS:**

Microsoft for Windows, Harvard Graphics, Word Perfect, Paradox, Lotus 123

ACTIVITIES:

College Marketing Association, President 1992-1993
VIA Pace, Volunteer, 1990-1992
Pace Press, Reporter, 1990-1992

REFERENCES:

Furnished upon request

29

SAMPLE FUNCTIONAL RESUME

KATHY JONES
451 E. 85th Street
New York, NY 11101
(212) 555-5902

OBJECTIVE Seeking position as an administrative assistant, utilizing my administrative, organizational, and computer skills

SKILLS

Administrative
- Organized major client's account for an advertising agency
- Managed funds in excess of $80,000 for a non-profit corporation
- Coordinated two rental properties.

Organizational
- Set up procedure for assigned experiments and procured equipment for a research laboratory
- Planned course syllabi to assess weaknesses of individual students to facilitate learning

Computer
- Developed data input system and generated monthly report
- Completed courses in FORTRAN and BASIC

EMPLOYMENT

Computer Operator, Wilco, Queens, NY   1990-Present

Trouble-shooter in accounting, Cargill,
  Wilson, and Acree, Stamford, CT   1988-90

Instructor, Math Dept., Hofstra University,
  Hempstead, NY   1986-88

EDUCATION

Hofstra University, M.S. Mathematics   1988

Penn State University, B.A. Mathematics   1986

REFERENCES   Furnished upon request

SAMPLE COMBINATION RESUME

SUSAN SKINNER
40-34 35th Avenue
Astoria, NY 11401
(718) 555-0011

OBJECTIVE: Software development position, utilizing software and computer skills

EDUCATION: LONG ISLAND UNIVERSITY, GPA 3.7/4.0
M.S., Information and Computer Science 6/93

CORNELL UNIVERSITY, GPA 3.5/4.0
A.B., Mathematics 6/88

QUALIFICATIONS:
Career-related projects:
- Designed and implemented multi-tasking operating system for the IBM-PC.
- Devised compiler system for Pascal-like language.
- Utilized mainframe to simulate proposed projects.
- Developed electronic mail system using PSL/PSA specification language.
- Coordinated menu-based interface for beginning UNIX users.

Languages and operating systems:
- Proficient in Ada, Modula-2, Pascal, COBOL.
- Familiar with C, Fortran, Lisp, Prolog, dBaseIII, SQL, QBE.
- Working knowledge of IBM-PC hardware and 8088 assembly language.

Hardware:
- IBM-PC (MS-DOS, Xenix), Pyramid 90x (UNIX), Cyber 990 (NOS).

WORK EXPERIENCE:
Neil Araki Programming Services—Astoria, NY 6/90-Present
- UNIX Programmer—Transferred MS-DOS database applications to IBM-PC/AT running Xenix System V. System administration.

Strathmore Systems—Newark, NJ 6/88-6/90
- Computer Programmer—Performed daily disk backup on Burroughs B-1955 machine.
- Executed database update programs and checks. Provided user assistance.

REFERENCES: Furnished upon request

SAMPLE COVER LETTER

133 Elm Street
Valley Stream, NY 11580
November 1, 1993
(516) 555-6886

Ms. Alice Kehoe
Wide World Publishing Company
1400 Forest Square, Suite #250
Norwalk, CT 06832

Dear Ms. Kehoe:

As an honors graduate of Pace University with two years of copy editing and feature writing experience with the *Chronicle*, I am confident that I would make a successful editorial assistant with Wide World.

Besides my strong editorial background, I offer considerable business experience. I have held summer jobs in an insurance company, a law firm, and a data processing company. My familiarity with word processing should prove particularly useful to Wide World now that you're about to become fully automated.

I would like to interview with you as soon as possible and would be happy to check in with your office about an appointment. If you prefer, your office can contact me between the hours of 11:00 a.m. and 3:00 p.m. at (516) 555-6886.

Sincerely,

Samantha Holland

SAMPLE COVER LETTER

70 Gates Avenue
Somers, NY 10589
May 15, 1993

Advertiser
Box 1826
The New York Times
229 W. 43rd Street
New York, NY 10036

Dear Employer:

Your advertisement in the May 13 issue of the *Times* for an experienced accountant seems perfect for someone with my background. My five years of experience in a small accounting firm in Stamford, Connecticut, has prepared me to move on to a more challenging position.

As you can see from my resume, my work experience includes not only basic accounting work but also some consulting with a few of our firm's bigger clients. This experience combined with an appetite for hard work, an enthusiastic style, and a desire to succeed makes me a strong candidate for your consideration.

I would appreciate the opportunity to discuss how my background could meet your needs.

Sincerely,

James Alles
(914) 555-4414

SAMPLE COVER LETTER

228 Meadow Road
Stamford, CT 06832

November 17, 1993

Dear Mike:

Just when everything seemed to be going so well at my job, the company gave us a Christmas present that nobody wanted— management announced that half the department will be laid off before the end of the year. Nobody knows yet just which heads are going to roll. But whether or not my name is on the list, I am definitely back in the job market.

I have already lined up a couple of interviews. But knowing how uncertain job hunting can be, I can use all the contacts I can get.

You know my record, both from when we worked together at BMI and since then. But in case you've forgotten the details, I've enclosed my resume.

I know that you often hear of job openings as you wend your way about New York and the suburbs. I'd certainly appreciate your passing along any leads you think might be worthwhile.

My best to you and Fran for the Holidays.

Cordially,

Ruth Blackburn
(203) 555-7888

Seven ways to ruin a cover letter

1. Spell the name of the firm incorrectly.
2. Don't bother to find out the name of the hiring authority. Just send the letter to the president or chairman of the board.
3. If the firm is headed by a woman, be sure to begin your letter, "Dear Sir." Otherwise, just address it "To Whom It May Concern."
4. Make sure the letter includes a couple of typos and sloppy erasures. Better yet, spill coffee on it first, then mail it.
5. Be sure to provide a phone number that has been disconnected, or one at which no one is ever home.
6. Tell the firm you'll call to set up an appointment in a few days; then don't bother.
7. Call the firm at least three times the day after you mail the letter. Get very angry when they say they haven't heard of you. ■

Researching the New York Job Market

To a large extent, the success of your job search will depend on how well you do your homework. Once you've figured out what kind of job you want, you need to find out as much as you can about which specific companies might employ you. Your network of personal contacts can be an invaluable source of information about what jobs are available where. But networking can't do it all; at some point, you'll have to do some reading. This chapter fills you in on the directories, newspapers, and magazines you'll need in your search and notes the libraries where you can find them.

Libraries

Public libraries are an invaluable source of career information, everything from books on resume writing to *Standard and Poor's Register of Corporations, Directors, and Executives* can usually be found in the business and economics sections.

Save time by checking with reference librarians on what is available and where to find it. These staff members will be especially cooperative if you first ask them when their "slow" periods are. These are the times when they can give you their undivided attention.

The public library system in New York City is very large and can be confusing. There are hundreds of libraries in the system. The New York Public Library system includes libraries in the Bronx, Staten Island, and Manhattan. The Brooklyn Public Library System and the Queens Borough Public Library system oversee the libraries in those boroughs. You are welcome to use the reference section in any library regardless of your place of residence, but you are not permitted to borrow any materials unless you are a resident of that borough.

Most of the suburban libraries in Westchester and Nassau counties make interlibrary loans. Again, you can use the reference sections in the libraries but are not permitted to remove any material unless you are a county resident.

The libraries listed here all have job-information centers or some kind of special job services. Rather than list all of the branches in the library system, we have given detailed information about those branches that offer special assistance to job seekers.

MANHATTAN

The Job Opportunities Information Center of the New York Public Library is located on the second floor of the mid-Manhattan branch at Fifth Avenue and 40th Street. The Center includes a vast collection of general career and employment information. Also available is the Civil Service Study Handbook (for civil service exams). There are on-line computer databases with more extensive information to be found in the fourth floor business section, which carries assorted CD ROM products for company and other business information searches. The Center also posts classified ads of local papers! The telephone number for the Center is (212) 340-0836. It is the largest and most comprehensive center in the New York Public Library system.

BROOKLYN

The main branch of the Brooklyn Public Library, located at Grand Army Plaza, includes a Job Information Center. To make an appointment with a counselor, call (718) 780-7777.

A special business library is located at 280 Cadmen Plaza West. For information, call (718) 780-7800. If you need background information about a potential employer, this is the place to go. It has the most comprehensive business library reference section in the borough.

QUEENS

The main library of the Queens Borough Public Library system is located at 89-11 Merrick Boulevard in Jamaica. It operates an Adult

Learning Center, which offers career counseling and job information. There is no fee for use of the Center, and no appointment is necessary. For more information, call (718) 990-0800.

BRONX

The main library in the Bronx is located at 2556 Bainbridge Avenue near Fordham Road. This library has a career counselor on staff to assist with job and career information as well as help with resume writing. And you can print your new resume on the library's laser printer at no charge! This library has the most extensive job information center in the Bronx system. For more information, call (718) 220-6573.

STATEN ISLAND

There is no job center at any of the Staten Island libraries. You should check with one of the other borough libraries or the main mid-Manhattan library.

NASSAU COUNTY

Nassau County's public library system includes a variety of branches, but no main library. The Hempstead Public Library (115 Nichols Court, Hempstead, NY 11550) has a Job Information Center. The Center offers a variety of career-related resources and services. Resources include listings of job openings, out-of-town newspapers, and civil service lists and examinations. The center also offers group workshops on career exploration, resume writing, and interviewing skills. Services are free to Nassau County residents, including career counseling sessions. For an appointment, call (516) 481-6990.

The following Nassau County libraries offer job information materials:

> East Meadow (516) 794-2570
> Hempstead (516) 481-6990
> Long Beach (516) 432-7200

Other libraries with job services include Levitown, Manhasset, Massapequa, and Oceanside.

WESTCHESTER COUNTY

The Westchester library system has 38 branch libraries, all of which have job information centers. Specialty librarians offer assistance with career planning, resume writing, interviewing, and career changes. These libraries also have Infotrac/Magazine Collection CD Rom Index to magazines and newspapers with full text on microfilm, as well as access to on-line networks for database searches. For information about these libraries call the Westchester Library System at (914) 592-8214.

In addition, the county's Westchester Educational Brokering Service (WEBS) offers free career counseling seminars. WEBS focuses on people who are considering a career change, those interested in job advancement, and those entering the job market for the first time. Group as well as private sessions are offered. For information on schedules and locations, contact WEBS at (914) 592-8791.

Job Links, an on-line database listing employment possibilities by field, location, and number of positions, is available at no cost at the Yonkers Library (914-337-1500) and the Mount Vernon Library (914-668-1840).

UNIVERSITY LIBRARIES AND CAREER RESOURCE CENTERS

Local university and community college libraries may also offer resources for job seekers. In New York, most private and state schools have large reference libraries that are well equipped with career resource information and job directories that you can use even if you are not an alumnus.

Many colleges offer vocational testing and career guidance and placement through the school's career services office. While these services are often available to alumni only, many colleges have reciprocal agreements and will see alumni from participating colleges. For a list of area colleges and universities, see Chapter 11.

Directories

When you're beginning your job search, whether you're researching an entire industry or a specific company, there are four major sources of information with which you should become familiar.

Standard and Poor's Register of Corporations, Directors, and Executives (Standard and Poor's Publishing Co., 25 Broadway, New York, NY 10004) is billed as the "foremost guide to the business community and the executives who run it." This three-volume directory lists more than 50,000 corporations and 70,000 officers, directors, trustees, and other bigwigs.

Each business is assigned a four-digit number called a Standard Industrial Classification (S.I.C.) number, which tells you what product or service the company provides. Listings are indexed by geographic area and also by S.I.C. number, so it's easy to find all the companies in New York that produce, say, industrial inorganic chemicals.

You can also look up a particular company to verify its correct address and phone number, its chief officers (that is, the people you might want to contact for an interview), its products, and, in many cases, its annual sales and number of employees. If you have an appointment with the president of XYZ Corporation, you can consult Standard and Poor's *Register* to find out where he or she was born and went to college—information that's sure to come in handy in an employment interview. Supplements are published in April, July, and October.

The **Thomas Register of American Manufacturers** and **Thomas Register Catalog File** (Thomas Publishing Co., One Penn Plaza, New York, NY 10119) is published annually. This 23-volume publication is another gold mine of information. You can look up a particular product or service and find every company that provides it. (Since this is a national publication, you'll have to weed out companies that are not in the New York area, but that's easy.) You can also look up a particular company to find out about branch offices, capital ratings, company officials, names, addresses, phone numbers, and more. The *Thomas Register* even contains five volumes of company catalogs. Before your appointment with XYZ Corporation, you can bone up on its product line using the *Thomas Register*.

Moody's Complete Corporate Index (Moody's Investor Service, 99 Church St., New York, NY 10007) gives you the equivalent of an encyclopedia entry on more than 20,000 corporations. This is the resource to use when you want really detailed information on a particular company. *Moody's* can tell you about a company's history—when it was founded, what name changes it has undergone, and so on. It provides a fairly lengthy description of a company's business and properties, what subsidiaries it owns, and lots of detailed financial information. Like the directories above, *Moody's* lists officers and directors of companies. It can also tell you the date of the annual meeting as well as the number of stockholders and employees.

Double-check names and numbers

Printed directories, even those that are regularly and conscientiously revised, go out of date as soon as someone listed in them gets promoted or changes companies. Always double-check a contact whose name you get from a directory or other printed resource, including this one, to make sure he or she is still in the same job. If necessary, call the company's switchboard to confirm the name and title of the person who heads the division or department you're interested in. Many directories also have on-line computer databases that can be accessed from a personal computer. ∎

The **Million Dollar Directory** (Dun & Bradstreet, 3 Century Drive, Parsippany, NJ 07054) is a three-volume listing of approximately 160,000 U.S. businesses with a net worth of more than half a million dollars. Listings appear alphabetically, geographically, and by product classification and include key personnel. Professional and consulting organizations such as hospitals, engineering services, credit agencies, and financial institutions other than banks and trust companies are not generally included.

So much for the Big Four directories. The following list contains dozens of additional directories and guides that may come in handy during your job search.

USEFUL DIRECTORIES

Accounting Firms and Practitioners
(American Institute of Certified Public Accountants, 1211 Avenue of the Americas, New York, NY 10036.) Covers about 25,000 certified public accounting firms belonging to the institute, as well as member accountants with independent practices.

Acon's Publicity Checker
(Bacon's Publishing Company, 332 S. Michigan Ave., Chicago, IL 60604.) Covers over 4,800 trade and consumer magazines, 1,700 daily newspapers, and 8,000 weekly newspapers in the United States and Canada.

AdWeek Agency Directory
(BPI/ASM, 49 E. 21st St., New York, NY 10010.) Directory of advertising agencies.

Associations' Publications in Print
(R.R. Bowker Company, 1180 Avenue of the Americas, New York, NY 10036.) Lists 13,000 associations with acronym cross-references, 82,000 publications, and audio-video materials.

Beauty Fashion—Fragrance Directory Issue
(Beauty Fashion, Inc., 530 5th Ave., New York, NY 10017.) Lists manufacturers of perfumes, colognes, and other fragrances for men and women. Arranged alphabetically.

Billion Dollar Directory: America's Corporate Families
(Dun and Bradstreet, 3 Century Drive, Parsippany, NJ 07054.)Lists 2,600 United States parent companies and their 24,000 domestic subsidiaries. Organized alphabetically by name of parent company.

Black Enterprise—Leading Black Businesses Issue
(Earl G. Graves Publishing Co., 130 5th Ave., New York, NY 10017.) Covers 100 black-owned or black-run businesses. Ranked by financial size.

Career Guide: Dun's Employment Opportunities Directory
(Dun's Marketing Services, 3 Sylvan Way, Parsippany, NJ 07054.) Designed for entry-level applicants; describes job prospects and career opportunities at hundreds of companies indexed geographically.

Career Guide to Professional Associations: A Directory of Organizations by Occupational Field
(Caroll Press, Squantum St., Evanston, RI 02920.) Covers over 2,500 organizations that are concerned with specific industries; coverage includes Canada.

Chemical and Engineering News
(Facts and Figures Issue, American Chemical Society, 1155 16th St., NW, Washington, DC 20036.) List of 100 largest chemical producers chosen by total chemical sales.

College Placement Annual
(College Placement Council, 62 Highland Ave., Bethlehem, PA 18017.) Directory of the occupational needs of over 1,200 corporations and government employers. Lists names and titles of recruitment representatives.

Complete Guide to Public Employment
(Impact Publications, 10655 Big Oaks Circle, Manassas, VA 22205.) List
of federal, state, and local government agencies and departments, trade
and professional associations, contracting and consulting firms and
support groups, and other organizations offering public employment
career opportunities.

Consultants and Consulting Organizations Directory
(Gale Research Co., 835 Penobscot Bldg., Detroit, MI 48226.) Contains
descriptions of 6,000 firms and individuals involved in consulting;
indexed geographically.

**Data Sources: Hardware Data Communications Directory and
Data Sources**: Software Directory
(Ziff-Davis Publishing Co., 20 Brace Rd., Suite 110, Cherry Hill, NJ
08034.) Two-volume guide to most products, companies, services, and
personnel in the computer industry.

Dictionary of Occupational Titles
(U.S. Dept. of Labor, 200 Constitution Ave., NW, Washington, DC
20210.) Occupational information on job duties and requirements;
describes almost every conceivable job.

Directories in Print
(Gale Research Co., 835 Penobscot Bldg., Detroit, MI 48226.) Contains
detailed descriptions of all published directories: what they list, who uses
them, and who publishes them.

Directory of Agencies
(National Assoc. of Social Workers, 1425 4th St., NW, Washington, DC
20212.) Provides information on over 300 U.S. and international volun-
tary intergovernmental agencies involved in social work.

Directory for the Arts
(Center for Arts Information, 625 Broadway, New York, NY 10013,
$6.75.) Covers 145 organizations and government agencies involved with
the arts; also includes New York State community arts councils as well
as video periodicals.

**Directory of Commerce and Industry—Nassau and Suffolk
Counties**
(L.I. Association of Commerce and Industry, 425 Broad Hollow Road,
Suite 205, Melville, NY 11747.) Lists 5,200 companies located in Nassau
and Suffolk counties. Arranged by product.

Directory of Construction Associations
(Metadata, Inc., Box 585, Locust, NJ 07760.) Lists about 2,500 local,
regional, and national professional societies, technical associations, trade
groups, manufacturer bureaus, government agencies, labor unions, and
other construction information sources. Arranged by topic.

Directory of Human Resource Executives
(Hunt-Scanlon Publishing Co., Two Pickwick Plaza, Greenwich, CT
06830.) Lists companies and their executives with concentration on the
human resource executive.

Directory of Human Resources in Health, Physical Education and Recreation
(ERIC Clearing House on Teacher Education, 1 DuPont Circle, Suite 616, Washington, DC 20036, $3.50.) Covers information centers in the U.S. and Canada concerned with health, physical education, and recreation. Geographic index.

Directory of Women Business Owners
(Westchester Association of Women Business Owners, 3 Wagner Place, Hastings, NY 10706.) Lists 120 member firms in Westchester, New York, and the surrounding area; at least 50 percent of each firm is owned by women. Arranged by line of business, town, or city.

Directory of Women-Owned Businesses
(National Association of Women Business Owners, 2000 P St., NW, Suite 511, Washington, DC 20036, free.) Lists women-owned businesses by state; describes products and services.

Dun's Consultants Directory
(Dun and Bradstreet Corporation, 3 Sylvan Way, Parsippany, NJ 07054.) Top 25,000 consulting firms in the U.S. indexed geographically.

Electronic News Financial Fact Book and Directory
(Fairchild Publications, 7 E. 12th St., New York, NY 10003.) Background and financial information about leading companies in the electronics industry.

Emerson's Directory of Leading U.S. Accounting Firms
(Emerson's Professional Services Review, Redmond, Washington.) Contains principal offices and branches.

Encyclopedia of Associations
(Gale Research Co., 835 Penobscot Bldg., Detroit, MI 48226.) Lists 30,000 local and national associations, professional clubs, and civic organizations by categories; includes key personnel. Indexed geographically.

Encyclopedia of Business Information Sources
(Gale Research Co., 835 Penobscot Bldg., Detroit, MI 48226.) Lists each industry's encyclopedias, handbooks, indexes, almanacs, yearbooks, trade associations, periodicals, directories, computer databases, research centers, and statistical sources.

Fairchild's Financial Manual of Retail Stores
(Fairchild Books, Fairchild Publications, 7 E. 12th St., New York, NY 10003.) Lists 550 publicly-held companies in the U.S. and Canada that deal partly or exclusively in retail sales. Arranged alphabetically.

Fairchild's Textile and Apparel Financial Directory
(Fairchild Books, Fairchild Publications, 7 E. 12th St., New York, NY 10003.) Lists 275 publicly-owned textile and apparel corporations. Arranged alphabetically.

Fortune Double 500 Directory
(Time, Inc., 1271 Avenue of the Americas, New York, NY 10020.) Lists 500 largest and 500 second largest industrial corporations, as well as the largest banking, financial, and utility firms in the U.S.

The Franchise Handbook
(Enterprise Magazine, 1020 North Broadway, Milwaukee, WI.) 1,700
franchises classified by business type.

Gale Directory of Publications and Broadcast Media
(Gale Research Company, 835 Penobscot Building, Detroit, MI 48226.)
Lists 35,000 publications and broadcast stations as well as the feature
editors of major daily newspapers. Alphabetically and by state.

Hotel and Motel Management—Buyer's Directory I
(Harcourt Brace Jovanovich, 757 3rd Ave., New York, NY 10017.) Lists
about 2,100 companies that supply goods and services to the lodging
market; includes separate sections for hotel chains, related associations,
manufacturers' representatives, franchise and referral organizations,
consulting firms, personnel agencies, publishers, and schools.

International Advertising Association—Membership Directory
(IAA, 342 Madison Ave., New York, NY 10017.) Covers 2,700 member
advertisers, advertising agencies, media, and other firms involved in
advertising. Arranged geographically and by function or service.

**International Association for Personnel Women—Membership
Roster**
(IAPW, P.O. Box 969, Andover, MA 01810.) Lists 2,000 members-at-large
and members of affiliated chapters.

International Television and Video Almanac
(Quigley Publishing Company, 159 W. 53rd St. New York, NY 10019,
$65.) Lists television networks, major program producers, major group
station owners, cable television companies, distributors, firms serving
the industry, equipment manufacturers, casting agencies, literary
agencies, advertising and publicity representatives, and television
stations.

Job Opportunities in Business
(Peterson's, P.O. Box 2123, Princeton, NJ 08543.) Profiles of 2,500
companies with more than 10,000 jobs in high-growth companies for
entry-level to experienced professionals. For financial services, management consulting, consumer products, media/entertainment.

Job Opportunities in Engineering and Technology
(Peterson's, P.O. Box 2123, Princeton, NJ 08543.) Profiles of over 2,500
companies with openings for entry-level to experienced professionals in
biotechnology, telecommunications, software engineering, consumer
electronics.

Job Opportunities in the Environment
(Peterson's, P.O. Box 2123, Princeton, NJ 08543.) Profiles of over 2,500
companies with openings in waste management companies, state and
federal agencies, advocacy groups, environmental design firms.

Job Opportunities in Health Care
(Peterson's, P.O. Box 2123, Princeton, NJ 08543.)
Profiles of over 2,500 companies with openings for entry-level to experienced professionals in skilled nursing care facilities, hospitals, medical
laboratories, home health care, pharmaceuticals.

Jobs in Arts and Media Management: What They Are and How to Get One!
(Drama Book Publishers, 260 5th Ave., New York, NY 10001.) Lists about 150 sources of information on job opportunities in the arts, including organizations offering graduate programs, internships, short-term study, and job listings.

Jobs '92
(Prentice Hall, 15 Columbus Circle, New York, NY 10023.) Good source of employers, professional associations, publications, and industry trends. Organized by state.

Knowledge Industry 200
(Knowledge Industry Publications, 701 Westchester Ave., White Plains, NY 10604.) Covers 200 major companies active in more than 3,000 broadcasting, publishing, and information services.

Literary Market Place
(R.R. Bowker Co., 121 Chanlon Road, New Providence, NJ 07974.) Covers book publishers in the U.S. and Canada who issued 3 or more books during the preceding year, plus book printers and binders, book clubs, book trade and literary associations. Also selected newspaper syndicates, periodicals, and radio and television programs that use book reviews or book publishing news; translators and literary agents; etc.

Macrae's State Industrial Directories: Connecticut, New York, New Jersey
(Macrae's Blue Books, 817 Broadway, New York, NY 10003.) Lists companies; includes key executives, number of employees, plant size, products, gross sales, bank references, and year established. Main section contains geographical listing of companies. Has alphabetical and industry indexes.

Madison Avenue Handbook
(Peter Glenn Publications, 17 E. 48th St., New York, NY 10017.) Lists advertising agencies and related services. Includes television producers, photographers, artists, models, actors and their agents, photographers and suppliers, sources of props and rentals, fashion houses, etc., for major cities.

National Trade and Professional Associations
(Columbia Books, 1212 New York Ave., NW, Washington, DC 20005.) Lists most associations and labor unions in the U.S. and Canada. Indexed geographically and by key words.

New Firms Listing Service
(L.I. Association of Commerce and Industry, 425 Broadhollow Road, Suite 205, Melville, NY 11746.) Lists new plants, expansions, relocations, and incorporations of firms in Nassau and Suffolk counties. Arranged geographically.

Newsletters In Print
(Gale Research, 835 Penobscot Bldg., Detroit, MI 48226.) Reference guide to newsletters, financial services, association bulletins.

New York Insurance Directory
(American Underwriter, Box 1056, Media, PA 19063.) Lists over 36,000

property and casualty brokers licensed in New York State. Includes partnerships, associations, and corporations.

New York Publicity Outlets
(Public Relations Plus, Box 327, Washington Depot, CT 06794.) Consumer media in New York metropolitan area, including over 100 radio and TV stations, about 200 radio and TV interview shows, and about 500 daily and weekly newspapers.

New York State Directory
(Cambridge Directories, Robert M. Walsh, Publisher, San Mateo, California.) Lists government agencies, key officials, federal government, New York state, county, and municipal governments; also political parties, lobbyists, news media.

New York State Foundations: A Comprehensive Directory.
(Foundation Center, 79 5th Ave., New York, NY 10003.) Lists 5,343 organizations located in New York that awarded grants of $1 or more in the latest fiscal year of record. Those who award more than $100,000 have complete descriptive entries. Also includes 310 out-of-state foundations with funding interests in New York.

Occupational Outlook Handbook
(U.S. Dept. of Labor, 200 Constitution Ave., NW, Washington, DC 20212.) Describes in clear language what people do in their jobs, the training and education they need, earnings, working conditions, and employment outlook.

O'Dwyer's Directory of Public Relations Firms
(J.R. O'Dwyer & Co., 271 Madison Ave., New York, NY 10016.) Describes 900 public relations firms in the U.S., their key personnel, local offices, and accounts; indexed geographically.

Official Museum Directory
(National Register Publications, 3004 Glenview Road, Wilmette, IL 60091.) Covers about 6,700 institutions of art, history, and science in the United States, including general museums, college museums, National Park nature centers, children's and junior museums, company museums, displays, highly specialized museums. Also includes several thousand suppliers of services and products to museums.

Pharmaceutical Manufacturers of the U.S.
(Noyes Data Corporation, 120 Mill Road, Park Ridge, NJ 07656.) Lists 500 manufacturers of pharmaceutical products.

Reference Book of Corporate Management
(Dun & Bradstreet, 3 Sylvan Way, Parsippany, NJ 07054.) National directory of 2,400 companies with at least $20 million in sales listed by name. Also lists biographies of key personnel and directors.

Regional Directory of Minority and Women Owned Business Firms.
(Business Research Services, 2 E. 22nd St., Lombard, IL 60148.) Eastern volume. 22,500 organizations listed, including contact information, minority group, number of employees, description of firm, etc.

Standard Directory of Advertising Agencies
(National Register Publishing Co., 3004 Glenview Road, Wilmette, IL

60091.) The *Red Book* of 4,000 advertising agencies and their 60,000 accounts.

Standard Periodical Directory
(Oxbridge Communications, 150 5th Ave., New York, NY 10011.) Profiles magazines by interest categories. Indexed by subject.

Theatre Directory
(Theatre Communications Group, 355 Lexington Ave., New York, NY 10017.) Lists over 275 resident, non-commercial theatrical companies and 45 related organizations.

Training and Development Organizations Directory
(Gale Research, 835 Penobscot Bldg., Detroit, MI 48226.) 2,300 organizations and their products, courses and training programs are described.

Travel Industry Personnel Directory
(Fairchild Publications, 7 E. 12th St., New York, NY 10003.) Lists air and steamship lines, tour operators, bus lines, hotel representatives, foreign and domestic railroads, foreign and domestic tourist information offices, and travel trade associations.

Who's Who in the Motion Picture Industry and Who's Who in Television
(Packard Publishing Co., 7623 Sunset Blvd., Hollywood, CA 90046.) Names and addresses of hundreds of directors, producers, production companies, and network executives.

Woman's Guide to Career Preparation: Scholarships, Grants and Loans
(Anchor Press, Doubleday Publishing Company, 245 Park Ave., New York, NY 10017, $5.95.) Lists organizations that provide counseling, scholarships, and other assistance to older women and minority women who are returning to work or seeking a career change.

Newspapers

Answering want ads is one of several tasks to be done in any job search, and it's generally among the least productive. According to *Forbes* magazine, only about 10 percent of professional and technical people find their jobs through want ads. Like any other long shot, however, answering want ads sometimes pays off. Be sure to check not only the classified listings but also the larger display ads that appear in the Sunday business sections of major papers. These ads are usually for upper-level jobs.

Help-wanted listings generally come in two varieties: open advertisements and blind ads. An open ad is one in which the company identifies itself and lists an address. Your best bet is not to send a resume to a company that prints an open ad.

Instead, you should try to identify the hiring authority (see Chapter 5) and pull every string you can think of to arrange an interview directly.

The personnel department is in business to screen out applicants. Of the several hundred resumes that an open ad in a major newspaper is likely to attract, the personnel department will prob-

47

ably forward only a handful to the people who are actually doing the hiring. It's better for you to go to those people directly than to try to reach them by sending a piece of paper (your resume) to the personnel department.

Blind ads are run by companies that do not identify themselves because they do not want to acknowledge receipt of resumes. Since you don't know who the companies are, your only option in response to a blind ad is to send a resume. This is among the longest of long shots and usually pays off only if your qualifications are exactly suited to the position that's being advertised. Just remember that if you depend solely on ad responses, you're essentially conducting a passive search, waiting for the mail to arrive or the phone to ring. Passive searchers usually are unemployed a long time.

Newspaper business sections are useful not only for their want ads but also as sources of local business news and news about personnel changes. Learn to read between the lines. If an article announces that Big Bucks, Inc., has just acquired a new vice president, chances are that he or she will be looking for staffers. If the new veep came to Big Bucks from another local company, obviously that company may have at least one vacancy, and possibly several.

MAJOR NEWSPAPER RESOURCES

The New York Times
229 W. 43rd St.
New York, NY 10036
(212) 556-1234
The *New York Times* is well known for its huge Sunday classified ad section. The paper also publishes a business section in its daily and Sunday editions. The *Times* is a highly-respected source of business information and will keep you up to date on all late-breaking news in the business community. In addition to a Manhattan edition, the *Times* also publishes editions for Long Island, Westchester, and New Jersey. The *Sunday Times* also includes in its business section employment opportunities for experienced professionals in a wide range of career fields. The editorial section lists employment opportunities in the fields of education, library, health care, hospital and medical.

The New York Daily News
229 E. 42nd St.
New York, NY 10017
(212) 949-1234
If you're concentrating your job search in Queens, you may have better luck with the *Daily News* than with the *New York Times*. But keep in mind that the *News* rarely runs ads for executive positions. Most of the positions it does list are for positions with companies in Queens. The paper's business section provides only a cursory look at the latest business news. The *News* publishes separate Long Island editions.

Crain's New York Business
Crain Communications
220 E. 42nd St.
New York, NY 10017
(212) 210-0100
Crain's New York Business, published weekly, covers only business news about New York or national news as it affects the New York business community.

The Wall Street Journal
22 Cortlandt St.
New York, NY 10007
(212) 416-2000
The Wall Street Journal is the nation's leading business newspaper. Its classified section usually carries ads for mid- to upper-level management positions. The *Journal* only covers news about the business community—everything from the economy to personnel changes in the country's major corporations. If you want to do your homework on the business community, the *Journal* is the place to start.

National Business Employment Weekly
Box 300
Princeton, NJ 08543
800-JOB-HUNT
This weekly is published by *The Wall Street Journal*. It includes the want-ad sections of the *Journal's* four regional editions, as well as articles and editorials about the business community.

Checking the want ads can pay off

Searching through classified job ads can be tedious and time consuming. But as Elizabeth Kaplan discovered, the classifieds can sometimes help you land the job you want.

"Before I began an intensive job search, I casually read the *Times* classified section each Sunday," says Elizabeth. "I was looking for a position as the assistant to a literary agent. At the time, I was a managing editor for a top New York publisher. In the publishing industry, the usual way to change positions is through networking. So when I noticed an ad in the *Times* one Sunday, I must admit I treated it rather casually.

"As it turned out, the job in the ad was with the Sterling Lord Agency, one of the most prestigious literary agencies in New York. I got the job as assistant to Sterling Lord and am learning the agenting business. Had I not checked the paper each week in addition to laying the groundwork for a networking search, I would have missed a golden opportunity." ■

New York Newsday
235 Pinelawn Road
Melville, NY 11747
(516) 454-2020
Newsday is Long Island's leading newspaper. It covers both
Nassau and Suffolk counties. While the daily business section
provides only a cursory look at the day's business news, the
Sunday business section provides a complete overview. The
classified section covers positions ranging from secretary through
mid- to upper-level management. In addition to the Nassau and
Suffolk editions, the paper also publishes a Queens edition with
job ads for that area.

The New York Post
210 South St.
New York, NY 10002
(212) 815-8000
The *New York Post* started a Sunday edition in 1989, which
includes employment section. The paper lists all level jobs and
provides coverage of the New York business scene. The *Post's*
recent financial condition has been shaky.

Amsterdam News
2340 Frederick Douglas Blvd.
New York, NY 10027
(212) 932-7400
The Amsterdam News is a weekly newspaper for the black community with employment opportunities.

Westchester Rockland Newspapers
1 Gannett Drive
White Plains, NY 10604
(914) 694-9300
The Westchester Rockland Newspapers chain consists of ten daily
newspapers and two weekly newspapers, eight of which are
published in Westchester. Each daily includes community news
as well as county and national news. The largest and most
complete classified ad section is found in *The White Plains Reporter Dispatch*. Many of these ads are repeated in local editions.
The following newspapers are part of this chain:

> Bronxville Review Press
> Fair Press-Connecticut
> The Mamaroneck Daily Times
> The Mt.Vernon Daily Argus
> The New Rochelle Standard-Star
> The Nyack Journal News (Rockland County)
> The Ossining Citizen Register
> The Peekskill Star
> The Portchester Daily Item
> The Tarrytown Daily News

The White Plains Reporter Dispatch
The Yonkers Herald Statesman

General Business Magazines

The smart job seeker will want to keep abreast of changing trends in the economy. These periodicals will help you keep up with the national business scene.

Barron's Magazine
420 Lexington Ave., Suite 2540
New York, NY 10170

Business Week
1221 Avenue of the Americas
New York, NY 10020
(212) 997-1221
Weekly.

Forbes
60 5th Ave.
New York, NY 10011
(212) 620-2200
Bi-weekly.

Fortune
1271 Avenue of the Americas
New York, NY 10020
(212) 522-1212
Published 26 times per year.

Inc.
488 Madison Ave.
New York, NY 10022
(212) 326-2600
The magazine for growing companies.

Money
Time Life Building
1271 Avenue of the Americas
New York, NY 10020
(212) 522-1212
Monthly.

Newsweek
444 Madison Ave.
New York, NY 10022
(212) 350-4000
Weekly.

Time Magazine
1271 Avenue of the Americas

New York, NY 10022
(212) 586-1212
Weekly.

Working Woman
209 Park Ave.
New York, NY 10169
(212) 551-9500
Monthly.

Worth
575 Lexington Ave.
New York, NY 10022
(212) 223-3100
Personal finances.

Trade and Special Interest Magazines

Almost every industry or service business has a trade magazine that covers specialized topics not found in general interest publications. You can approach a job interview better prepared by reading up on the latest developments in your field. Also, some trade magazines carry help-wanted sections and announcements of employee transfers and promotions, indicating potential job openings.

Trade magazines are usually expensive and available by subscription only. Many of the magazines listed below are available in the New York public libraries. For publications not found there, call the magazine's editorial or sales office and ask if you can look at the latest issue.

The following magazines have editorial offices in the New York area. In some industries, knowing about inside news as it happens can make the difference in a job interview. For a complete listing of the trade press, consult the *Gale Directory of Publications and Broadcast Media*, the "Business Publications" volume of *Standard Rate and Data Service*, and the *Standard Periodical Directory*.

TRADE MAGAZINES

ABA Banking Journal
345 Hudson St.
New York, NY 10014
(212) 620-7200
Monthly.

Advertising Age
(Crain's International Newspaper
of Marketing)
220 E. 42nd St.
New York, NY 10017
(212) 210-0725
Weekly.

Adweek/East
49 E. 21st St.
New York, NY 10010
(212) 995-7323
Weekly.

American Artist
1515 Broadway
New York, NY 10036
(212) 764-7300
Monthly.

American Banker
1 State St. Plaza
New York, NY 10004
(212) 943-6700
Daily.

American Bookseller
560 White Plains Road
Tarrytown, NY 10591
(914) 524-9200
Monthly.

American Funeral Director
1501 Broadway
New York, NY 10036
(212) 398-9266
Monthly.

**American Jewelry
Manufacturer**
827 7th Ave.
New York, NY 10019
(212) 245-7555
Monthly.

American Journal of Nursing
555 W. 57th St.
New York, NY 10019
(212) 582-8820
Monthly.

American Lawyer
600 3rd Ave.
New York, NY 10016
(212) 973-2800
10 issues per year.

American Photographer
1515 Broadway
New York, NY 10036
(212) 975-7911
Monthly.

American Salons
270 Madison Ave.
New York, NY 10016
(212) 951-6600
Monthly. Beauty and hair supply.

Apparel Merchandising
425 Park Ave.
New York, NY 10022
(212) 371-9400
Monthly.

Architectural Record
1221 Avenue of the Americas
New York, NY 10020
(212) 512-4686
Monthly.

Area Development
400 Post Ave.
Westbury, NY 11590
(516) 338-0900
Monthly. Industrial development.

Art Direction
10 E. 39th St.
New York, NY 10016
(212) 889-6500
Monthly.

**Aviation Week and Space
Technology**
1221 Avenue of the Americas
New York, NY 10020
(212) 512-2294
Weekly.

Back Stage
330 W. 42nd St.
New York, NY 10036
(212) 947-0020
Weekly.

Bankers Magazine
One Penn Plaza
New York, NY 10019
(212) 971-5226
Bi-monthly.

Barron's National
Business and Financial Weekly
200 Liberty St.
New York, NY 10281
(212) 416-2700
Weekly.

Beauty Fashion
530 5th Ave.
New York, NY 10036
(212) 687-6190
Published 10 times per year.

Beverage Media
100 Avenue of the Americas
New York, NY 10013
(212) 620-0100
Monthly.

Billboard
1515 Broadway
New York, NY 10036
(212) 764-7300
Weekly.

**Business and Incentive
Strategies**
1515 Broadway
New York, NY 10036
(212) 869-1300
Monthly.

Cablevision
827 7th Ave.
New York, NY 10019
(212) 887-8400
Bi-weekly.

Chain Store Age
425 Park Ave.
New York, NY 10022
(212) 756-5000
Monthly.

Chemical Week
888 7th Ave.
New York, NY 10019
(212) 621-4900
Weekly.

Chief Civil Service Leader
150 Nassau St.
New York, NY 10038
(212) 962-2690
Weekly. Federal and state civil
service.

Civil Engineering
345 E. 47th St.
New York, NY 10017
(212) 705-7463
Monthly.

CPA Journal
200 Park Ave.
New York, NY 10166
(212) 973-8300
Monthly.

Daily News Record
7 W. 34th St.
New York, NY 10003
(212) 630-4000
Daily. Men's fashions.

Data Communications
1221 Avenue of the Americas
New York, NY 10020
(212) 512-2699
Monthly.

D & B Reports Magazine
Dun and Bradstreet
299 Park Ave.
New York, NY 10171
(212) 593-6723
Bi-monthly. Small business
management.

Direct Marketing
224 7th St.
Garden City, NY 11530
(516) 746-6700
Monthly.

Discount Store News
425 Park Ave.
New York, NY 10022
(212) 756-5000

Drug Store News
425 Park Ave.
New York, NY 10022
(212) 371-9400
Bi-weekly.

Editor and Publisher
11 W. 19th St.
New York, NY 10011
(212) 675-4380
Weekly.

Electrical World
11 W. 19th St.
New York, NY 10011
(212) 337-4072
Monthly.

Electronic News
7 E. 12th St.
New York, NY 10016
(212) 741-4320
Weekly.

Engineering News-Record
1221 Avenue of the Americas
New York, NY 10020
(212) 512-2000
Weekly.

Entertainment Weekly
1675 Broadway
New York, NY 10019
(212) 522-4158
Weekly.

The Exporter
34 W. 37th St.
New York, NY 10018
(212) 563-2772
Monthly.

Facilities Design and Management
1515 Broadway
New York, NY 10036
(212) 869-1300
Monthly.

Financial Executive
Box 1938
Morristown, NJ 07960
(201) 898-4600
Bi-monthly.

Financial World
1328 Broadway
New York, NY 10001
(212) 594-5030
Semi-monthly.

Food and Beverage Marketing
505 8th Ave.
New York, NY 10018
(212) 695-0704
Monthly.

Food and Wine Magazine
1120 Avenue of the Americas
New York, NY 10036
(212) 382-5600
Monthly.

Fund Raising Management
224 7th St.
Garden City, NY 11530
(516) 746-6700
Monthly.

Fur Age Weekly
Box 868
Glenwood Landing, NY 11547
(516) 676-2918
Weekly.

Graphic Arts Monthly
249 W. 17th St.
New York, NY 10011
(212) 463-6834
Monthly.

Hotel and Resort Management
488 Madison Ave.
New York, NY 10022
(212) 888-1500
Monthly.

Industrial Equipment News
5 Penn Plaza
New York, NY 10001
(212) 695-1521
Monthly.

Institutional Investor
488 Madison Ave.
New York, NY 10022
(212) 303-3300
Monthly.

Insurance Advocate
P.O. Box 9001
Mt. Vernon, NY 10552
(212) 233-3768
Weekly.

International Business
500 Mamaroneck Ave.
Harrison, NY 10528
(914) 381-7700
Monthly.

Intimate Fashion News
309 5th Ave.
New York, NY 10012
(212) 679-6677
Bi-weekly.

Investment Dealer's Digest
2 World Trade Center
New York, NY 10048
(212) 227-1200
Weekly.

Knitting Times
386 Park Ave. S.
New York, NY 10016
(212) 683-7520
Monthly.

Library Journal Magazine
249 W. 17 St.
New York, NY 10011
(212) 463-6819
Semi-monthly.

Management Accounting
10 Paragon Drive
Montvale, NJ 07645
(201) 573-9000
Monthly.

Mechanical Engineering
345 E. 47th St.
New York, NY 10017
(212) 705-7782
Monthly.

Media Industry News
145 E. 49th St.
New York, NY 10017
(212) 751-2670
Weekly.

Metals Week
1221 Avenue of the Americas
New York, NY 10020
(212) 997-2823
Monthly.

MIS Week
7 E. 12th St.
New York, NY 10003
(212) 741-4000
Weekly.

New Accountant
36 Railroad Ave.
Glenhead, NY 11545
(516) 759-3484

New York Apparel News
110 E. 9th St.
Los Angeles, CA 90079
(213) 627-3737
Published 5 times per year.

New York Construction News
135 E. 65th St.
New York, NY 10021
(212) 472-6000
Weekly.

News Inc.
49 E. 21st St.
New York, NY 10010
(212) 979-4600
Monthly. Covers newspaper
business.

Opera News
Metropolitan Opera Guild
70 Lincoln Center Plaza
New York, NY 10023
(212) 769-7080
Published 17 times per year.

PC Magazine
Ziff-Davis Publishing
One Park Ave.
New York, NY 10016
(212) 503-5155
Bi-weekly.

Photo Business
1515 Broadway
New York, NY 10036
(212) 536-5193
Monthly.

Poet and Writers Magazine
72 Spring St.
New York, NY 10012
(212) 226-3586

Practical Accountant
1 Penn Plaza
New York, NY 10119
(212) 971-5556
Monthly.

Printing News/East
245 W. 17th St.
New York, NY 10011
(212) 463-6730
Weekly. Graphic art.

Publishers Weekly
249 W. 17th St.
New York, NY 10011
(212) 463-6758
Weekly. Books trade news.

Real Estate Weekly
One Madison Ave.
New York, NY 10010
(212) 679-1234
Weekly.

Risk Management
205 E. 42nd St.
New York, NY 10017
(212) 286-9364
Monthly.

Sales Executive
13 E. 37th St.
New York, NY 10016
(212) 683-9755
Bi-monthly.

Sales and Marketing Management
633 3rd Ave.
New York, NY 10017
(212) 986-2250
Published 15 times per year.

School and Library Journal
249 W. 17th St.
New York, NY 10017
(212) 463-6759
Monthly.

Sporting Goods Dealer
2 Park Ave.
New York, NY 10016
(212) 779-5556
Monthly.

Sportstyle
7 E. 12th St.
New York, NY 10003
(212) 741-4000
Published 20 times per year.

Stock Market Magazine
16 School St.
Yonkers, NY 10701
(914) 423-4566
Monthly.

Theater Week
28 W. 25th St.
New York, NY 10010
(212) 627-2120
Weekly.

Travel Agent
802 2nd Ave.
New York, NY 10017
(212) 370-5050
Bi-weekly.

TV News
80 8th Ave.
New York, NY 10011
(212) 243-6800
Weekly.

Variety
475 Park Ave. S.
New York, NY 10016
(212) 779-1100
Weekly.

Wall Street Journal
Magazine of Personal
Business
224 W. 57th St.
New York, NY
(212) 649-3751
Monthly.

Wall Street and Technology
1515 Broadway
New York, NY 10036
(212) 869-1300
Monthly.

Wall Street Transcript
99 Wall St.
New York, NY 10005
(212) 747-9500
Weekly.

Westchester Commerce
222 Mamaroneck Ave.
White Plains, NY 10605
(914) 948-2110
Bi-monthly

Women's Wear Daily
7 W. 34th St.
New York, NY 10003
(212) 630-4000
Daily.

Local Feature Magazines and Newspapers

In your job search you'll find it helpful to know as much about the New York area as possible. The following periodicals do not necessarily cover local business news, but they are valuable sources of information on the New York community. Reading these publications will help you to become a well-informed New Yorker.

Brooklyn Heights Press
129 Montague St.
Brooklyn, NY 11201
(718) 624-0536
Weekly.

Connecticut Magazine
789 Reservoir Ave.
Bridgeport, CT 06606
(203) 374-3388
Monthly.

Manhattan
330 W. 56th St.
New York, NY 10019
(212) 265-7970
Monthly.

The New Yorker
25 W. 43rd St.
New York, NY 10036
(212) 840-3800
Weekly.

New York Magazine
755 2nd Ave.
New York, NY 10017
(212) 880-0700
Weekly.

Spotlight Magazine
126 Library Lane
Mamaroneck, NY 10543
(914) 381-4740
Monthly.
Six regional editions: Southern Westchester, Mid Westchester, Long
Island, Connecticut, Manhattan, New Jersey Rockland.

Staten Island Advance
950 Fingerboard Road
Staten Island, NY 10305
(718) 981-1234
Daily.

The Village Voice
842 Broadway
New York, NY 10003
(212) 475-3300
Weekly.

**Job
opportunities
for blacks**

Black Employment and Education magazine lists career opportunities nationwide. They'll even place your resume on their database for employer access. The publisher, S. Barry Hamdani, offers two tips to business management career seekers:

"Before the interview, make sure you know more about the company than the interviewer—research the firm. Second, be sure several key people within the organization already know your qualifications; you'll need all the inside influence you can get." If you need help, call the magazine:

Black Employment & Education
2625 Piedmont Road 56-282
Atlanta, GA 30324
(404) 469-5891 ■

Developing a Strategy:
The ABCs of Networking

The successful job search doesn't happen by accident. It's the result of careful planning. Before you rush out to set up your first interview, it's important to establish a strategy, that is, to develop a plan for researching the job market and contacting potential employers.

This chapter and Chapter 7 will cover specific techniques and tools that you'll find useful in your search. But before we get to them, a few words are in order about your overall approach.

It's Going to Take Some Time

Looking for a new job is no easy task. It's as difficult and time-consuming for a bright young woman with a brand-new MBA as it is for a fifty-year-old executive with years of front-line experience. Every once in a while someone lucks out. But most people should plan on two to six months of full-time job hunting before they find a position they'll really be happy with.

According to *Forbes* magazine, the older you are and the more you earn, the longer it will take to find what you're looking for—in fact, up to six months for people over 40 earning more than $50,000. People under 40 in the $20,000-$50,000 bracket average two to four months.

Your line of work will also affect the length of your search. Usually, the easier it is to demonstrate tangible, bottom-line results, the faster you can line up a job. Lawyers, public relations people, and advertising executives are harder to place than accountants and sales people, according to one top personnel specialist.

Be Good to Yourself

Whether or not you're currently employed, it's important to nurture your ego when you're looking for a new job. Rejection rears its ugly head more often in a job search than at most other times, and self-doubt can be deadly.

Make sure you get regular exercise during your job search to relieve stress. You'll sleep better, feel better, and perhaps even lose a few pounds.

Take care of your diet and watch what you drink. Many people who start to feel sorry for themselves tend to overindulge in food or alcohol. Valium and other such drugs are not as helpful as sharing your progress with your family or a couple of close friends.

Beef up your wardrobe so that you look and feel good during your employment interviews. There's no need to buy an expensive new suit, especially if you're on an austerity budget, but a new shirt, blouse, tie, pair of shoes, or hairstyle may be in order.

Maintain a positive outlook. Unemployment is not the end of the world; few people complete a career without losing a job at least once. Keep a sense of humor, too. Every job search has its funny moments. It's OK to joke about your situation and share your sense of humor with your friends and family.

Life goes on despite your job search. Your spouse and kids still need your attention. Try not to take out your anxieties, frustrations, and fears on those close to you. At the very time you need support and affirmation, your friends may feel that they should stay at arm's length. You can relieve their embarrassment by being straightforward about your situation and by telling them how they can help you.

Tax deductible job-hunting expenses

A certified public accountant offers the following tips on deducting job-hunting expenses on the income tax form. To qualify for certain deductions, you must hunt for a job in the same field you just left or in the field that currently employs you. For example, someone who has worked as a public school teacher could not deduct the cost of getting a real estate license and seeking a broker's job.

If you are unemployed or want to switch jobs, expenses can be deducted on the Income Tax Statement of Employee Business Expenses or itemized on Schedule A of Form 1040 regardless of whether or not employment is secured. Expenses you might be able to deduct include preparing, printing, and mailing resumes; vocational guidance counseling and testing; travel and transportation expenses. Telephone, postage, and newspaper expenses may also be deductible. While seeking work out of town, additional deductions might be allowed for transportation, food, and lodging. ■

Put Yourself on a Schedule

Looking for work is a job in itself. Establish a schedule for your job search and stick to it. If you're unemployed, work at getting a new job full-time—from 8:30 a.m. to 5:30 p.m. five days a week, and from 9 a.m. to 12 noon on Saturdays. During a job search, there is a temptation to use "extra" time for recreation or to catch up on household tasks. Arranging two or three exploratory interviews will prove a lot more useful to you than washing the car or cleaning out the garage. You can do such tasks at night or on Sundays, just as you would if you were working.

Don't take a vacation during your search. Do it after you accept an offer and before you begin a new job. You might be tempted to "sort things out on the beach." But taking a vacation when you're unemployed isn't as restful as it sounds. You'll spend most of your time worrying about what will happen when the trip is over.

Even if you're currently employed, it's important to establish regular hours for your job search. If you're scheduling interviews, try to arrange several for one day so that you don't have to take too much time away from your job. You might also arrange interviews for your lunch hour. You can make phone calls during lunch or on your break time. You'd also be surprised at how many people you can reach before and after regular working hours.

Watch Your Expenses

Spend what you have to spend for such basic needs as food, transportation, and housing. But watch major expenditures that could be delayed or not made at all. The kids will still need new shoes, but a $200 dinner party at a fancy place could just as well be changed to sandwiches and beer at home.

Keep track of all expenses that you incur in your job search, such as telephone and printing bills, postage, newspapers, parking, transportation, tolls, and meals purchased during the course of interviewing. These may all be tax deductible.

Networking Is the Key to a Successful Job Search

The basic tasks of a job search are fairly simple. Once you've figured out what kind of work you want to do, you need to know which companies might have such jobs and then make contact with the *hiring authority*. These tasks are also known as researching the job market and generating leads and interviews. *Networking*, or developing your personal contacts, is a great technique for finding out about market and industrial trends and is unsurpassed as a way to generate leads and interviews.

Networking is nothing more than asking the people you already know to help you find out about the job market and meet the people who are actually doing the hiring. Each adult you know has access to at least 30 people you do not know. Of course, a lot of them will not be able to do much in the way of helping you find a job. But if you start with, say, 20 or 30 people, and each of them tells you about 3 other people who may be able to help you, you've built a network of 60 to 90 contacts.

Mark S. Granovetter, a Harvard sociologist, reported to *Forbes* magazine that "informal contacts" account for almost 75 percent of all successful job searches. Agencies find about 9 percent of new jobs for professional and technical people, and ads yield another 10 percent or so.

How to Start

To begin the networking process, draw up a list of all the possible contacts who can help you gain access to someone who can hire you for the job you want. Naturally, the first sources, the ones at the top of your list, will be people you know personally: friends, colleagues, former clients, relatives, acquaintances, customers, and club and church members. Just about everyone you know, whether or not he or she is employed, can generate contacts for you.

Don't forget to talk with your banker, lawyer, insurance agent, dentist, and other people who provide you with services. It is the nature of their business to know a lot of people who might help you in your search. Leave no stone unturned in your search for contacts. Go through your Christmas card list, alumni club list, and any other list you can think of.

On the average, it may take 10 to 15 contacts to generate one formal interview. It may take 5 or 10 of these formal interviews to generate 1 solid offer. And it may take several offers before you uncover the exact job situation you've been seeking. You may have to talk to several hundred people before you get the job you want.

Don't balk at talking to friends, acquaintances, and neighbors about your job search. In reality, you're asking for advice, not charity. Most of the people you'll contact will be willing to help you, if only you tell them *how*.

Here's an example of a networking letter

Box 7457
Pace University
New York, NY 11550
April 11, 1994

Dr. Norman Hartman, President
Combined Opinion Research
200 Madison Ave., Suite 500
New York, NY 10008

Dear Dr. Hartman:

Dr. Carol Hernandez, with whom I have studied these past two years, suggested that you might be able to advise me of opportunities in the field of social and political research in the New York area.

I am about to graduate from Pace University with a B.A. in American History, and I am a member of Phi Beta Kappa. For two of the last three summers, I have worked in the public sector as an intern with Citizens for a Better Government in New York and with Senator Claghorn in Washington. Last summer I worked as a desk assistant at *Newsweek's* New York office.

I am eager to begin to work and would appreciate a few minutes of your time to discuss employment possibilities in the field of social and political research. I will be finished with exams on May 24 and would like to arrange a meeting with you shortly thereafter.

I look forward to hearing from you, and in any case I will be in touch with your office next week.

Sincerely,

Carlos Ponti
(212) 555-2636 ■

The Exploratory Interview

If I introduce you to my friend George at a major New York bank, he will get together with you as a favor to me. When you have your meeting with him, you will make a presentation about what you've done in your work, what you want to do, and you will ask for his advice, ideas, and opinions. That is an exploratory interview. As is true of any employment interview, you must make a successful sales presentation to get what you want. You must convince George that you are a winner and that you deserve his help in your search.

You've already got lots of contacts!

Networking paid off for Liz, a young woman eager to make her way in banking or a related industry. She told us why she's glad she took the time to talk with her friends and neighbors about her job search.

"I was having dinner with close friends and telling them about my job search," says Liz. "During the conversation, they mentioned a banker friend they thought might be hiring. As it turned out, the friend didn't have a job for me. But he suggested I come in, meet with him, and discuss some other possibilities. He put me in touch with an independent marketing firm servicing the publishing industry. The owner of the firm was looking for someone with my exact qualifications. One thing led to another, and pretty soon I had landed exactly the position I wanted." ■

The help the interviewer provides is usually in the form of suggestions to meet new people or contact certain companies. I introduce you to George. Following your successful meeting, he introduces you to Tom, Dick, and Mary. Each of them provides additional leads. In this way, you spend most of your time interviewing, not staying at home waiting for the phone to ring or the mail to arrive.

A job doesn't have to be vacant in order for you to have a successful meeting with a hiring authority. If you convince an employer that you would make a good addition to his or her staff, the employer might create a job for you where none existed before. In this way, networking taps the "hidden job market."

To make the most of the networking technique, continually brush up on your interviewing skills (we've provided a refresher course in Chapter 7). Remember, even when you're talking with an old friend, you are still conducting an exploratory interview. Don't treat it as casual conversation.

Developing Professional Contacts

Friends and acquaintances are the obvious first choice when you're drawing up a list of contacts. But don't forget professional and trade organizations, clubs, and societies—they are valuable sources of contacts, leads, and information. In certain cases, it isn't necessary for you to belong in order to attend a meeting or an annual or monthly lunch, dinner, or cocktail party.

Executive networking

The higher your rung on the corporate ladder, the greater the chances that networking with executives outside your own field will pay off. If you're looking for a top spot in electronics, don't pass up a chance to discuss your credentials and employment needs with the recruiting executive of an advertising firm. He or she just might have the hidden connection that could land you a great job.

One hiring exec from a large corporation reports: "I network with recruiters from more industries than most people would think, both industries that are related to ours and those that are not. It helps to find out what talent is available. If one of my contacts has someone in a file he doesn't need and I do, he's happy to tell me about that person. And I work the same way." ■

Many such groups also publish newsletters, another valuable source of information on the job market and industry trends. Some professional associations offer placement services to members, in which case it may be worth your while to join officially. At the end of this chapter, we've provided a list of selected organizations that might prove useful for networking purposes.

Your college's alumni office and career office are also helpful places to make and maintain contacts. These offices serve alumni at all career stages and coordinate events that facilitate networking opportunities.

Keep Yourself Organized

The most difficult part of any job search is getting started. A pocket calendar or engagement diary that divides each work day into hourly segments will come in handy.

You will also want to keep a personal log of calls and contacts. You may want to develop a format that's different from the one shown here. Fine. The point is to keep a written record of every person you contact in your job search and the results of each contact.

Your log (it can be a notebook from the drug store) will help keep you from getting confused and losing track of the details of your search. If you call someone who's out of town until Tuesday, your log can flag this call so it won't fall between the cracks. Your log may also come in handy for future job searches.

Your log's "disposition" column can act as a reminder of additional sources of help you'll want to investigate. You'll also have a means of timing the correspondence that should follow any interview.

CALLS AND CONTACTS

Date	Name & Title	Company	Phone	Disposition
2/10	J. Booth, V.P. Sales	Atlas Corp.	(718)277-5500	Interview 2/15
2/10	E. Franklin Sales Manager	Worldwide	466-0303	Out of town until 2/17
2/10	L. Duffy Dir. Marketing	Global Inc.	826-6112	Out of office. Call in aft.
2/10	A. Atkinson Sls. Dir.	Oceans Ent.	386-9100	Busy to 2/28 Call then.
2/10	S. Stanton Mktg. & Sales	Asian Co.	(914)338-1055	Call after 2

If you're unemployed and job hunting full time, schedule yourself for three exploratory interviews a day for the first week. Each of these meetings should result in at least three subsequent leads. Leave the second week open for the appointments you generated during the first. Maintain this pattern as you go along in your search.

We can't emphasize too strongly the importance of putting yourself on a job-searching schedule, whether or not you're currently employed. A schedule shouldn't function as a straitjacket, but it ought to serve as a way of organizing your efforts for greatest efficiency. Much of your job-hunting time will be devoted to developing your network of contacts. But you should also set aside a certain portion of each week for doing your homework on companies that interest you (see Chapter 4) and for pursuing other means of contacting employers (we'll get to these in a minute).

As you go through your contacts and begin to research the job market, you'll begin to identify certain employers in which you're interested. Keep a list of them. For each one that looks particularly promising, begin a file that contains articles about the company, its annual report, product brochures, personnel policy, and the like. Every so often, check your "potential employer" list against your log to make sure that you're contacting the companies that interest you most.

Go for the Hiring Authority

The object of your job search is to convince the person who has the power to hire you that you ought to be working for him or her. The person you want to talk to is not necessarily the president of the company. It's the person who heads the department that could use your expertise. If you're a salesperson, you probably want to talk with the vice president of sales or marketing. If you're in data processing, the vice president of operations is the person you need to see.

How do you find the hiring authority? If you're lucky, someone you know personally will tell you whom to see and introduce you. Otherwise, you'll have to do some homework. Some of the directories listed in Chapter 4 will name department heads for major companies in the New York area. If you cannot otherwise find out who heads the exact department that interests you, call the company and ask the operator. (It's a good idea to do this anyway, since directories go out of date as soon as a department head leaves a job.)

Use an introduction wherever possible when first approaching a company—that's what networking is all about. For those companies that you must approach "cold," use the phone to arrange a meeting with the hiring authority beforehand. Don't assume you can drop in and see a busy executive without an appointment. And don't assume you can get to the hiring authority through the personnel department. If at all possible, you don't want to fill out any personnel forms until you have had a serious interview. The same goes for sending resumes (see Chapter 3). In general, resumes are better left behind, after an interview, than sent ahead to generate a meeting.

Telephone Tactics

Cold calls are difficult for most job seekers. Frequently, a receptionist or secretary, sometimes both, stands between you and the hiring authority you want to reach. One way around this is to call about a half-hour after closing. There's a good chance that the secretary will be gone, and the boss will still be finishing up the XYZ project report. Only now there will be no one to run interference for him or her.

Generally, you're going to have to go through a support staffer, so the first rule is to act courteously and accord him or her the same professional respect you'd like to be accorded yourself. This person is not just a secretary. Often, part of his or her job is to keep unsolicited job hunters out of the boss's hair. You want this intermediary to be your ally, not your adversary. If possible, sell what a wonderfully qualified person you are and how it is to the company's advantage to have you aboard.

If you're not put through to the hiring authority, don't leave your name and expect a return call. Instead, ask when there's a convenient time you might call back. Or allow yourself to be put on hold. You can read job-search literature or compose cover letters while you wait. Be sure to keep your target's name and title and the purpose of your call on a card before you, however. You don't want to be at a loss for words when you're finally put through.

Other Tactics for Contacting Employers

Direct contact with the hiring authority—either through a third-party introduction (networking) or by calling for an appointment directly—is far and away the most effective job-hunting method. Your strategy and schedule should reflect that fact, and most of your energy should be devoted to direct contact. It's human nature, however, not to put all your eggs in one basket. You may want to explore other methods of contacting potential employers, but these should take up no more than a quarter of your job-hunting time.

68

Calling or writing to personnel offices may occasionally be productive, especially when you know that a company is looking for someone with your particular skills. But personnel people, by the nature of their responsibility, tend to screen out rather than welcome newcomers to the company fold. You're always better off going directly to the hiring authority.

Meetings are for meeting people

Laid off during a real estate slump, one enterprising 42-year-old escrow officer decided she would keep her finances flourishing by doing something she enjoyed—gardening. After a few phone calls to friends and former business associates, her newly formed Landscape Redecorating Service was in full bloom. At the same time, she attended every possible escrow association meeting, dinner, and other professional event.

"I set a goal," she recalls, "to contact at least three escrow company executives at each meeting, to let them know I was looking and available. Then I'd drop them a note to give them my phone number in case they wanted to get in touch right away."

About two months after her first dinner meeting, an officer from one of the larger title companies called her for an interview. "He couldn't get me working on that desk fast enough," she remembers. "The $15 I'd spent on that dinner ticket was the best investment I ever made." ■

Consider the case of a company that runs an ad in *The Wall Street Journal*. The ad may bring as many as 600 responses. The head of personnel asks one of the secretaries to separate the resumes into three piles according to experience: "under 3 years," "3-5 years," and "over 5 years." The personnel chief automatically eliminates two of the three stacks. He or she then flips through the third and eliminates all but, say, eight resumes. The personnel specialist will call the eight applicants, screen them over the phone, and invite three for a preliminary interview. Of those three, two will be sent to the hiring authority for interviews. That means that 598 applicants never even got a chance to make their case.

Statistically, fewer than one out of four job hunters succeed by going to personnel departments, responding to ads (either open or blind, as described in Chapter 4), or using various employment services. Some do find meaningful work this way, however. We repeat, if you decide to use a method other than networking or direct contact, don't spend more than 25 percent of your job-hunting time on it.

As you might expect, many books have been written on job-hunting strategy and techniques. Here is a list of selected resources.

SELECTED BOOKS ON JOB-HUNTING STRATEGY

(See also Chapter 2 for a list of career-strategy books)

Bolles, Richard N. *The Three Boxes of Life and How to Get Out of Them.* Berkeley, CA: Ten Speed Press, 1983.

Bolles, Richard N. *What Color Is Your Parachute?* Berkeley, CA: Ten Speed Press, annual updates.

Camden, Thomas M. *The Job Hunter's Final Exam.* Chicago: Surrey Books, 1990.

Davidson, Jeffrey P. *Blow Your Own Horn: How To Market Yourself and Your Career.* New York: American Management Association, 1987.

Figler, Howard. *The Complete Job Search Handbook.* New York: H. Holt & Co., 1988.

Fowler, Julianne. *How to Get the Job You Want in Tough Times.* Los Angeles: Lowell House, 1991.

Half, Robert. *How To Get a Better Job in This Crazy World.* New York: Crown, 1990.

Harkavy, Michael. *101 Careers: A Guide to the Fastest Growing Opportunities.* New York: John Wiley & Sons, 1990.

Kalt, Meil C., Ph.D., and William B. Helmreich, Ph.D. *Flight Path: How to Get the Job That Launches Your Career After College.* Saint Louis, MO, 1989.

Kisiel, Dr. Marie. *Design for a Change—A Guide to New Careers.* New York: Franklin Watts, 1980.

Kleiman, Carol. *Women's Networks.* New York: Ballantine, 1981.

Krannich, Ronald, and Caryl R. *Network Your Way to Job & Career Success: Your Complete Guide to Creating New Opportunities.* Manassas, VA: Impact, 1989.

Leeds, Dorothy. *Marketing Yourself: The Ultimate Job Seeker's Guide.* New York: Harper, Collins, 1991.

Lott, Catherine, and Lott, Oscar. *How to Land a Better Job.* Lincolnwood, IL: National Textbook Co., 1989.

Mast, Jennifer Arnold. *The Job Seekers Guide to the 1000 Top Employers.* Detroit: Visible Ink, 1993.

Petras, Kathryn and Ross. *Jobs'93.* New York: Simon & Schuster, 1993.

Rust, H. L. *Job Search: The Complete Manual for Job Seekers.* New York: Amacom, 1991.

Wallace, Phyllis Ann. *MBAs on the Fast Track.* New York: Ballinger, 1989.

Wendleton, Kate. *Through the Brick Wall.* New York: Villard Books, 1992.

There follows a selected list of organized groups ready-made for networking. Pick those that best fit into your career game plan, and work through them in search of the job you want.

SELECTED NEW YORK AREA PROFESSIONAL ORGANIZATIONS, TRADE GROUPS, NETWORKS, CLUBS, AND SOCIETIES

Advertising Club of New York
235 Park Ave. S., 6th Floor
New York, NY 10003
(212) 533-8080
Contact: Elaine Schacter
Members are professionals in advertising, publishing, marketing, and business. Holds semi-annual meetings. Four times a year, publishes a

newsletter that contains job listings and news of personnel changes in the industry. Offers educational seminars and workshops, social events, and public service campaigns. Salutes creative/communication excellence annually through the ANDY awards.

The Advertising Council
261 Madison Ave.
New York, NY 10016-2303
(212) 922-1500
President: Ruth A. Wooden
Creates national public service advertising campaigns. Publishes bi-monthly advertising bulletin as well as many educational materials. Holds annual meetings.

Advertising Women of New York
153 E. 57th St.
New York, NY 10022
(212) 593-1950
Executive Director: Nancy Megan
Organization of women whose members are executives in the communications industry: advertising, marketing, merchandising, research, promotion, public relations, and the media. Offers seminars and luncheon programs. Holds support sessions twice a month for members and acts as a job search clearinghouse. Sponsors annual career conference for professionals and students; awards scholarships and runs public service programs.

American Association of Advertising Agencies
666 3rd Ave.
New York, NY 10017
(212) 682-2500
President: John O'Toole
Organization of advertising agencies. The association acts as an information clearinghouse. Gathers statistics and conducts surveys on public relations, media, and related subjects. Operates a secondary research library, containing information on the advertising industry.

American Association of Exporters and Importers
11 W. 42nd St.
New York, NY 10036
(212) 944-2230
President: Eugene J. Milosh
Organization of U.S. exporters and importers. Members are customs brokers, freight forwarders, trading companies, banks, attorneys, insurance firms, and manufacturers. Conducts seminars and workshops. Publishes weekly trade alert and special information bulletins.

American Association of Retired Persons
919 3rd Ave.
New York, NY 10022
(212) 758-1411
Aims to promote independence and enhance the quality of life for persons aged 50 and older. Offers consumer aid, employment service, tax information; life, health, and auto insurance plans. Referrals to local groups for above services as well as for vocational training.

American Association of University Women
111 E. 37th St.

New York, NY 10016
(212) 684-6068
Contact: Anne Velesaris
National organization for women college graduates. Advocacy action and
research. Publishes monthly newsletter with job listings.

American Book Producers Association
160 5th Ave., Suite 604
New York, NY 10010-7000
(212) 645-2368
President: Stephen Eltlinger
Association of book production houses. Publishes semi-annual newsletter
and annual directory; holds monthly meetings.

American Booksellers Association
560 White Plains Road
Tarrytown, NY 10591
(914) 631-7800
National association of retail booksellers. Publishes weekly newswire
and monthly magazine. Annual convention is one of the most important
events of the publishing year. Also runs a booksellers' school.

American Cloak and Suit Manufacturers Assn.
450 7th Ave.
New York, NY 10123
(212) 244-7300
Contact: Peter Conticelli
Organization of contractors producing women's coats and suits for
wholesalers and other manufacturers.

American Federation of Arts
41 E. 65th St.
New York, NY 10021
(212) 988-7700

American Federation of School Administrators
110 E. 42nd St.
New York, NY 10017
Contact: Ted Elsberg
Membership includes school principals, vice principals, directors,
superintendents, and other administrators. Publishes newsletter 7 times
a year.

American Finance Association
44 W. 4th St., Suite 9-190
New York, NY 10012
(212) 285-6000
Exec. Secretary/Treasurer: Mike Keenan
Research organization consisting of professors in universities and
financial economists, bankers, treasurers, analysts, and others in
finance. Includes individual and corporate members. Publishes journal 5
times a year.

American Fur Industry
363 7th Ave.
New York, NY 10001
(212) 564-5133
Executive Vice Pres.: Sandy Blye

Association of fur manufacturers and retailers. Operates consumer hotline. Publishes various booklets and quarterly newsletter. Holds meetings at least twice a year.

American Fur Merchants' Association
101 W. 30th St.
New York, NY 10001
(212) 736-9200
Contact: Dorothy Banculli
Local association of fur merchants dealing in raw materials; brokers, silk and supply houses, banks, auction companies, wholesalers, and fur importers and exporters. Performs financial services for members. Holds annual meeting.

American Institute of Architects
457 Madison Ave.
New York, NY 10017
(212) 838-9670

American Institute of Certified Public Accountants
1211 Avenue of the Americas
New York, NY 10036
(212) 596-6200
Contact: Philip B. Chenok
Association of practicing certified public accountants in the private, government, and educational sectors. Offers seminars and workshops. Local chapters publish weekly newsletters; national association publishes a host of bulletins and letters. Holds annual meeting.

American Institute of Chemical Engineers
345 E. 47th St.
New York, NY 10017
(212) 705-7338
Executive Director: Richard Emmert
National association of chemical engineers. Maintains a job placement service for members; offers continuing education courses. Publishes monthly magazine, bi-monthly journal, and quarterly progress reports.

American Institute of Physics
335 E. 45th St.
New York, NY 10017
(212) 661-9404
Director: Kenneth Ford
Organization of nine physics societies affiliated to maintain communications among physicists. Publishes several semi-monthly and monthly newsletters.

American Insurance Association
85 John St.
New York, NY 10038
Office Manager: Kevin Kennedy
(212) 669-0400
Association of individual property and casualty insurance companies. Offers seminars and workshops to members; holds annual meeting.

American Management Association
135 W. 50th St.
New York, NY 10020

(212) 586-8100
President: David Fagiano
Organization of professional managers. Provides members with the latest
information about their fields; offers educational and training courses in
the area of management development. Members include individuals as
well as companies. Publishes newsletters and books; operates a management bookstore and information systems library.

American Paper Institute
260 Madison Ave.
New York, NY 10016
(212) 340-0600

American Society of Civil Engineers
345 E. 47th St.
New York, NY 10017
(212) 705-7496
Director: Dr. Edward Pfrang
National association of civil engineers. Membership categories include
student, associate, affiliate, and full member. Conducts educational
workshops and seminars.

American Society of Composers, Authors and Publishers (ASCAP)
1 Lincoln Plaza
New York, NY 10023
(212) 595-3050
President: Morton Gould
National association of composers, lyricists, and publishers. Publishes
newsletter and directory.

American Society of Interior Designers (ASID)
200 Lexington Ave.
New York, NY 10016
(212) 685-3480
New York chapter of association of practicing professional interior
designers and associate members in allied design fields. Largely a
networking organization; local chapters maintain placement services and
job round ups. Publishes bi-monthly report and student career guide.

American Society of Mechanical Engineers
345 E. 47th St.
New York, NY 10017
(212) 705-7722

American Society of Training and Development
1534 E. 94th St.
Brooklyn, NY 11236
(718) 531-8554
Contact: Prudence Scordino

American Society of Women Accountants
New York Chapter
500 Ft. Washington Ave.
New York, NY 10033
(212) 928-3055
Contact Joan Clark (212) 837-6600
Professional society of women accountants, educators, and others in the

accounting field. Publishes monthly and quarterly newsletter. Holds
semi-annual conference.

American Sportscasters Association
5 Beekman St.
New York, NY 10038
(212) 227-8080
President / Director: Louis O. Schwartz
Association of radio, network, and cable television sportscasters. Main-
tains job bank and publishes monthly sportsletter. Sponsors an annual
Hall of Fame dinner.

Apparel Guild
450 7th Ave., Suite 3002
New York, NY 10123-0101
(212) 279-4580
Chairman: Leon Newman
Local chapter of the national parent organization, Bureau of Wholesale
Sales Representatives. Members are salespeople servicing small local
retail stores. Offers financial services; acts as a networking group to
promote communication within the industry. Publishes monthly newsletter with advertisements from manufacturers and salespeople.

Architectural League of New York
457 Madison Ave.
New York, NY 10022
(212) 753-1722
Contact: Rosalie Genezro
National association of architects and architectural firms. Largely an
educational organization that sponsors lectures, exhibitions, and other
educational activities. Focuses on contemporary architecture in the areas
of city planning, mural decoration, sculpture landscape, interior design,
and photography.

Arts and Business Council
25 W. 45th St.
New York, NY 10016
(212) 819-9287

Associated Fur Manufacturers
363 7th Ave.
New York, NY 10001
(212) 736-4858
Association of manufacturers of fur wearing apparel. Publishes monthly
bulletins and newsletter. Annual meeting.

Association of American Publishers
220 E. 23rd St.
New York, NY 10010-4606
(212) 689-8920
President: Nicholas Veliotes
Confederation of more than 300 publishing houses; the major voice of the
U.S. publishing industry. Members are producers of hardbound and
softbound general, educational, trade, and reference materials, as well as
computer software. Publishes general monthly newsletter and newsletters for specific liaison groups.

Turning volunteer work into a job

After spending many years working as a volunteer for various organizations, Simone Marian's daughters advised her to "stop giving it away." She decided to look for paid employment. But because she had never held a paid job, Simone was not sure how to begin her job search.

"As a woman in my middle years, I wondered where in the world I would go," says Simone. "I had a good education and a great deal of volunteer experience. I had planned and orchestrated large benefits and had done an inordinate amount of fund-raising over the years. I also had done community work in the South Bronx.

"I talked to some people at a local college. They told me I was well qualified and that I should just go out and look for a job. But I didn't know where 'out' was. Later, career counselors at another local college helped me put together a resume. Then I began to talk to people I knew. I was offered various jobs, none of which thrilled me.

"Then I happened to mention my job search to the president of a hospital where I had done a great deal of volunteer work," says Simone. "He asked me not to take a job until I talked to him. Later, he hired me as his special assistant, with the charge to 'humanize the hospital.' Over a period of time, I developed a patient representative department.

"When I began the job 11 years ago, I was a one-person operation. As time went on, I added staff. I currently supervise a staff of 9, plus about 25 volunteers. The job of patient representative is now a full-fledged profession. Many women in the field began as volunteers. They knew a lot about the hospital where they were volunteering, and thus made the transition into a paid position more easily."

We asked Simone what advice she has for volunteers who want to move into the paid work force. "Go to the career counseling departments of some of the small colleges. Ask them to review your background and tell you what kinds of jobs you may be qualified for. If they suggest that you need additional training, get it. But before you go back to school, investigate the kinds of jobs available in your chosen field. Think about how you can use your volunteer experience in a paid position. Take what you've done and build from it." ■

Association of Business Publishers
675 3rd Ave.
New York, NY 10017-5704
(212) 661-6360
Sr. Vice President: Terry Lynn McGovern
Association of publishers of specialized business publications. Polices industry; publishes newsletter. Also publishes booklets offering tips to various groups, such as editors and salespeople. Operates an employment round-up.

Association for Computing Machinery
1515 Broadway
New York, NY 10036
(212) 575-1520 or (212) 869-7440
Executive Director: Joseph DeBlasi
Members are computer scientists, engineers, physical scientists, business system specialists, analysts, and social scientists interested in computing and data processing. Publishes several monthly newsletters. Holds annual conference.

Association of Consulting Chemists and Chemical Engineers
295 Madison Ave., 27th Floor
New York, NY 10017-6304
(212) 983-3160
A national association that acts to advance the practice of independent consultants and their organizations in the fields of chemistry and chemical engineering. Refers members to companies interested in hiring engineering consultants. Publishes directory of consulting services that includes resumes and histories. Also publishes monthly newsletter. Membership includes individual chemists as well as partners or executives of consulting organizations. Holds an annual meeting.

Association of Executive Search Consultants
230 Park Ave.
New York, NY 10169
(212) 949-9559
Accrediting organization for executive search firms.

Association of Independent Commercial Producers
42-22 22nd St.
Long Island City, NY 11101-4927
Contact: Stephen Steinbrecher
Association of independent producers of television commercials. Associate members include suppliers of editorial and payroll services, set designers, optical houses, labs, and others involved in commercial filmmaking. Semi-annual meeting.

Association of Investment Brokers
49 Chambers St., Suite 820
New York, NY 10007
Contact by mail only
Publishes newsletter 10 times a year. Annual meeting.

Association for Investment Management and Research
200 Park Ave.
New York, NY 10166
(212) 953-5700

Association of Management Consulting Firms (ACME)
521 5th Ave.
New York, NY 10175
(212) 697-9693
President: Edward B. Hendricks
Organization of professional management consulting firms that service
corporate and institutional clients.

Attorneys Group
292 Madison Ave., 4th Floor
New York, NY 10017
(212) 949-5900
Contact: Sinaid Doherty, Supervisor Membership
National association that acts largely as a networking group. Membership includes practicing attorneys and law students. Offers members
economic benefits and financial services. Provides seminars and workshops. Publishes bi-monthly newsletter and quarterly news report.

Business and Professional Women's Club
(212) 769-8206
Contact by phone only
Works to advance women toward equal participation in business,
industry, and the professions. Provides a forum for executive-level
women to discuss areas of common interest. Encourages women to
assume leadership roles and develop their own businesses. Offers
educational workshops and seminars.

**How to
distinguish
yourself**

A senior employment relations representative for
a large firm headquartered in Manhattan offers
the following tip for standing out in a crowd of
interviewees. "Almost everybody will show up
well dressed, with a neatly printed resume and
as professional a manner as he or she can
muster. You have to show an employer that
you're someone special. Try bringing a backup
book with you to every interview, one that
contains examples of your work. If you're a
secretary, bring some samples of your most
beautiful typing. If you're a research chemist,
perhaps you've published something that you
can show or maybe articles have appeared
about your work or you can bring along a product
that utilizes your research. It all depends on
what you do for a living, of course, but use your
imagination." ■

Cable Television Advertising Bureau
757 3rd Ave.
New York, NY 10017
(212) 751-7770
President: Thomas McKinney
Promotes advertising in the cable television industry. Members are
individuals involved in cable television, including sales and sales management, personnel, network sales representatives, and systems management personnel. Publishes monthly newsletter that often posts personnel

changes within the industry. Also publishes a membership directory and semi-annual and annual cable factbook. Holds an annual meeting.

Chemists' Club of New York
295 Madison Ave., Suite 808
New York, NY 10017
(212) 532-7649
Manager: Charles Dorn
Organization of chemists and chemical engineers. Works to advance the interests of chemists and those interested in the science, practice, and applications of chemistry and chemical engineering. Publishes monthly newsletter; holds annual meeting.

Childrenswear Manufacturers Association
Two Greentree Centre, Suite 225
Marlton, NJ 08053
(609) 985-2878
Contact: William MacMillan
Members are manufacturers of children's apparel. Publishes quarterly newsletter; holds annual meeting.

Club of Printing Women of New York
P.O. Box 8, Village Station
New York, NY 10014
(212) 532-6222
President: Annette Wolf Bensen
Members are women at the executive or middle-management level in printing plants and such allied fields as publishing, advertising, and printing supplies. Membership also includes plant owners, production managers, bindery workers, salespeople, printing and paper buyers, estimators, cost accountants, mill representatives, and designers.

Cosmetic Executive Women
217 E. 85th St., Suite 214
New York, NY 10028
(212) 759-3283
President: Lee MacCallum
Organization of women who have served more than 3 years in executive positions in the cosmetic industry or allied fields. Publishes newsletter and membership roster.

Cosmetic Industry Buyers and Suppliers
Graphic Prose Inc.
570 7th Ave.
New York, NY 10018
(212) 398-6444
President: Stephen Berman
National association of buyers and suppliers of goods related to the cosmetic industry. Holds monthly meetings.

Council of Fashion Designers of America
1412 Broadway
New York, NY 10018
(212) 302-1821

Council of Sales Promotion Agencies
750 Summer St.
Stamford, CT 06901-1020

(203)325-3911
Executive Director: Marilyn N. Esposito
Trade association of sales promotion agencies that have been in business at least 3 years.

CPA Associates
201 Route 17 North, 4th Floor
Rutherford, NJ 07070-2574
(201) 804-8686
President: James F. Flynn
Association of independent certified public accounting firms offering professional accounting, auditing, tax, and management advisory services. Publishes a monthly newsletter, annual calendar, and recruiting brochure. Holds annual meeting.

Direct Marketing Association
11 W. 42nd St.
New York, NY 10036-8096
(212) 768-7277

Drug, Chemical and Allied Trades Association
2 Roosevelt Ave., Suite 301
Syosset, NY 11791
(516) 496-3317
Executive Director: Richard Lerman
Organization of manufacturers and distributors of drugs, chemicals, cosmetics, toiletries, essential oils, flavors, and fragrances. Offers seminars for management development. Publishes bi-monthly newsletter. Sponsors annual dinner and annual meeting, as well as periodic regional meetings.

Environmental Defense Fund
257 Park Ave. S.
New York, NY 10010
(212) 5052100

Financial Analysts Federation
200 Park Ave.
New York, NY 10166
(212) 957-2860

Financial Women's Association of New York
215 Park Ave. S., Suite 2014
New York, NY 10003
(212) 533-2141
Contact: Nancy Sellar
Organization of women and men involved in investment and commercial banking; securities research, sales, and trading; portfolio management; corporate financial analysis and planning; business journalism; and investor relations. Provides monthly job listings, internship program for college students and career guidance seminars. Publishes monthly newsletter. Holds monthly luncheon meetings.

Forty Plus Club of New York
15 Park Row
New York, NY 10038
(212) 233-6086
Contact: Bernard See

Networking organization that functions as a job-search club for unemployed managers over 40. Seminars and workshops offered to members
during and after their job search. Publishes quarterly newsletter; holds
annual meeting.

Greater New York Hospital Association
555 W. 57th St.
New York, NY
(212) 246-7100

Greenpeace Action
462 Broadway
New York, NY
(212) 941-0994

Hospitality Industry Foundation of New York
505 8th Ave.
New York, NY 10035
(212) 714-1330

Hotel Credit Managers Association
40 W. 38th St.
New York, NY 10018
(212) 869-4600
Contact: Joseph Spinnato
Members are credit managers of hotels and hotel credit-collection
agencies. Maintains job placement service for members.

Human Resource Planning Society
41 E. 42nd St., Suite 1509
New York, NY 10017
(212) 490-6387
Executive Director: Dr. Steven J. Noble
National association of human resource planning professionals: manpower planning and development professionals; staffing analysts;
business planners; and others concerned with employee recruitment,
development, and utilization. Publishes quarterly newsletter and
biennial membership directory.

Institute of Electrical and Electronics Engineers
345 E. 47th St.
New York, NY 10017
(212) 705-7900

Institute of Management Accountants
10 Paragon Drive
Montvale, NJ 07645
(201) 573-9000
Executive Director: Gary Scopes, CAE
International association with local chapters throughout the United
States. Acts as a networking group to improve communication among
accountants and educate them on changing trends in the industry.
Publishes monthly magazine; local chapters publish frequent newsletters. Offers seminars and workshops as well as continuing education
classes.

Institute of Management Consultants
230 Park Ave.

New York, NY 10169
(212) 697-8262

Insurance Information Institute
110 William St., 24th Floor
New York, NY 10038
(212) 669-9200
President: Gordon C. Stewart
Organization of property and liability companies and insurance companies. Publishes monthly newsletter and weekly letter.

Insurance Society of New York
101 Murray St.
New York, NY 10007
(212) 962-4111
President: Ellen Thrower
Parent organization of the College of Insurance. Maintains insurance-related library of books, pamphlets, and historic documents. Publishes annual bulletin.

Investment Counsel Association of America
20 Exchange Pl.
New York, NY 10005
(212) 344-0999

Jewelers of America
1185 Avenue of the Americas, 30th Floor
New York, NY 10036
(212) 768-8777
Chairman: Michael D. Roman
Organization of retailers of jewelry, watches, silver, and allied merchandise.

Ladies Apparel Contractors Association
450 7th Ave.
New York, NY 10123
(212) 564-6161
Contact: Sydney Reiff
Established to handle labor relations for apparel contractors. Offers seminars and workshops on labor relations. Publishes newsletter; holds annual meeting.

Licensing Industry Merchandisers' Association
350 5th Ave., Suite 6210
New York, NY 10018-0110
(212) 244-1944
Executive Director: Murray Altchuler
National association of individual licensees and licensing companies. Publishes annual membership directory.

**Women
helping
women**

The New York City Commission on the Status of Women is a city-run agency that publishes a 144-page directory of women's organizations. Some of these organizations offer personal and vocational counseling as well as referrals to other agencies in the self-help network. In addition, there are lists of agencies that can help with day care, education, legal and financial advice.

To obtain a copy of the directory, you must first send for the Commission's information packet. Write to:

The New York City Commission on the Status of Women
52 Chambers St., Room 207
New York, NY 10007.

To get a copy of the directory, return the mail order coupon from the information packet. For more information about the directory, contact Lisa Castle at **(212) 566-3830.** ▨

Long Island Women's Network
P.O. Box 280
Port Jefferson, NY 11776
(516) 378-3441
Contact: Betty Schlein
Organization of Long Island women cooperating to form an influential power structure of women leaders. Works to direct women into policy-making positions, share information regarding high-level career opportunities, and build professional and personal contacts. Serves as a resource bank by matching individuals with opportunities.

Magazine Publishers Association
575 Lexington Ave., Suite 540
New York, NY 10022
(212) 752-0055

Master Furriers Guild of America
101 W. 30th St.
New York, NY 10001
(212) 244-8570
Contact: Connie Karopoulos
Organization of retailers of custom furs; associate members represent allied branches of the fur industry.

Men's Fashion Association of America
475 Park Ave. S., 17th Floor
New York, NY 10016
(212) 683-5665
Executive Director: Norman Karr
Organization of textile mills, apparel manufacturers, yarn producers, and retailers of men's and boys' apparel. Brings together the fashion press, designers, and manufacturers through two annual press previews.

Metropolitan Area Apparel Association
150 5th Ave., Suite 407
New York, NY 10011
(212) 243-6425
Contact: Jack Barnes
Organization of contractors of children's apparel. Holds annual meeting.

National Academy of Television Arts and Sciences
111 W. 57th St., Suite 1020
New York, NY 10019
(212) 586-8424
President: John Cannon
Persons engaged in almost all facets of television performing and production. Confers Emmy awards. Has film and tape library at UCLA, California. Sponsors workshops and seminars; bi-monthly newsletter *(NATAS News)*.

National Association of Environmental Professionals
815 2nd Ave.
New York, NY 10017

National Association for Female Executives
127 W. 24th St.
New York, NY 10011
(212) 645-0770
Contact: George Tunick
National association that functions as a networking group for women executives from all phases of business. Offers resume service and aptitude testing. Publishes bi-monthly magazine; holds annual meeting.

National Association of Media Women
157 W. 126th St.
New York, NY 10027
Contact: Jean Wright
Networking group of women professionals in all phases of mass communications. Holds meetings and seminars; works to create opportunities for women in mass media and to inspire young women to seek careers in the field. Local parent chapters also organize student chapters. Publishes annual journal. Holds annual meeting.

National Association of Milliners, Dressmakers, and Tailors c/o Harlem Institute of Fashion
157 W. 126th St.
New York, NY 10027
(212) 666-1320
Secretary: Laura James
Organization of designers, dressmakers, tailors, milliners, fashion commentators, coordinators, and others engaged in the fashion business. Publishes monthly newsletter and semi-annual journal. Holds semi-annual meetings.

National Association of Social Workers
New York City Chapter
545 8th Ave.
New York, NY 10018
(212) 947-5000
Contact: Nita Henick

Organization of professional social workers. Focus is on social issues; association sets professional standards.

National Association of Women Artists
41 Union Square West, Room 906
New York, NY 10003
(212) 675-1616
Office Secretary: Ann Hermanson Chennault
National association of women painters, sculptors, and printmakers. Acts as a forum for women in the arts; sponsors exhibitions nationally and worldwide. Publishes annual membership catalog and newsletter. Holds semi-annual meetings.

National Cartoonists Society
157 W. 57th St., Suite 904
New York, NY 10019
(212) 333-7606
Contact: Arnold Roth
National organization of professional cartoonists. Associate members include editors, writers,and others interested in cartooning. Publishes annual magazine.

National Conference of Black Lawyers
2 W. 125th St., 2nd Floor
New York, NY 10027
(212) 864-4000
National organization of attorneys in the U.S. and Canada united to use legal skills in the service of black and poor communities. Publishes quarterly newsletter; holds annual meeting.

National Council of Salesmen's Organizations
303 5th Ave., Room 1303
New York, NY 10016
(212) 835-4591
President: Michael Gale
Wholesale commissioned salespeople in all industries. Publishes quarterly magazine. Holds annual meeting.

National Customs Brokers and Forwarders Association of America
1 World Trade Center, Suite 1153
New York, NY 10048
(212) 432-0050
Exec. Vice President: John Hammon
National organization of customhouse brokers and independent ocean freight forwarders. Offers workshops and seminars. Publishes monthly bulletin and annual membership directory.

National Lawyers Guild
55 Avenue of the Americas, 3rd Floor
New York, NY 10013
(212) 966-5000
Executive Director: Rick Best
Members are lawyers, law students, and legal workers dedicated to seeking economic justice and social equality, as well as ensuring the right to political dissent. Publishes monthly and bi-monthly newsletters. Meetings are held every 18 months.

National League for Nursing
350 Hudson St.
New York, NY 10014
(212) 989-9393
Contact: Pamela Maraldo
Main purpose is to advance nursing education and nursing practice while providing affordable, quality health care. Membership includes individuals, agencies, and nursing education institutions. Publishes several journals and service journals and newsletters. Offers educational programs. Holds biennial meeting.

National Retail Federation
100 W. 31st St.
New York, NY 10001
(212) 244-8780
Executive Director: John J. Schultz
National association of retail merchants. Membership includes merchants of all sizes, as well as manufacturers, distributors, and consultants.

Newswomen's Club of New York
15 Grammercy Park S.
New York, NY 10003
(212) 777-1610
President: Virginia Byrne
Largely a social group focused on networking. Members are journalists with the daily newspapers; wire services; syndicates; national news and news/feature magazines; and radio and television stations. Publishes monthly bulletin; holds monthly workshops.

New York Association for New Americans
225 Park Ave. S.
New York, NY 10003
(212) 674-7400
Contact: Mark Handelman
Organization aids the resettlement of Jewish newcomers in the greater New York area. Also acts as a rehabilitation agency. Holds an annual meeting.

New York City Commission for the United Nations and for the Consular Corps
809 UN Plaza
New York, NY 10017
(212) 319-9300
Contact: Gillian Martin Sorensen
The mayor's official 'iaison between the city of New York and the diplomatic community.

New York Clothing Manufacturers Association
c/o Sidney Orenstein
Solomon and Rosenbaum, Dreschler and Leff
100 E. 42nd St.
New York, NY 10017
(212) 867-5524
Contact: Sidney Orenstein
Networking group for manufacturers of men's tailored clothing. Holds frequent meetings. Member of the Clothing Manufacturers Association of the USA. Parent organization often holds workshops and seminars.

New York Credit and Financial Management Association
520 8th Ave.
New York, NY 10010
(212) 268-8711
Contact: John G. Kosman
Organization of credit and financial executives of manufacturing firms,
wholesalers, banks, advertising agencies, insurance companies, and
accounting firms. Publishes bi-monthly newsletter, books, and pamphlets.

New York Financial Writers Association
P.O. Box 21
28 Robert Circle
Syosset, NY 11791
(516) 921-7766
Contact: Ben Weberman
Established to further the professionalism of business and financial
journalists. Most members are staff members of New York-based independent publications. Operates job clearing committee; holds annual
seminars for graduate students. Holds monthly meetings.
Publishes newsletter.

New York League of Savings Institutions
700 White Plains Road
Scarsdale, NY 10583
(914) 472-3500
Representing New York's savings and loan industry.

Internships can lead to permanent relationships

"Working as an intern for ABC Television during
my senior year in college proved to be one of the
most valuable experiences of my life," says Bill.
Bill's close-up internship proved to be very
rewarding.

"I was in the office five days a week working
for a top-rated network show," he says. "I
learned how to focus my goals, manage my
time, and work under pressure. When a full-time
position opened up, I was first in line. When the
producer realized that I had been doing a lot of
the work anyway, knew the ropes, and knew the
people, my internship ended with an offer for a
permanent job."

Although Bill was not paid for his work as an
intern, many interns are salaried. Keep in mind
also that internship programs are not necessarily limited to students. For more information,
check the *Directory of Internships* available at
the public library. ■

New York Society of Independent Accountants
24 W. 40th St.
New York, NY 10018
(212) 768-8323

New York Society of Security Analysts
71 Broadway, 2nd Floor
New York, NY 10006
(212) 344-8450
Contact: A. Wm. Bodine
Non-profit educational organization. Members include analysts employed
by brokerage houses, banks, insurance companies, mutual funds, and
other financial institutions. Holds daily meetings for analysts; also holds
seminars and workshops. Publishes a monthly newsletter with calendar
of events.

New York State Society of Certified Public Accountants: Foundation for Accounting Education
200 Park Ave.
New York, NY 10166
Executive Director: Robert L. Gray

New York Women's Bar Association
245 5th Ave.
New York, NY 10016
(212) 889-7873

Promotion Marketing Association of America
322 8th Ave., Suite 1201
New York, NY 10001
(212) 206-1100
Executive Director: Christopher Sutherland
Organization of promotion service companies, sales incentive organizations, and companies using various promotion programs. Associate
members include manufacturers of premium merchandise, consultants,
and advertising agencies. Holds annual meeting.

Public Relations Society of America
33 Irving Place, 3rd Floor
New York, NY 10003-2376
(212) 995-2230
Contact: Elizabeth Ann Kovacs, CAE
Professional society of public relations practitioners in business and
industry, counseling firms, trade and professional groups, government,
education, and health and welfare organizations. Publishes monthly
journal and annual register. Holds annual meeting.

Promotion Marketing Association of America
322 8th Ave.
New York, NY 10001
(212) 206-1100

Public Securities Association
40 Broad St., 12th Floor
New York, NY 10004-2373
(212) 809-7000
President: Heather L. Ruth
Organization of dealers and dealer banks who sell and trade federal,
state, and local government bonds.

Publisher's Ad Club
Franklin Spier, Inc.
650 1st Ave.

New York, NY 10016
(212) 679-4441
Contact: Ken Atkatz
Networking group that includes book publishers, book ad agencies, and media representatives. Holds monthly luncheon meetings with guest speakers. Sponsors seminars and workshops, scholarship funds, and charity functions. Publishes monthly newsletter with job postings.

Publishers' Publicity Association
c/o Farrar, Straus & Giroux
19 Union Square West
New York, NY 10003
(212) 206-5323
President: Helene Atwan
Networking group made up of publicity directors and staff members. Holds monthly meetings featuring guest speakers from the electronic and print media. Offers workshops and seminars. Publishes monthly newsletter and maintains job exchange service.

Radio Advertising Bureau
304 Park Ave. S.
New York, NY 10010
(212) 387-2100
President: Gary Fries
National association that includes radio stations, radio networks, and station representatives. Publishes monthly sales letter and radio facts annual. Holds annual meeting.

Sales Association of the Graphic Arts (SAGA)
c/o James W. Prendergast Associates
220 E. 42nd St., Suite 402
New York, NY 10017-5858
Networking group of sales and marketing professionals from the graphic arts industry. Holds bi-monthly meetings featuring guest speakers. Offers seminars and workshops.

Sales Executives Club of New York
13 E. 37th St.
New York, NY 10016
(212) 683-9755
Contact: Edward B. Flanagan
Networking group of company executives interested in improving marketing and selling techniques. Sponsors educational workshops and seminars as well as social outings. Publishes a bi-weekly newsletter and special research reports. Holds annual meeting.

Securities Industry Association
120 Broadway, 35th Floor
New York, NY 10271
(212) 608-1500
President: Edward I. O'Brien
Association of investment bankers, securities underwriters, and dealers in stocks and bonds. Publishes monthly newsletter, bi-monthly report, and annual directory and guide.

Security Traders Association
1 World Trade Center, #4511

New York, NY 10048
(212) 524-0484

Service Corporation of Retired Executives (SCORE)
400 County Seat Drive South
Mineola, NY 11501
(516) 571-3303
SCORE is an organization of retired executives who volunteer their time
and expertise to small business owners. Federally funded. Several offices
through the metropolitan area.

Service Employers Association
60 E. 42nd St.
New York, NY 10165
(212) 682-1030
Contact: Arthur M. Marin
Association of office, industrial, and general cleaning contracting firms in
the New York City metropolitan area. Publishes monthly bulletin.

Society of Women Engineers
345 E. 47th St., Room 305
New York, NY 10017
(212) 705-7855
Executive Director: B.J. Harrod
Educational service society of women engineers. Membership is also open
to men. Publishes journal 6 times a year. Holds annual meeting.

Special Interest Group for Business Data Processing
(c/o Association for Computing Machinery)
1515 Broadway
New York, NY 10036
(212) 869-7440
Primary goal is to promote the use of computers in business. Publishes
quarterly newsletter.

Special Interest Group on Programming Languages
c/o Association for Computing Machinery
1515 Broadway
New York, NY 10036
(212) 869-7440
Association of computer professionals interested in programming
languages. Publishes monthly newsletter. Holds annual symposium.

Special Interest Group for System Documentation
c/o Association for Computing Machinery
1515 Broadway
New York, NY 10036
(212) 869-7440
Executive Director: Joseph DeBlasi
Group of individuals involved in data processing, information processing,
and data entry. Members include students, instructors, and executives.
Holds annual meeting.

Sportswear Apparel Association
450 7th Ave.
New York, NY 10123
(212) 564-6161

Station Representatives Association
230 Park Ave.
New York, NY 10169-0175
(212) 687-2482
Managing Director: Jerome Feniger
Association of sales representatives who sell spot advertising for radio and television stations. Holds annual convention.

Textile Distributors Association
45 W. 36th St., 3rd Floor
New York, NY 10018
(212) 563-0400
Executive Director: Bruce F. Roberts
Association of converters and distributors of fabrics who sell mainly to apparel manufacturers and to the over-the-counter trade. Holds annual meeting.

Type Directors Club
60 E. 42nd St., Suite 721
New York, NY 10165-0721
(212) 983-6042
Executive Director: Carol Wahler
Professional society of typographic designers, type directors, teachers of typography, and those with an interest in typographic education. Holds annual meeting.

Typographers Association of Greater New York
408 8th Ave.
New York, NY 10001
(212) 629-3232
Contact: John Trieste
Association of firms producing composition using direct impression, photocomposition, and computerized typesetting. Also includes firms that provide such services as layout, paste-up, mechanicals, art, and forms. Publishes bi-monthly newsletter. Holds monthly meetings.

United Engineering Trustees
345 E. 47th St., Suite 304
New York, NY 10017-2330
(212) 705-7828
Secretary/General Manager: Jerome Fishel
Federation of five major national engineering societies: American Society of Civil Engineers; American Institute of Mining, Metallurgical and Petroleum Engineers; American Society of Mechanical Engineers; Institute of Electrical and Electronics Engineers; American Institute of Chemical Engineers.

Vietnam Veterans of America
Local New York Chapter
346 Broadway
New York, NY 10010
(212) 349-8214
Contact: Robert Muller
First nationwide group formed specifically to help Vietnam veterans adjust to post-war life. Offers counseling and job placement programs. Lobbies for the group in legislative matters. Publishes monthly newsletter; holds annual meeting.

The Westchester County Association
235 Mamaroneck Ave.
White Plains, NY 10605
(914) 948-6444
Organization of business and civic leaders.

Wings Club
52 Vanderbilt Ave., 18th Floor
New York, NY 10017
(212) 867-1770
Contact: Doris H. Renninger-Brell
Maintains a meeting place in New York City for persons connected with
aviation and foreign and domestic aeronautics. Publishes monthly
bulletin.

Women in Communications
New York Chapter
245 5th Ave.
New York, New York 10017
(212) 532-3669
Contact: Ellen Rekant
Professional group for women in all areas of communications. Publishes
newsletter with job listings: seminars, monthly meetings.

Women in Data Processing
15 Maiden Lane
New York, NY 10017
(212) 227-2010
Contact: Denise L. Hassman
Networking group of male and female technical personnel, managers,
and students in the field of data processing. Maintains placement service
for members. Sponsors networking socials, lecture series, and educational workshops and seminars.

Women Executives in Public Relations
200 Park Ave.
New York, NY 10017
(212) 683-5438
Contact: Barbara Hannan
Organization of women executives in the field of communications,
primarily public relations.

Women in Production
347 5th Ave., Suite 1008
New York, NY 10016
(212) 481-7793
Membership committee: (212) 503-4734
Contact: Vicki Hudspith
Organization of individuals involved in all phases of print and graphics,
including those working in magazine and book publishing, agency
production, print manufacturing, print-related vending and buying, and
advertising production.

Young Menswear Association
1328 Broadway
New York, NY 10001
(212) 594-6422
Contact: Theodore M. Kaufman

Established to encourage young people to explore the potential of the menswear industry. Members are individuals associated with any aspect of the men's apparel industry. Publishes quarterly newsletter.

Using Professional Employment Services

Conducting a job search is no easy task. When the pressure is on, many a job seeker's first instinct is to turn to professional employment services for relief. "After all," he or she reasons, "everyone knows that professional services have all the job listings." Wrong!

It's smart to use every available resource to generate leads and interviews. But professional employment services vary from agencies that specialize in temporary clerical help to executive recruiters who deal primarily with top-management types.

Employment agencies, career consultants, and executive recruitment firms differ greatly in the kinds of services they offer and in how—and by whom—they get paid. You can save yourself a lot of time, effort, and perhaps even money and anguish by informing yourself about the advantages and disadvantages of the various kinds of professional employment services. One handbook that might prove useful is the *Directory of Approved Counseling Services* (American Personnel and Guidance Assoc., 5201 Leesburg Pike 400, Falls Church, VA 22041).

Employment Agencies

The thousands of employment agencies that have succeeded through the years have done so by acting as intermediaries in the job market between buyers (companies with jobs open) and sellers (people who want jobs). An employment agency obtains a fee when a person it refers to a company is hired by that company. The fee may be paid by the company, but in some cases it is paid by the worker. Agencies that specialize in restaurant and domestic help, for example, often charge the worker a fee. Usually the placement fee amounts to a certain percentage of the worker's annual salary.

Seldom will an employment agency place a candidate in a job that pays more than $30,000 a year. Most employment agencies concentrate on support jobs. Supervisory openings also may be listed, but employment agencies usually don't handle middle- or upper-management positions. In the computer field, for example, computer operators, programmers, and perhaps systems analysts could find work through an agency. But directors of data processing or MIS (management information systems) would go to an executive search firm or would job hunt on their own.

A company that's looking for a secretary gains certain advantages by going to a reputable agency. It doesn't have to advertise or screen the hundreds of resumes that would probably pour in from even a small want ad in the Sunday *New York Times*. A good employment agency will send over only qualified applicants for interviews. Referrals are made quickly, and there is no cost to the company until it hires the secretary. For many companies, it's worth it to pay an agency fee to avoid the hassle of prescreening dozens, if not hundreds, of applicants.

The advantage to the agency of a successful placement (besides the fee) is repeat business. After two or three referrals work out well, an employment agency can generally count on receiving future listings of company vacancies.

The value to the job seeker of using an employment agency depends on a number of factors, including the quality of the agency, the kind of work you're looking for, how much experience you have, and how broad your network of personal and business contacts is.

In general, an agency's loyalty will be to its source of income. Agencies are more interested in making placements than in seeing to it that applicants land in jobs that are really fulfilling.

**Who's good?
Who's not?**

A listing in this book does not constitute an endorsement of an employment agency or career consultant. In New York State, all employment agencies must be licensed by the state. Temporary employment agencies must be licensed by the State Department of Labor. New York City agencies must be licensed by the Department of Consumer Affairs. But career consultants placing people in jobs paying over $20,000 a year need not be licensed at all. Before engaging these professional services, check with the Better Business Bureau and other resources listed in Chapter 2. ■

An agency is likely to put pressure on its applicants to accept jobs that they don't really want just so it can collect its fee. With certain exceptions, unless you're just starting out, new in town, or switching to a field in which you have no experience, an agency probably can't do much more for you than you could do for yourself in an imaginative and energetic job search. If a company has to pay a fee to hire you, you're at a disadvantage compared with applicants who are "free." Also, giving an employment agency your resume could be a serious mistake if you're trying to conduct a confidential job search.

On the other hand, a good agency can help its candidates develop a strategy and prepare for employment interviews. This training can be very valuable to people who are inexperienced in job-hunting techniques. Agency pros know the market, screen well, and provide sound advice. A secretary who tries to investigate the metropolitan job market on his or her own will take up to six times longer to get the "right" job than someone who uses a quality agency.

Historically, certain employment agencies engage in practices that can only be called questionable at best, and the field as a whole is trying to polish up a somewhat tarnished image. There are many highly respected and successful employment agencies able and willing to help qualified job seekers. But as in any profession, there are also crooks. It's still a practice in some agencies to advertise nonexistent openings to attract applicants for other, less desirable positions.

So much for the pros and cons of employment agencies. If you decide to try one, be sure it's a reputable firm. Ask people in your field to recommend a quality agency, and consult the Better Business Bureau and other resources listed in Chapter 2 to see if there have been any complaints about the agency you're considering.

Most important, *be sure to read the contract thoroughly*, including all the fine print, before you sign it. If you have any questions, or if there's something you don't understand, don't be afraid to ask. It's your right. Make sure you know who is responsible for paying the fee and what the fee is. Remember that in some cases, *an agency's application form is also the contract*.

Here, then, is a selective listing of New York area employment agencies, including their areas of specialization.

EMPLOYMENT AGENCIES

Manhattan

Accountants and Auditors Agency
30 E. 42nd St.
New York, NY 10017
(212) 687-5656
Accountants and auditors.

Ayers Group
370 Lexington Ave.
New York, NY 10017
(212) 889-7788
General.

Career Blazers
590 5th Ave.
New York, NY 10110
(212) 719-3232
General. Offices also at 230 Park Ave. in Manhattan.

Cohen, Irene, Personnel
475 5th Ave.
New York, NY 10017
(212) 725-1666
General.

Cosmopolitan Personnel Systems
290 Madison Ave.
New York, NY 10017
(212) 725-9200
General. Offices also at 150 Broadway in Manhattan.

Eden Personnel
280 Madison Ave.
New York, NY 10017
(212) 685-8600
General.

Engineering Employment Service
217 Broadway
New York, NY 10007
(212) 267-5640
Engineers, construction specialists, electricians, and computer programmers.

Fortune Personnel
505 5th Ave.
New York, NY 10017
(212) 557-8500
Hospitality and food service consultants.

Fry Group
18 E. 41st St.
New York, NY 10017
(212) 532-8100

Half, Robert, of New York
522 5th Ave.
New York, NY 10036
(212) 221-6500
Accounting and bookkeeping personnel; controllers.

Homer, J.B., Associates
521 5th Ave.
New York, NY 10017
(212) 697-3300
Human resources.

Interlangue Ltd. Agency
41 E. 42nd St.
New York, NY 10017
(212) 949-0170
Bilingual and international specialists.

Interspace Personnel
380 Lexington Ave., Suite 1700
New York, NY 10168
(212) 481-6600
Telecommunications.

Medical and Dental Personnel by Larkin
25 W. 42nd St.
New York, NY 10036
(212) 695-2668
Hospital and private practice personnel.

Olsten Legal Professions
1270 Avenue of the Americas
New York, NY 10020
(212) 262-1980

Olsten Professional Accounting Services
20 E. 46th St.
New York, NY 10017
(212) 370-0063

Palmer, Lynne, Associates
14 E. 60th St.
New York, NY 10022
(212) 759-2942
Publishing and media personnel.

Planned Staffing
575 Madison Ave.
New York, NY 10022
(212) 371-9850

Remer-Ribolow Employment Agency
230 Park Ave.
New York, NY 10016
(212) 808-0580
Book and magazine publishing.

Sloan, Howard, Associates
545 5th Ave.
New York, NY 10017
(212) 661-5250
Advertising sales, management-marketing, public relations, and direct
marketing.

Sloan Personnel
1 E. 42nd St.
New York, NY 10017
(212) 949-7200
General.

Stanton Personnel
189 Broadway
New York, NY 10017
(212) 962-4020
General.

Tax Network Resources
521 5th Ave.
Suite 1725
New York, NY 10017
(212) 983-7555
Tax and accounting.

Winston Personnel Agency
535 5th Ave.
New York, NY 10017
(212) 557-5000
General.

Temps are hot

Temp workers used to be thought of as low-skilled fill-ins for companies, but no longer. Professionals and other highly skilled people are working in temporary positions today, including doctors, lawyers, and engineers.

With many companies unable to pay full-time salaries and benefits, the need for temps is on the rise. Temp work can be very rewarding in advancing your career through work experience (and keeping food on the table). Drawbacks include no benefits and a very unstable position. See Chapter 8 for a list of temporary agencies.

A new book covering this topic is *The Temp Track: Make One of the Hottest Job Trends for the 90's Work for You* by Peggy Justice. ■

Queens

Employment Recruiters
118-21 Queens Blvd., Suite 312
Forest Hills, NY 11375
(718) 263-2300
General.

Kent, Lyra, Personnel Agency
118-21 Queens Blvd.
Forest Hills, NY 11375
(718) 544-1077
Executive placement for accounting, programming, systems analysis, chemistry, and engineering.

Queens Employment Service
29-27 41st Ave.
Long Island City, NY 11101
(718) 784-1010

Snelling and Snelling
39-15 Main St., Room 201
Flushing, NY 11354
(718) 961-1900
General.

Vintage Personnel
118-21 Queens Blvd., Suite 503
Forest Hills, NY 11375
(212) 544-3100
Office; general.

Bronx

Floringdale Employment Agency
1439 E. Gunhill Road
Bronx, NY
(212) 320-1160
Nursing.

Monroe Business Institute
2449 Morris Ave.
Bronx, NY 10468
(212) 933-7065
General.

Brooklyn

Aim Personnel Agency
44 Court St.
Brooklyn, NY 11201
(718) 834-8600
Office personnel, skilled industrial personnel.

Olsten Services
16 Court St.
Brooklyn, NY
(718) 522-2600
General.

PSP Agency
188 Montegue
Brooklyn, NY 11201
(718) 596-9155
Banking, secretarial, sales, data processing.

Be firm with an agency

A friend of ours had this to say about her experience with employment agencies during her recent job search. "I've been working as a secretary for 25 years," says Marietta Raio. "When I decided to change jobs, I knew my qualifications supported my desire to work at a higher level. Unfortunately, I went on a lot of job interviews that I knew were not right for me. The salaries, job descriptions, and locations were all wrong. But I went because the agency suggested I do so.

"Now that I've found a job as administrative assistant to the president of an internationally based manufacturing firm, I'd like to offer this advice to fellow job searchers. Don't hesitate to be assertive with an agency. Demand that they arrange interviews that suit your qualifications and your needs. If they can't, take your business elsewhere. Your time is valuable and should not be wasted on mismatched job interviews." ■

Nassau County

ADS Personnel Agency, Ltd.
11 Pondview Court
Jericho, NY 11753
(516) 248-6000
Data processing, accounting, banking, financial, insurance, engineering, and office personnel.

Alpha Personnel Placement Systems
600 Old Country Road
Garden City, NY 11530
(516) 228-9600
Office services, data processing, and insurance.

Career Blazers
445 Broadhollow Road
Melville, NY 11747
(516) 756-2400
Office, law, finance, data processing, publishing.

Westchester County

Bailey Employment Services
188 E. Post Road
White Plains, NY 10603
(914) 946-1383
Banking, EDP auditing, technical and secretarial personnel.

Career Blazers
202 Mamaroneck Ave.
White Plains, NY 10604
(914) 949-1166
General.

Half, Robert, of Westchester
701 Westchester Ave., #2A2
White Plains, NY 10604
(914) 682-8842
Accounting, finance, bookkeeping, data processing, banking.

Professional Placement Associates
14 Rye Ridge Plaza
Rye Brook, NY 10573
(914) 251-1000

Sales Recruiters International
371 S. Broadway
Tarrytown, NY 10591
(914) 631-0090

Snelling Personnel Services
345 Broadway
White Plains, NY 10604
(914) 965-3757
General.

Vantage Careers
180 E. Post Road
White Plains, NY 10601
(914) 761-1120
Corporate relocation specialists plus general office services personnel.

For women in Westchester

The Westchester County Office for Women (112 E. Post Road, White Plains, NY 10601) offers several programs designed to help women in Westchester County lead fuller lives. Operation Talent Bank tries to match women county residents with available positions throughout Westchester and occasionally in Manhattan. Call **(914) 285-5972** to request a personal data form to which you can attach a resume. After you return the form with your resume, you are automatically placed in the talent bank. In addition, a career counselor is available for appointments each Wednesday. All services are free. ■

Executive Search Firms

An executive search firm is compensated by a company to locate a person with specific qualifications that meet a precisely defined employment need. Most reputable executive search firms belong to an organization called the Association of Executive Recruiting Consultants (AERC). The association, listed in Chapter 5, publishes a code of ethics for its membership.

A search firm never works on a contingency basis. Only employment agencies do that. The usual fee for a search assignment is 30 percent of the annual salary of the person to be hired, plus out-of-pocket expenses. These are billed on a monthly basis. During hard times, many companies forgo retaining search firms because it's so expensive.

It's difficult to get an appointment to see a search specialist. Executive search consultants have only their time to sell. If a specialist spends time with you, he or she can't bill that time to a client. If you can use your personal contacts to meet a search professional, however, by all means do so. Executive specialists know the market and can be very helpful in providing advice and leads.

Search firms receive dozens of unsolicited resumes every day. They seldom acknowledge receipt and usually retain only a small portion for future search needs or business development. They really can't afford to file and store them all. Sending your resume to every search firm in the New York area will be useful only if one firm coincidentally has a search assignment to find someone with exactly your background and qualifications. It's a long shot, similar to answering blind want ads.

If you are ever contacted by an executive search firm, says A. Robert Taylor, author of *How to Select and Use an Executive Search Firm*, take the time to listen to what the consultant has to offer. Even if it isn't the job for you, establishing rapport with the consultant is important. You never know when a more appealing job might become available.

The following is a selected list of executive search firms in the New York area.

MAJOR EXECUTIVE SEARCH FIRMS

Battalia Winston International
275 Madison Ave.
New York, NY 10016
(212) 683-9440
Domestic and international search firm.

Boyden International
260 Madison Ave.
New York, NY 10016
(212) 685-3400
Connecticut office:
1290 E. Main St.
Stamford, CT 06902
(203) 324-4300
Also: Morristown, NJ (201) 267-0980
Generalists.

Gardiner Stone Hunter International
70 E. 55th St.
New York, NY 10022
(212) 644-7177
General and financial services.

Gilbert Tweed Assoc.
630 3rd Ave.
New York, NY 10017

(212) 697-4260
Generalists.

Heidrick and Struggles
245 Park Ave.
New York, NY 10001
(212) 867-9876
104 Field Point Road
Greenwich, CT 06830
(203) 629-3200
Generalists, upper and middle echelon executives.

Korn-Ferry International
237 Park Ave.
New York, NY 10017
(212) 687-1834
Generalists.

Mines, Herbert, Associates
399 Park Ave., 27th Floor
New York, NY 10022
(212) 355-0909
Retail, fashion manufacturing, consumer products, direct marketing.

Meta/Mat, Ltd.
120 Wood Ave. S.
Iselin, NJ 08830
(branch)
237 Park Ave.
New York, NY 10017
(212) 551-1472
Finance, high technology, and consumer products businesses.

Nordeman Grimm
717 5th Ave.
New York, NY 10022
(212) 935-1000
Generalists.

Peck Consultancy
17 W. 54th St.
New York, NY 10019
(212) 757-2688
Generalists for profit and not-for-profit institutions.

Reynolds, Russel, Inc.
200 Park Ave.
New York, NY 10166
(212) 351-2000
General.

Werbin Associates Executive Search
521 5th Ave.
New York, NY 10175
(212) 953-0909
Computer and research professionals.

Witt Associates
575 Madison Ave.
New York, NY 10022
(212) 605-0245
Health care, insurance, pharmaceutical.

Career Consultants

If you open the employment section of the Sunday *New York Times*, *Newsday*, or check out the classifieds of the daily *Wall Street Journal*, you'll see ads placed by career consultants (also known as career counselors and private outplacement consultants). The ads are generally directed to "executives" earning yearly salaries anywhere between $30,000 and $300,000. Some ads suggest that the consultants have access to jobs that are not listed elsewhere. Others claim, "We do all the work." Most have branch offices throughout the country.

Career consultants vary greatly in the kind and quality of the services they provide. Some may offer a single service, such as vocational testing or resume preparation. Others coach every aspect of the job search and stay with you until you accept an offer. The fees vary just as broadly and range from $100 to several thousand dollars. You, not your potential employer, pay the fee.

A qualified career consultant can be a real asset to your job search. *But no consultant can get you a job.* Only you can do that. You are the one who will participate in the interview, and you are the one who must convince an employer to hire you. A consultant can help you focus on an objective, develop a resume, research the job market, decide on a strategy, and train you in interviewing techniques. But you can't send a consultant to interview in your place. It just doesn't work that way.

Don't retain a career consultant if you think that the fee will buy you a job. The only reason you should consider a consultant is that you've exhausted all the other resources we've suggested here and still feel you need expert and personalized help with one or more aspects of the job search. The key to choosing a career consultant is knowing what you need and verifying that the consultant can provide it.

There are many reputable consulting firms in the New York area. But as is true of employment agencies, some career consultants have been in trouble with the law. Before engaging a career consultant, check with the Better Business Bureau and other resources listed in Chapter 2. Has anyone lodged a bona fide complaint against the firm you're considering?

Check references. A reputable firm will gladly provide them. Before you sign anything, ask to meet the consultant who will actually provide the services you want. What are his or her credentials? How long has the consultant been practicing? Who are the firm's corporate clients?

Read the contract carefully before you sign it. Does the contract put the consultant's promises in writing? Has the consultant told you about providing services that are not specified on the contract? What does the firm promise? What do you have to promise? Are all fees and costs spelled out? What provisions are made for refunds? For how long a time can you use the firm's or the consultant's services?

Be sure to do some comparison shopping before you select a consultant. A list of New York area firms you might want to investigate is provided in Chapter 2.

Social Service Agencies

Unlike professional employment agencies, career consultants, and executive search firms, social service agencies are not-for-profit organizations. They offer a wide range of services, from counseling and vocational training to job placement and follow-up, and their services, in general, are free.

How do you locate these agencies? The most comprehensive guide is *The Sourcebook: Social and Health Services in the Greater New York Area* (Oryx Press, 4041 N. Central Avenue, Suite 700, Phoenix, AZ 85012-3397, (800) 279-6799). This directory is indexed by both key word and agency names. Each directory listing includes the agency's name, address, phone number, fees (if any), and a brief description of all programs offered.

The following social service agency listings include resources for women, minorities, seniors, handicapped, and young people.

SOCIAL SERVICE AGENCIES

Manhattan

All-Craft Foundation
19-23-25 St. Mark's Place
New York, NY 10003
(212) 228-6421
Provides training programs in the building trades, home improvement, building maintenance, and related skills. Offers job referral service for women, minorities in construction and other skilled trades.

American Woman's Economic Development Corp.
60 E. 42nd St.
New York, NY 10165
(212) 692-9100
Provides one-to-one counseling, in-house and over the phone, in virtually all phases of small business development and operation.

Help for vets

The work of the **Vietnam Veterans of America** in establishing memorials to Vietnam veterans is well known. But many people do not realize that the group has also established over 100 outreach centers nationwide. The main objective of these centers is to help men and women veterans of the Vietnam War readjust to civilian life.

The centers offer a variety of services. They solicit job listings from both the public and private sectors. Veterans who need additional

help are referred to appropriate counseling
groups, health agencies, and other organizations. The New York Outreach Center at 166 W.
75th St., (212) 944-2917, is open Monday
through Friday. No appointment is necessary. ■

Catalyst
14 E. 60th St.
New York, NY 10022
(212) 759-9700
National organization that works for the full participation of women in
corporate and professional life. Works to expand women's career options,
further their upward mobility, and help to reconcile the needs of the
workplace and the family. Affiliated with 224 career counseling and
resource centers. Offers a comprehensive library and information center.

Employment Program for Recovered Alcoholics
225 W. 34th St.
New York, NY 10122
(212) 947-1471
Offers job training and comprehensive vocational training.

Epilepsy Institute
67 Irving Place
New York, NY 10003
(212) 677-8550
Offers vocational and career counseling, testing, and evaluation. Serves
only those with epilepsy.

Federation of the Handicapped
154 W. 14th St.
New York, NY 10011
(212) 727-4200
Offers vocational and office skills training, work experience, and job
training programs.

Madison Group
Career Planning
342 Madison Ave., Suite 1060
New York, NY 10017
(212) 599-0032
Offers vocational and career counseling, placement, and job development.
Serves primarily women, ages 20-65.

Mayor's Office for the Handicapped
250 Broadway, Room 1414B
New York, NY 10017
(212) 788-4636
Offers educational, vocational, and career counseling. Also provides a job
training program, employment counseling, and job placement.

New York Junior League
130 E. 80th St.
New York, NY 10021
(212) 288-6220
Involved in a variety of community projects and services. Programs

include a speakers' bureau, career planning workshops, and management training.

New York League for the Hard of Hearing
71 W. 23rd St., 18th Floor
New York, NY 10010
(212) 741-7650
Offers vocational and career counseling, evaluation, testing, and assessment. You must be hearing-impaired to participate in the programs.

92nd St. YM-YWCA
Group Services Department
1395 Lexington Ave.
New York, NY 10028
(212) 427-6000
Offers workshops, seminars, and support groups for women and men considering various life options.

Vietnam Veterans of America
Outreach Center
166 W. 75th St.
New York, NY 10023
(212) 944-2917
Veterans can receive numerous job referrals through corporate postings solicited by the agency. No appointment necessary. Postings from both the public and private sector.

Vocational Foundation
902 Broadway
New York, NY 10010
(212) 777-0700
Offers vocational evaluation, testing, and assessment. Also provides employment services, job training, education counseling, and information.

Women's Action Alliance
370 Lexington Ave., Room 603
New York, NY 10017
(212) 532-8330
Offers job postings, resource bibliography, career counseling, vocational testing, and job referrals.

YWCA of Greater New York
610 Lexington Ave.
New York, NY 10022
(212) 755-4500
Offers vocational guidance counseling.

Queens

Goodwill Industries of Greater New York
4-21 27th Ave.
Astoria, NY 11102
(718) 728-5400
Offers vocational evaluation, testing and assessment, job training, sheltered employment, and on-the-job training program.

Women's Counseling Center of Queens
c/o Sandra Fishman
112-11 68th Drive
Forest Hills, NY 11375
(718) 268-3077
Provides resources and self-help opportunities. Sponsors workshops, support groups, rap sessions, and individual counseling for self-aware-ness, career and job development, and life crisis situations.

Brooklyn

Flatbush Development Corporation
1418 Cortelyou Road
Brooklyn, NY 11226
(718) 469-8990
Offers vocational and career counseling, pre-job skills counseling, and job development and placement.

Independent Living for the Handicapped
408 Jay St.
Brooklyn, NY 11201
(718) 625-7500
Offers vocational and career counseling, reviews career options, explains Office of Vocational Rehabilitation system and makes referrals for emotional, mental, and physical handicaps.

Industrial Home for the Blind
57 Willoughby St.
Brooklyn, NY 11201
(718) 522-2122
Offers employment services, health counseling, and information rehabili-tation service.

YWCA of Brooklyn
30 3rd Ave.
Brooklyn, NY 11217
(718) 875-1190
Offers personal and job counseling.

Bronx

Altro Health and Rehabilitation Services
3600 Jerome Ave.
Bronx, NY 10467
(212) 881-7600
Offers vocational evaluation, testing, and assessment.

Nassau County

Central Long Island Family Counseling Services
225 Jericho Turnpike
Floral Park, NY 11101
(516) 354-8926
Offers vocational, career, educational, and generic counseling.

Nassau County Medical Center-Rehabilitation Counseling
240 Old Country Road
Mineola, NY 11501
(516) 542-2227
Offers vocational evaluation, personal adjustment training, and appropriate referral services.

Yours, Ours, Mine Community Center
Center Lane, Village Green
Levittown, NY 11756
(516) 796-6633
Offers career counseling as well as other support counseling. For an appointment with an employment counselor, call (516)796-6633.

Westchester County

YWCA of White Plains and Central Westchester
515 N. White Plains
White Plains, NY 10603
(914) 949-6227
Offers career counseling and vocational testing.

Government and County Agencies

Most job seekers do not take advantage of the employment listings available through city, state, and federal government agencies because the caliber of these jobs is often disappointing. These listings are free, however. So you may as well stop in at one or more of the following offices and see what is available.

Civil Service Department of New York City
Department of Personnel
49 Thomas St.
New York, NY 10013
(212) 566-8700

Civil Service Division of Nassau County
140 Old Country Road
Mineola, NY 11501
(516) 535-2511

Mayor's Office of Second Careers Volunteer Programs
51 Chambers St.
New York, NY 10007
(212) 566-1808

Nassau County Department of Senior Citizen Affairs
222 Willis Ave.
Mineola, NY 11501
(516) 535-5862
Senior citizen job exchange.

**Nassau County Department of Social Services—
Employment Programs Information**
County Seat Drive
Mineola, NY 11501
(516) 535-5757

Nassau County Office of Employment and Training
9000 Ellison Ave.
Westbury, NY 11590
(516) 683-3320

New York City Senior Action Line
Municipal Building
1 Centre St.
New York, NY 10007
(212) 669-7670
Health, employment, social services, and complaint referrals. Also crime and transportation assistance.

New York State Civil Service Department Announcement and Application
2 World Trade Center
New York, NY 10048
(212) 488-4248

New York State Veteran's Affairs Counseling Service 80 Centre St.
New York, NY 10007
(212) 417-4826

Office of Personnel Management—Federal Job Information and Testing Center
26 Federal Plaza
New York, NY 10278
(212) 264-0422

United States Government, Department of Labor, Job Corps
201 Varick St.
New York, NY 10014
(212) 337-2287

Veteran's Employment and Training Services
1515 Broadway
New York, NY 10036
(212) 944-3259

Veteran's Services of Nassau County
320 Old Country Road
Mineola, NY 11501
(516) 535-3218

Westchester County Department of Employment and Training
150 Grand St.
White Plains, NY 10603
(914) 285-3910

Westchester County Office of Personnel Planning
Office Building 1
White Plains, NY 10603
(914) 285-2117
Civil service examinations.

How to Get a Job

Westchester County Operation Talent Bank
Office for Women
112 E. Post Road, Room 216
White Plains, NY 10601
(914) 285-5972

Westchester Veteran's Agency
150 Grand St.
White Plains, NY 10603
(914) 285-2146

Women's Office for Information and Referral
170 E. Post Road
White Plains, NY 10604
(914) 285-5972

Women's Services of Nassau County
1425 Old Country Road
Plainview, NY 11803
(516) 420-5101

Youth Board of Nassau
400 County Seat Drive
Mineola, NY 11501
(516) 535-5892

JOB LISTINGS AT THE NEW YORK STATE JOB SERVICE

The New York State Job Service is a state-operated agency that fills positions and screens applicants for jobs in the private sector. The agency operates a number of offices throughout the city of New York and suburbs. You can visit any of the offices. We suggest you consult your local listings for offices nearest your home. Some of these offices service specific fields or professions. Job listings change daily.

Manhattan

Apparel Industries Personnel
238 W. 35th St.
New York, NY 10001
(212) 971-0500
Apparel industry personnel.

Health Services Placement Center
238 W. 35th St.
New York, NY 10001
(212) 971-0500
Registry of doctors, dentists, and nurses.

Queens

Flushing Placement Center
42-09 Main St.
Flushing, NY 11355
(718) 321-6307

Queens State Employment Office
97-45 Queens Blvd.
Rego Park, NY 11374
(718) 706-2190
Apparel, industrial, office, professional, and sales personnel.

Bronx

Bronx Employment Office
60 Bond St.
New York, NY 10005
(718) 780-9352
Professional, technical, clerical, sales, and industrial personnel.

Bronx Employment Office
501 Cortlandt Ave.
Bronx, NY 10451
(718) 292-0164

Staten Island

Staten Island
1139 Hyland Blvd.
Staten Island, NY 10305
(718) 447-2931
Office, professional, industrial, service, and sales personnel.

Nassau County

Nassau County Employment Office
84 N. Main St.
Freeport, NY 11520
(516) 623-1950

Westchester County

New York State Job Service
161 Gramatan Ave.
Mt. Vernon, NY 10550
(914) 664-7900

New York State Job Service
201 S. James St.
Peekskill, NY 10566
(914) 737-3490

New York State Job Service
5 Prospect Ave.
White Plains, NY 10601
(914) 997-9588

New York State Job Service
3 Prospect Ave.
Yonkers, NY 10704
(914) 965-9500

How To Succeed In an Interview

If you've read straight through this book, you already know that networking (see Chapter 5) is one of the most important and useful job-hunting techniques around. Networking is nothing more or less than using personal contacts to explore the job market and to generate both exploratory and formal job interviews.

Networking and interviewing go hand in hand; all the contacts in the world won't do you any good if you don't handle yourself well in an interview. No two interviews are ever identical, except that you always have the same goal in mind: to convince the person to whom you're talking that he or she should help you find a job or hire you personally. An interview is also an exchange of information. But you should never treat it as you would a casual conversation, even if the "interviewer" is an old friend.

Preparing for the Interview: The 5-Minute Resume

Whether you're talking to the housewife next door about her brother-in-law who knows someone you want to meet or going through a final, formal interview with a multinational corporation, you are essentially making a sales presentation—in this case, selling yourself. Your goal is to convince the interviewer that you have the ability, experience, personality, maturity, and other characteristics required to do a good job and to enlist the interviewer's help in getting you that job.

In an informal interview you'll be talking first to friends and acquaintances. Most of the people you'll be talking to will want to help you. But they need to know who you are, what you've done, what you want to do, and most important, *how they can help you.*

To prepare for any interview, first perfect what we like to call the five-minute resume. Start by giving a rough description, not too detailed, of what you're doing now (or did on your last job) so that when you're telling your story, the listener isn't distracted by wondering how it's going to end.

Then go all the way back to the beginning—not of your career, but of your life. Talk about where you were born, where you grew up, what your folks did, whether or not they're still living, what your brothers and sisters do, and so on. Then trace your educational background briefly and, finally, outline your work history from your first job to your latest.

"What!" say many of our clients. "Drag my PARENTS into this? Talk about my crazy BROTHER and the neighborhood where we grew up?"

Yes, indeed. You want to draw the listener into your story, to make him or her interested enough in you to work for you in your search. You want the interviewer to know not only who you are and what you have achieved but also what you are capable of. You also want to establish things in common with the listener. The more you have in common, the harder your listener will work for you.

Co-author Tom Camden, we are not ashamed to admit, is a master of the five-minute resume. Here's how he would begin a presentation to someone like the neighbor down the street:

"Would it be all right with you if I gave you a broad-brush review of my background? Let you know what I've done, what I'd like to do? That'll give us some time to talk about how I should go about this job search. Maybe I could pick your brain a little about how you can help me. OK?

"Currently, I have my own career consulting business.

"Originally, I'm from the Southwest Side of Chicago, near Midway Airport. I'm 54 years old, married with five grown children.

"My father was a security guard at IIT Research Institute; my mother is retired. She used to work for Walgreens—made aspirins, vitamins, and other pills. I'm the oldest of four children. My brother John does the traffic 'copter reports for a Chicago radio station. My sister Connie is a consultant for an industrial relations firm.

"I went to parochial schools. When I was 14, I left home and went into a monastery. I stayed there until I was 19. Then I went to Loyola University, studied psychology, got my degree in '59. I was also commissioned in the infantry.

"I started my graduate work in Gestalt psychology. In 1960 Kennedy called up troops for the Berlin crisis. That included me, so I spent a year on active duty. Following that, I came back and continued my graduate work in industrial relations..."

Tom took exactly a minute and a half to make this part of his presentation, and he's already given his neighbor several areas in which they may have something in common. He's volunteered enough information not only to get the neighbor interested in his story but to let the neighbor form judgments about him. People don't like to play God, says Tom. Yet it's a fact of life that we constantly form judgments about each other. In an interview—even an exploratory, informal one—you may as well provide enough information to be judged on who you are rather than on what someone has to guess about your background. What does it mean to be the oldest of four kids? What can you deduce from Tom's middle-class background?

The typical personnel professional will tell you that the number of brothers and sisters you have has nothing to do with getting a job. Technically, that's true. The law says that an employer can't ask you how old you are, your marital status, and similar questions. Yet anyone who's considering hiring you will want to know those things about you.

The typical applicant begins a presentation with something like, "I graduated from school in June, nineteen-whatever, and went to work for so-and-so." Our task in this book is to teach you how *not* to be typical. Our experience has convinced us that the way to get a job offer is to be different from the rest of the applicants. You shouldn't eliminate the first 20 years of your life when someone asks you about your background! That's the period that shaped your basic values and personality.

Neither should you spend too much time on your personal history. A minute or two is just about right. That gives you from three to eight minutes to narrate your work history. Most exploratory interviews, and many initial employment interviews, are limited to half an hour. If you can give an oral resume in 5 to 10 minutes, you have roughly 20 minutes left to find out what you want to know (more on that shortly).

The five-minute resume revisited

Psychologist and career expert Gayle Roberts has her own slant on the five-minute resume. She believes that "while nothing works every time, you should try to emphasize those aspects of your personal history that have a bearing on your current qualifications for the job you're seeking.

"For example, I am one of those rare creatures who always liked school. I got along fine with the teachers. I even liked studying and taking tests. I liked to learn, and I still do. That's part of why I choose to work in an academic setting. I think it's helpful to mention my long history as a book worm any time I'm applying for a position that requires research, writing, or critical thinking skills. I don't think I'd mention it if I were going for a sales position.

"I personally wouldn't recommend saying too much about your past unless you can connect it to the present in a way that makes you look like a better job candidate. Everybody has a number of revealing personal anecdotes. The trick is to pick the right ones." ■

A word about your work history. If you've done the exercises in Chapter 2, or written your own resume, you ought to be able to rattle off every job you've had, from the first to the latest, pretty easily. In the oral resume you want especially to *emphasize your successes and accomplishments* in each job. This will take some practice. We are not accustomed to talking about ourselves positively. From childhood we're conditioned that it's not nice to brag. Well, we are here to tell you that if you don't do it in the interview, you won't get the offer.

We repeat: *the interview is a sales presentation*. It's the heart of your job search, your effort to market yourself. In an exploratory interview, the listener will be asking, "Should I help this person?" In a formal interview, the employer will be asking, "Should I hire this person?" In either case, the answer will be "yes" only if you make a successful presentation, only if you convince the interviewer that you're worth the effort.

So, the first step in preparing for any interview, formal or informal, is to practice your five-minute resume. Go through it out loud enough times so that you're comfortable delivering it. Then work with a tape recorder and critique yourself. Try it out on a couple of friends.

When you're preparing for a formal employment interview, do your homework on the company. This advice is merely common sense. But it's surprising how many candidates will ask an interviewer, "What does this company do?" Don't be one of them. Before you go in for an employment interview, find out everything you can about the company—its history, organization, products and services, and growth expectations. Get hold of the company's annual report, catalogs, and brochures. Consult your networking contacts, and use the resources in Chapter 4.

Steps to a Successful Interview

Before the Interview
- Self-assessment: identify strengths, goals, skills, etc.
- Research the company.

- Rehearse what you plan to say. Practice answers to common questions.
- Prepare questions to ask employer.

During the Interview
- Make sure you arrive a few minutes early.
- Greet the interviewer by his/her last name; offer a firm handshake and a warm smile.
- Be aware of non-verbal communication. Wait to sit until you are offered a chair. Sit up straight, look alert, speak clearly and forcefully but stay relaxed. Make good eye contact, avoid nervous mannerisms, and try to be a good listener as well as a good talker. Smile.
- Follow the interviewer's lead, but try to get the interviewer to describe the position and duties to you fairly early in the interview so you can then relate your background and skills in context.
- Be specific, concrete, and detailed in your answers. The more information you volunteer, the better the employer gets to know you.
- Offer examples of your work that document your best qualities.
- Answer questions as truthfully and as frankly as you can. Do not appear to be "glossing over" anything. On the other hand, stick to the point and do not over-answer questions. The interviewer may steer the interview into ticklish political or social questions. Answer honestly, trying not to say more than is necessary.

Closing the Interview
- Don't be discouraged if no definite offer is made or specific salary discussed.
- If you get the impression that the interview is not going well and that you have already been rejected, do not let your discouragement show. Once in a while, an interviewer who is genuinely interested in you may seem to discourage you to test your reaction.
- A typical interviewer comment toward the close of an interview is to ask if you have any questions. Prepare several questions in advance, and ask those that weren't covered during the interview.
- At the conclusion of your interview, ask when a hiring decision will be made. Also thank your interviewer for his or her time and express your interest in the position.

After the Interview
- Take notes on what you feel you could improve upon for your next interview.
- If you are interested in the position, type a brief thank-you letter to the interviewer, indicating your interest.

- If offered the position, one to two weeks is a reasonable amount of time to make a decision. All employment offers deserve a written reply whether or not you accept them.

How to dress

A young friend of ours who wanted to break into real estate finally landed her first big interview— with Coldwell Banker. It was fairly easy for her to do her homework on a company of that size. Two days before the interview, however, it suddenly dawned on her that she had no idea how to dress. How did she solve her problem?

"It was pretty easy, actually, and fun, too," says Susan. "All I did was go and hang around outside the office for 15 minutes at lunchtime to see what everyone else was wearing."

However, we recommend that even if the office attire is casual, one should still dress professionally. One career counselor recommends that one should "always dress one step above the attire of those in the office where you are interviewing." ■

What Interviewers are Looking For

General Personality: Ambition, poise, sincerity, trustworthiness, articulateness, analytical ability, initiative, interest in the firm. (General intelligence is assumed.) Different firms look for different kinds of people—personalities, style, appearance, abilities, and technical skills. Always check the job specifications. Don't waste time talking about a job you can't do or for which you do not have the minimum qualifications.

Personal Appearance: A neat, attractive appearance makes a good impression and demonstrates professionalism.

Work Experience: Again, this varies from job to job, so check job specifications. If you've had work experience, be able to articulate the importance of what you did in terms of the job for which you are interviewing and in terms of your own growth or learning. Even if the work experience is unrelated to your field, employers look upon knowledge of the work environment as an asset.

Verbal Communication Skills: The ability to express yourself articulately is very important to most interviewers. This includes the ability to listen effectively, verbalize thoughts clearly, and express yourself confidently.

Skills: The interviewer will evaluate your skills for the job, such as organization, analysis, and research. It is important to emphasize the skills that you feel the employer is seeking and to give specific examples of how you developed them. This is the main reason why it is important to engage in self-assessment prior to the interview.

Goals/Motivation: Employers will assess your ability to articulate your short-term and long-term goals. You should seem ambitious, yet realistic about the training and qualifications needed to advance. You should demonstrate interest in the functional area or industry and a desire to succeed and work hard.

Knowledge of the Interviewer's Company and Industry: At a minimum, you really are expected to have done some homework on the company. Don't waste interview time asking questions you could have found answers to in printed material. Know the firm's position and character relative to others in the same industry. General awareness of media coverage of a firm and its industry is usually expected.

Handling the Interview

In an exploratory, or informal, interview most of the people you'll talk with will want to help you. But they need to know how. After you've outlined your personal and work history, ask your contact how he or she thinks your experience fits into today's market. What companies should you visit? Specifically, what people should you contact?

When someone gives you advice or a recommendation to call someone else, do it! Few things can be more irritating than to provide free counsel to someone who then ignores it. If your contact suggests that you call Helen Smith, call her!

In a formal employment interview, there are several typical questions you can expect to encounter, though not necessarily in this order:

Tell me about yourself. (This is your cue for the five-minute resume.)

Why do you want to change jobs?

What kind of job are you looking for now?

What are your long-range objectives?

What are your salary requirements?

When could you be available to start here?

Tell me about your present company.

What kind of manager are you?

How would you describe yourself?

What are your strengths and weaknesses?

(In the course of his career, Tom Camden has posed this last question to untold numbers of applicants. "They'll list two or three strengths," he says, "and then can't wait to tell me about their weaknesses." Don't be one of those people! Accentuate the positive. Remember, this is a competitive interview.)

Describe your present boss.

To whom can I talk about your performance?

Are you open to relocation?

How long have you been looking for a new job?

Why are you interested in this company? (This is your golden opportunity to show the interviewer that you've done your homework on the company.)

Practice your answers to these questions before you go in for the interview. Anticipate other questions you might be asked, and develop answers for them. In general, keep your responses positive. Never volunteer a negative about yourself, another company, or a former employer. Even if you hate your present boss, describe your areas of disagreement in a calm, professional manner. You are selling yourself, not downgrading others. Even if you're not particularly interested in the company, always conduct the interview as if you were dead set on getting the job.

The interviewer will apply your responses to the questions he or she really wants answered:

Does the applicant have the ability to do the job?

Can he or she manage people?

How does he or she relate to people?

What kind of person is this? A leader? A follower?

What strengths does he or she have that we need?

Why the number of job changes so far?

Where is he or she weak?

How did the applicant contribute to present and past companies?

What are his or her ambitions? Are they realistic?

Is he or she too soft or too tough on subordinates?

What is this person's standard of values?

Does he or she have growth potential?

Is there a health problem anywhere?

What is the nature of the "chemistry" between us?

What will the department manager think of this applicant as opposed to the others?

Should this person get an offer?

The interview should not be a one-sided affair, however. Questions that you should ask the interviewer are equally important in this exchange of information. For example, you have to know about the job, the company, and the people in your future employment situation. It's necessary to use your judgment to determine how and when to ask questions in an interview. But without the answers, it will be next to impossible for you to make a sound decision if you receive an offer. Some of the questions you want answered are:

What are the job's responsibilities?

What is the company's recent history? Its current objectives? Its market position?

Where are its plants located? What distribution systems does it use?

121

To whom will I report? What's his or her background?
How much autonomy will I have to get the job done?
Why is the job available?
Where does the job lead?
What about travel requirements?
Where is the job located?
Are there any housing, school, or community problems that will develop as a result of this job?
What is the salary range? (Do not raise the question of explicit salary at this point.)
What is the detailed benefit picture?
What is the company's relocation policy?
When will an offer decision be made?
What references will be required?
When would I have to start?
What is the personality of the company?
Do the job and company fit my plan for what I want to do now?
What's the next step?

Following the Interview

Many job seekers experience a kind of euphoria after a good interview. Under the impression that a job offer is imminent, a candidate may discontinue the search. This is a serious mistake. The decision may take weeks, or may not be made at all. On the average, about six weeks elapse between the time a person makes initial contact with a company and when he receives a final answer. If you let up on the search, you will prolong it. Maintain a constant sense of urgency. Get on with the next interview. Your search isn't over until an offer is accepted and you actually begin the new job.

Always follow up an interview with a thank you letter which should be written within 48 hours of the interview. The following form provides the points to be covered.

100 Your Street
Hometown, State 01000
Date, Month, Year

Mr. John Doe
President
XYZ Company
500 Fortune Street
City, State 01000

Dear Mr. Doe:

Your first paragraph thanks the interviewer for his/her time and consideration. You may also express how much you enjoyed the meeting and learning more of the position at his/her firm.

The second paragraph could sum up some important qualifications you possess which make you a good candidate for the position. For example, "I believe my organizational abilities would make me particularly effective in this position," or "I am quite interested in the accounting with XYZ Company because it complements my experience in taxes and auditing." Be enthusiastic and sincere with your comments. The notes you jotted down after your interview will help you formulate comments for this second paragraph.

The last paragraph thanks the employer once again for his/her interest in you as a candidate. You may also write something to the effect of "I look forward to learning of your decision" or "I am excited about gaining more knowledge of your advertising objectives" or "The finance position at your firm sounds like an outstanding opportunity."

Sincerely,

(Your Name typed)

P.S. Keep it short and sweet (1 page typed on white bond paper). Be sure to check your spelling and typing!

A recruiter from a Fortune 500 company told us that what often makes the difference between a job offer and a rejection letter is evidence that the candidate has researched the company and written a thoughtful thank-you letter.

If you think you could benefit from professional counseling in interviewing skills, consider the resources suggested in Chapter 2 and in Chapter 6. You may also find it helpful to refer to some of the following books.

BOOKS ON INTERVIEWING

Allen, Jeffrey. *How to Turn an Interview Into a Job Offer*. New York: Simon & Schuster, 1988.

Biegelein, J.I. *Make Your Job Interview a Success*. New York: Arco, 1991.

Danna, Jo. *Winning the Job Interview Game: Tips for the High-Tech Era*. Briarwood, NY: Palomino Press, 1986.

Fear, Richard A. *The Evaluation Interview*, 4th ed. New York: McGraw-Hill, 1990.

Fry, Ron. *Your First Interview: Everything You Need to Know to "Ace" the Interview Process and Get Your First Job*. Hawthorne, NJ: The Career Press, 1991.

Goodale, James G. *The Fine Art of Interviewing*. Englewood Cliffs, NJ: Prentice-Hall, 1982.

Kennedy, Joyce Lain. *Job Interviews: How to Win the Offer*. Cardiff, CA: Sun Features, 1990.

Kohlmann, James D. *Make Them Choose You*. Englewood Cliffs, NJ: Prentice Hall, 1988.

Marcus, John J. *The Complete Job Interview Handbook*, 2nd ed. New York: Harper & Row, 1988.

Smart, Bradford D. *The Smart Interviewer*. New York: John Wiley & Sons, 1989.

Stoodley, Martha. *Informational Interviewing: What It Is and How To Use It in Your Career*. Garrett Park, MD: Garrett Park Press, 1990.

Yate, Martin John. *Knock 'em Dead with Great Answers to Tough Questions*. Boston: Bob Adams, 1991.

How to get the most from your references

References should be kept confidential and never revealed until a company is close to making you an offer and you want to receive one. Always brief your references before you supply an interviewer with their names and numbers. Tell your references what company you're interviewing with and what the job is. Give them some background on the company and the responsibilities you'll be asked to handle. Your references will then be in a position to help sell your abilities. Finally, don't abuse your references. If you give their names too often, they may lose enthusiasm for your cause. ∎

What To Do If Money
Gets Tight

Any job search takes time. One particularly pessimistic career counselor we know suggests you plan to spend about two weeks of search time for every thousand dollars you want to earn per year. (Pity the poor soul who wants to make $60,000!) A more optimistic estimate for a job search is around three months, provided the search is conducted full time.

If you already have a full-time job, it will take you longer to find a new one. But at least you will be receiving a paycheck while you're looking. This chapter is intended for those who are unemployed and facing the prospect of little or no income during the search.

When the financial squeeze is on, the first thing to do is make a thorough review of your liquid assets and short-term liabilities. Ask yourself how much cash you can expect to receive during the next three months from the following sources, plus any others you might come up with:

Savings

Securities

Silver and gold

Insurance loan possibilities

Second mortgage possibilities

Unemployment compensation

Severance pay

Accrued vacation pay

Personal loan sources (relatives, friends)

Sale of personal property (car, boat, stamp collections, etc.)

Next you should consider exactly what bills absolutely must be paid. Don't worry about your total outstanding debt. Many creditors can be stalled or might be willing to make arrangements to forgo principal as long as interest payments are made. Talk to each of your creditors to see if something can be worked out.

The final step is easy—if sometimes painful. You compare the amount of money you have on hand or expect to receive, with the amount you know you'll have to spend. The difference tells you exactly what kind of financial shape you're in.

The old adage has it that it's better to be unemployed than underemployed. If you can afford it, it's wise not to take a part-time or temporary job. The more time you spend looking for a good full-time position, the sooner you're likely to succeed. But if the cupboard looks pretty bare, it may be necessary to supplement your income any way legally possible in order to eat during the search.

Try to find part-time or temporary work that leaves you as free as possible to interview during the day. For this reason, many people choose to drive a cab at night or work in a bar or restaurant during the evenings or work for a security service. This kind of job gives you the advantage of flexible hours, but the pay is not always desirable. Commissioned sales positions, especially telemarketing, abound in almost every industry. But if your personality isn't suited to sales work, don't pursue it. You'll find it very frustrating.

It's best if you can locate part-time work in your chosen field. The pay is usually more attractive, and you can continue to develop your network of contacts. Many professionals can freelance. An administrative assistant, for example, might be able to find part-time work at a law firm. An accountant might be able to do taxes on a part-time basis and still gain access to new referrals.

Here are some additional sources to consider when the money is really tight and you need part-time or temporary work.

Part-time work can mean more than just money

If you're a student, working part time in your chosen field can be a great way to make contacts and gain valuable experience. Part-time work may even lead to a full-time position, as it did for our friend Christine Alles. Chris was attending New York's Fashion Institute of Technology when she decided to get an insider's look at the fashion industry.

"I could type and take stenography," says Chris. "I felt my best shot at getting a job in the fashion industry would be to use my practical skills." Through a mutual friend, Chris was hired as a part-time clerical worker at Evan Picone Leg Fashions.

Chris put a lot of effort into her job. "I took on extra work and began visiting accounts to make stock checks and to meet the buyers," says Chris. "About two months before graduation, I was hired as a full-time employee. I became a national sales representative for specialty accounts."

If you're lucky enough to get a part-time job in your field, make it work for you. Get to know everyone you work for and everyone who works with you. Many companies like to promote part-time staffers. They feel they've got a loyal employee who's learned the ropes from the ground up. ■

TEMPORARY WORK SERVICES

Accountants Executive Search
535 5th Ave., Suite 1901
New York, NY 10017
(212) 682-5900
Senior-level accounting and finance.

Accountemps
522 5th Ave.
New York, NY 10036
(212) 221-6500
Accountants, bookkeepers, EDP experts, word processors.
Westchester office: (914) 682-8842. Connecticut office: (203) 324-3399.

Allied Temporary Personnel
295 Madison Ave.
New York, NY 10017
(212) 599-6171
Data entry, word processing, keypunch, and clerical personnel.

ALTCO Temporary Services
100 Menlo Park
Edison, NJ 08837
(908) 549-6100

Burns International Security
1501 Broadway
New York, NY 10036
(212) 764-3110
Armed guard service.

Cantor Concern Interim Services
33 W. 58th St.
New York, NY 10019
(212) 333-3000
PR and communications professionals.

Career Blazers Temporary Services
590 5th Ave.
New York, NY 10017
(212) 719-3232
Finance, insurance, computers, legal, advertising, personnel, and office services.
Melville, Long Island office: (516) 756-2400. Westchester: (914) 949-1166.

Career Employment Services
1600 Stewart Ave.
Westbury, NY 11590
(516) 683-3000
Health care and related areas.

CoverTemp
(Gateway Careers
235 Main St.
White Plains, NY 10601
(914) 946-2300

Kelly Temporary Services
1212 Avenue of the Americas
New York, NY 10020
(212) 704-2040
Secretarial and clerical personnel.
Other offices include: Queens, (718) 898-3550; Bronx, (212) 298-7878; Brooklyn, (718) 855-7505; Nassau, (516) 741-0262; and Westchester, (914) 761-5885.

Kling Custom Temps and Consulting
Borrow-A-Banker
180 Broadway, Suite 801
New York, NY 10038
(212) 964-3640
Banking and finance professionals.

Manpower Temporary Services
50 Main St.
White Plains, NY 10606
(914) 428-0155
New York City office: 100 E. 42nd St.
(212) 557-9110
General.

MB Inc.
Interim Executive Division

505 5th Ave.
New York, NY 10017
(212) 661-4937
Managers in various marketing areas.

Metro Systems Corporation
30-17 40th Ave.
Long Island City, NY 11101
(718) 786-0640
Taxicab leasing.

Olsten Temporary Services
30 E. 42nd St.
New York, NY 10017
(212) 687-5100
General office, word processing, records management, accounting,
marketing, and light industrial. Offices in Queens, (718) 459-8300;
Brooklyn, (718) 522-2600; Staten Island, (718) 438-9448; Nassau,
(516) 997-6666; and Westchester, (914) 948-2591.

Sloan Personnel Agency
1 E. 42nd St.
New York, NY 10017
(212) 949-7200
Secretarial and general office services.

Temp Force
1 Old Country Road
Carle Place, NY 11514
(516) 794-9700
Office personnel: secretaries, typists, clerks, bookkeepers, word processors, and keypunch operators. Day, night, and weekend work available.
Eight locations on Long Island.

Tempo Temporary Personnel
Sunrise Highway and Rockaway Ave.
Valley Stream, NY 11580
(516) 872-8080
Office, industrial, and medical personnel. Five locations on Long Island.

Temporary Service
295 Madison Ave.
New York, NY 10017
(212) 683-0165
Several different areas of specialization.

Wells Fargo Guard Services
135 W. 41st St.
New York, NY 10018
(212) 840-1884
Security guard service.

Wintemps
535 5th Ave.
New York, NY 10017
(212) 687-7890
General office services.

**Fast talk nets
big part-time
$$$**

People who need to earn money while job hunting might consider the telemarketing, or telephone sales, industry. Debra Schwartz, who has worked as a telemarketing manager, feels that the field offers a variety of challenges and rewards. We asked Debra what telemarketing managers look for in the people they hire.

"The crucial element is the person's voice. Telemarketers must speak clearly and have pleasing voices. They also must use standard English grammar. Previous sales experience is a plus, although it's not necessary. Managers also look for people who can handle rejection. A person might get rejected 25 or 30 times before making a sale."

According to Debra, most telemarketers work in four-hour shifts. "You can't work on the phone for more than four hours without becoming ineffective. Also, many firms operate only in the afternoons and evenings. But some firms do have morning hours—those involved in corporate sales, for example."

How much can a telemarketer expect to make?

"Top people can make over $10 per hour," says Debra. "The average telemarketer makes about $4-$8 per hour. The pay varies depending on whether you are working on a straight commission basis or are being paid a base hourly wage plus commissions."

Debra suggests investigating a telemarketing firm carefully before accepting a job since there are quite a few fly-by-night operations. ■

SELECTED BOOKS ON PART-TIME AND FLEXIBLE EMPLOYMENT

Arden, Lynie. *The Work-at-Home Sourcebook*. Boulder, CO: Live Oak Publications, 1987.

Canape, Charlene. *The Part-Time Solution: The New Strategy for Managing Motherhood*. New York: Harper Collins, 1990.

Justice, Peggy. *The Temp Track: Make One of the Hottest Job Trends for the 90's Work for You*. Princeton, NJ: Petersons, 1993.

Lee, Patricia. *The Complete Guide to Job Sharing*. New York: Walker, 1983.

Magid, Renee Y. *When Mothers and Fathers Work: Creative Strategies for Balancing Career and Family*. New York, NY: AMACOM, 1987.

Marsh, DeLoss L. *Retirement Careers: Combining the Best of Work and Leisure*. Williamson, Susan, and Roger Griffith, eds. Charlotte, VT: Williamson Publ. Co., 1991.

O'Hara, Bruce. *Put Work in Its Place*. Victoria, BC, Canada: Work Well, 1988.

Olmsted and Smith. *The Job Sharing Handbook*. Walnut Creek, CA: Ten Speed Press, 1983.

Rothberg and Cook. *Part-Time Professional*. Washington, DC: Acropolis Books, 1985.

Government and Private Assistance Programs

If you've exhausted all your resources and can't find part-time or temporary work, you might consider state, federal, or private assistance. Many people bridle at the mere mention of "charity" or "welfare."

But the help you receive may be needed—and temporary. It's a way of bridging the gap until you land a job. More people take advantage of these sources of assistance than you might imagine. In the case of state and federal aid, your tax dollars have helped to provide the benefits. Your taxes have also paid the salaries of the people distributing the benefits.

Don't pass judgment on the merits of the following sources until you talk with the professionals who administer their respective programs. Pros can advise you on eligibility, benefits, and can also provide you with other ideas and resources.

GOVERNMENT AID SOURCES

Human Resources Administration—Department of Income Maintenance, City of New York
250 Church St.
New York, NY 10013
(212) 274-5400
Provides emergency financial assistance. Monday through Friday, 9:00 a.m. to 5:00 p.m. There are 59 service sites in New York City. Check your local phone book for the site nearest you.

Nassau County Department of Social Services
County Seat Drive
Mineola, NY 11501
(516) 535-4817
Makes referrals to such county-wide agencies as the following:

Employment Programs Information (516) 535-5100

Food Stamps Information (516) 535-4613

Public Assistance Information (516) 535-4817
Rent, food, and utility vouchers distributed based on need.

New York City Food Stamp Program
(718) 291-1900
Call this number for the names and addresses of offices distributing food stamp applications in the five boroughs. You must make an appointment to pick up an application. Eligibility requirements are the same for Nassau and Westchester counties.

New York City Senior Action Line
1 Centre St.
Municipal Building
New York, NY 10004
(212) 669-7670
Hot-line for senior citizens. Provides free information and referrals regarding food stamps, social security payments, health services, city agencies, and crime assistance. Open 11:00 a.m. to 1:00 p.m., Monday through Friday.

Veteran's Administration Regional Office
252 7th Ave.
New York, NY 10001
(212) 620-6901
Offers financial assistance in the form of loans, educational benefits, veterans' compensations. Also provides vocational and career counseling.

Veteran's Employment and Training Service
201 Varick St.
New York, NY
(212) 337-2300

Westchester County Department of Social Services
85 Court St.
White Plains, NY 10601
(914) 285-5000
After hours emergency: (914) 592-3791
Makes referrals to other county agencies, including public assistance and food stamps.

GETTING UNEMPLOYMENT BENEFITS

You can file for unemployment benefits at any state unemployment office. To be eligible for benefits, you must have worked 20 out of the last 52 weeks. You will need proof of identification, including a photo ID, your social security card, and a list of all the companies you have worked for in the last 52 weeks.

If your application is approved, you should receive your first unemployment check in about four weeks depending on the office. The size of your check depends on how much you were earning at your last job or jobs. Unemployment benefits last a maximum of 26 weeks. Be aware of changes in New York State law affecting unemployment benefits and requirements.

Here are the addresses and phone numbers of a few of the centrally located unemployment offices. Office hours vary, so it's best to call in advance to make sure a counselor will be available.

New York State
Department of Labor,
Unemployment Division
50 Park Place
New York, NY 10048
(212) 791-1400

New York State
Department of Labor,
Unemployment Division
14 Bank St.
Peekskill, NY 10605
(914) 737-3490

New York State
Department of Labor,
Unemployment Division
5 Prospect Ave.
White Plains, NY 10604
(914) 997-9588

New York State
Department of
Unemployment Insurance
84 Main St.
Freeport, NY 11520
(516) 623-1950

New York State
Department of
Unemployment Insurance
344 Fulton Ave.
Hempstead, NY 11550
(516) 486-3435

PRIVATE CHARITABLE ORGANIZATIONS

The Bowery Mission Ministries
227 Bowery
New York, NY 10002
(212) 674-3456
Provides free food and shelter; offers drug and alcohol counseling.
Assistance lasts 90 days; recipients must stay at the Mission.

Catholic Charities of the Archdiocese of NY
1011 1st Ave.
New York, NY 10022
(212) 371-1000
Offers counseling. Provides referrals to city and privately run agencies
offering short-term financial assistance. Branch offices located throughout the metropolitan area and Nassau and Westchester counties.

Catholic Youth Organization—Archdiocese of New York
1011 1st Ave.
New York, NY 10022
(212) 371-1000
Offers vocational and career counseling, clothing and food provisions,
meals, work experience programs, and on-the-job training programs.

Federation of Protestant Welfare Agencies
666 Broadway
New York, NY 10010
(212) 777-4800
Local branch offices offer food, clothing, and shelter on a short-term
basis. Call the main office for the number of the office nearest you.

Legal Aid Society
Administration, 22nd Floor
15 Park Row
New York, NY 10038
(212) 513-0071

How to Get a Job

Offers free legal assistance if income eligibility requirements are met. Assistance in all legal matters.

St. Vincent De Paul Society
1011 1st Ave.
New York, NY 10022
(212) 755-8615
Consists of local parish conferences. Most offer food programs and make referrals for shelter. One of largest organizations of its kind in the New York metropolitan area. Operates a clothing and household goods distribution center in the Bronx at 402 E. 152nd St., Bronx, NY 10455.

Salvation Army
221 E. 52nd St.
New York, NY 10022
(212) 758-0763
Offers food and clothing distribution programs. Branch offices in the five boroughs as well as Nassau and Westchester counties.

United Way of New York City
99 Park Ave.
New York, NY 10016
(212) 973-3800
The Greater New York Fund division of the United Way of New York City provides emergency food and shelter.

Volunteers of America
340 W. 85th St.
New York, NY 10024
(212) 873-2600
Offers special assistance programs.

Where To Turn If Your
Confidence Wilts

Recently a bank fired a loan officer who had worked there for more than ten years. The employee was 58 years old, about 5 feet, 6 inches tall, weighed almost 300 pounds, and did not have a college degree. His written communication skills were negligible. His poor attitude and appearance, lack of enthusiasm, and dismal self-esteem suggested he would be unemployed a long time.

The bank decided to use Tom Camden's services to help the person get another job. "There wasn't much we could do about changing his age, education, size, or communication skills," Tom recalls. "But we certainly could—and did—work with him on improving his self-esteem and changing his attitude toward interviewing for new jobs."

After a four-month search, the loan officer succeeded in landing a position that exactly suited his needs. His new job even was located in the neighborhood where he lived. It seemed like a typical success story—until the bank informed Tom Camden about how dissatisfied that person was with the counsel he had received. The man told the bank that they would have been better off paying him the consulting fee instead of retaining outside help.

"He was really angry," Tom recalls, "and also full of stress, guilt, fear, anxiety, desire for vengeance, and a host of other emotions."

Such feelings, unfortunately, are not at all unusual. In fact, they're a normal part of any job search, particularly for those who have been laid off or fired. That's because rejection, unfortunately, is inevitable in any job search.

If you've read Chapter 5, you know that you may speak with as many as 300 people on a formal or informal basis while you're looking for suitable work—and a healthy percentage of those people will be unable or unwilling to help you. Every job seeker must anticipate rejection—it comes with the territory. Being turned down in an interview is a painful experience, and it's normal to feel hurt. The trick is to keep those hurt and angry feelings from clouding your judgment or affecting your behavior.

Danger and opportunity: Career transition issues

"A job search, like the Chinese character for crisis, contains both danger and opportunity," according to Burt Kirson, a licensed psychotherapist who works with clients dealing with career transition issues. "The danger is rejection, failure, and dissatisfaction. The opportunity is a chance to go after what you want or need." Kirson defines seven key issues that most people confront during a job hunt:

Self-esteem: Do you feel good about yourself, your daily life, and your future? Are you self-accepting? Do you have a positive self-image?

Self-validation: Do you validate yourself both from without and within? Do you have an inner sense of your own worth? Are you able to learn from the feedback you get from others during the job hunt?

Risk and control: Are you willing to take the risks needed to get what you want? Are you willing to reveal yourself even in a situation such as a job interview when you're not completely in control?

Sadness or depression: Can you feel sad about loss but still bounce back? Can you learn from failure even as you feel good about success?

Internalized anger: Can you recognize when you feel angry? If you are angry, can you identify which of your needs are not being met? Can you discover effective and appropriate ways to express your anger?

Goal setting: Are your goals appropriate to who you are and what you need? Are your goals and expectations realistic in terms of the current job market and your own training and expertise?

Phase of life issues: How have your goals changed over time? Has your self-image changed as you have changed and grown? Are you flexible enough to change as your life changes? ■

If you're beginning to feel your confidence wilt, reread the tips for treating yourself well in Chapter 5. Put yourself on a regular schedule. Make sure you're eating healthy foods and getting enough rest and exercise. Don't punish yourself for being unemployed or losing a job offer.

One of the worst things that can happen in any job search is to let rejection undermine your self-confidence. Like the little boy at the door who asks, "You don't want to buy a magazine, do you?" a person who doesn't feel good about himself will not easily convince an employer that he should be hired. Each new rejection further erodes self-esteem, and the job search stalls or takes a nose dive: "Maybe I am a loser. Perhaps I was lucky to have my old job as long as I did. Maybe my sights are set too high. I suppose I should look for something less responsible at a lower salary."

Thoughts such as these cross most people's minds at some time or other in the job search. As we've said, it's normal to feel hurt, angry, and depressed after a series of rejections. It's important, however, to recognize these feelings and learn to work them out in some non-destructive way. It is not normal to let such feelings sabotage your job search. Just because you're unemployed or looking for a new job doesn't mean you're a bad or worthless person. The only thing "wrong" with you is that you haven't found the offer that you want.

When your confidence starts to wilt, turn to a trusted friend or relative. Talk about your feelings frankly. Get mad or sad or vengeful. Then get back to work on your job search. Don't let fear of rejection keep you from making that next call. It may be just the lead you're looking for.

There are no hard and fast rules on when to seek professional counseling and support, but we can offer certain guidelines. If you seriously think you need professional help, you ought to investigate two or three sources. Besides the ones we've listed below, check with your minister, priest, or rabbi. Many clerics are trained counselors, and their help is free.

If you feel you have nowhere else to turn, or if you don't want to share your feelings with anyone you know, you should consider psychiatric or psychological counseling. If you're not making calls, not preparing for interviews, or not doing what you know you have to do to get the job you want, you could probably use some counseling.

Everybody feels bad about being rejected. But if you allow those feelings to overwhelm you, or if they're interfering with finding a job, it's probably time to talk with a professional. Another sure sign of the need for help is to wake up most mornings too sick or lethargic from overeating, overdrinking, or abusing some other substance to do what you have to do.

Where To Find Help for Emotional Problems

A listing in this book does not constitute an endorsement of any institution, therapist, or school of therapy. Therapy depends a great deal on the "chemistry" between therapist and patient—something only you can evaluate. A basic rule of thumb is that if you're not comfortable with or confident in a particular therapist, it may not be wise to continue seeing him or her.

Therapy is offered by quite a variety of people, from psychiatrists and psychologists with years of post-graduate training, to those with considerably lower levels of education and experience. Before engaging a therapist, check his or her credentials. Where was the therapist trained? What degrees does the therapist hold? How long has the therapist been practicing? Does he or she belong to any professional associations?

There are some rules and regulations governing the mental health professions in New York State that you should be aware of before settling on a therapist.

Psychologists and psychiatrists must pass a written examination given by the New York State Board of Education, Division of Professional Licenses, to obtain a license and be accredited to practice in New York State. Licensed practicing psychiatrists are listed (along with other medical doctors) in the *Medical Directory of New York State*. You should be able to find a copy of the *Directory* at your local library, or you can contact the **Medical Society of New York** at (516) 488-6100, 420 Lakeville Road, Lake Success, NY 11042.

Social workers are required to have a Master's degree in social work in addition to a Certificate of Social Work (CSW). Most social workers in the metropolitan area are members of one or both of the following professional organizations: **The National Association of Social Workers**, (212) 947-5000, and the **Society of Clinical Social Workers**, (800) 288-4279. The National Association of Social Workers provides a directory of all certified social workers in the United States. Call the Association for information about obtaining a copy. The Society of Clinical Social Workers publishes a register containing the names and addresses of its members. Most public libraries have a copy of this register. You can also call the society for more information. In Nassau County, the society provides a free 24-hour information and referral service at (516) 783-3999.

If you'd like to check the credentials of a particular social worker you plan to visit, contact the State Board for Social Work Education in Albany at (518) 474-4974. The Board can give you information about a social worker's background, professional affiliations, and certification.

Many social workers who are also marriage and family counselors are accredited through the **American Association for Marriage and Family Therapy**. The Association's national headquarters is at 1717 K Street, NW, Washington, DC 20006, or call (202) 429-1825.

To check on the licenses of any health professional, call the **New York State Department of Education**, Professional Licensing Division, in Albany. The toll-free number is (800) 342-3729.

SELECTED COUNSELING CENTERS AND INSTITUTIONS

Manhattan

Al-Anon Family Intergroup
200 Park Ave. S.
New York, NY 10003
(212) 254-7230
Free referrals to area Al-Anon meetings for families of alcoholics. Meetings and counseling sessions are also free.

Alcoholics Anonymous
15 E. 26th St.
New York, NY
(212) 683-3900
Open 24 hours a day, 7 days a week. Phone for an appointment. Free referrals to area AA meetings.

Catholic Charities
1011 1st Ave.
New York, NY 10022
(212) 371-1000
Staff members provide crisis intervention counseling and assessment for individuals and families. Counseling billed on a sliding scale.

New York State Division of Substance Abuse
80 Center St.
New York, NY 10013
(212) 870-8362
Free referral service for drug-related problems. Supports and polices private drug programs. Also does individual and family therapy, counseling, and referrals. Fees based on a sliding scale.

Vietnam Veterans Outreach Center
166 W. 75th St.
New York, NY 10023
(212) 944-2917
Individual, group, and family counseling for Vietnam veterans and their families. Appointments necessary. All services are free.

Women's Counseling Project
3001 Broadway
New York, NY 10027
(212) 854-3963
Individual counseling. Free referrals to legal and social services. Also offers short-term peer counseling. Referrals for family counseling. Affiliated with Columbia University.

Queens

Central Queens Psychotherapy Center
89-15 Parsons Blvd.

Jamaica, NY 11432
(718) 658-4880
Individual, marriage, and family counseling by certified counselors.
Hourly fee of $45.

Staten Island

Family Forum of Staten Island
500 Seaview
Staten Island, NY 10306
(718) 979-1355
Offers crisis intervention, generic and specialty counseling. Also provides
outpatient psychiatric counseling and self-help group services.

Nassau County

Community Counseling of West Nassau
1200 Hempstead Turnpike
Franklin Square, NY 11010
(516) 328-1717
Individual, family, and group counseling. Referrals to outside medical
agencies, vocational rehabilitation, and testing services, as well as in-
patient hospitalization programs for in-depth counseling. Fees based on
client's net income.

Gwaltney Enterprises
Human Consultants to Business
10 Cuttermill Road
Great Neck, NY 11021
(516) 829-8143
Family, individual, and group counseling. Also accepts referrals from
corporate employee-assistance programs.

Long Island Jewish
Medical Center Mineola Family Consultation Service
366 Jericho Turnpike
Mineola, NY 11550
(516) 742-4015
Comprehensive alcohol treatment program for the alcoholic and his/her
family. Individual group, marital, family, and children's sessions.
Psychiatric consultation; detoxification; vocational and occupational
services; weekly Alcohol Education Series for adults and children.

Mental Health Association of Nassau County
Information and Referral Service
186 Clinton St.
Hempstead, NY 11550
(516) 489-2322
Free information, counseling, and referral service for individuals or
families who need help with problems related to mental health. Social
workers give telephone counseling free.

Nassau County Department of Health
240 Old Country Road
Mineola, NY 11501
(516) 535-3410
(516) 681-3454 (Nights and weekends; emergencies)

Referrals for psychiatric counseling. Fees are on a sliding scale according to income. Nassau County residents only; all referrals are made to county health centers. The names and addresses of a few area clinics are listed below.

Nassau County Department of Health—
Health Centers and Clinics
Elmont Health Center
Elmont Road and Village Ave.
Elmont, NY 10003
(516) 354-3604

Freeport–Roosevelt Health Center
460 N. Main St.
Freeport, NY 11520
(516) 378-7310

Inwood–Lawrence Health Center
270 Lawrence Ave.
Lawrence, NY 11559
(516) 571-7874

Nassau County Medical Services Information
Department of Social Service
County Seat Drive
Mineola, NY 11501
(516) 535-4817

Westchester County

Westchester Counseling Center
3 Old Mamaroneck Road
White Plains, NY 10106
(914) 761-9038
Individual, group, and family counseling. Limited outside referral service. Fees based on a sliding scale.

Westchester County Department of Health
19 Bradhurst Ave.
Hawthorne, NY 10532
(914) 593-5100
Makes psychiatric and general health referrals to neighborhood health centers. Fees based on a sliding scale.

Westchester County Medical Center
Route 100
Crisis Intervention-Psychiatric
Valhalla, New York 10595
(914) 285-7000
Individual, couple, and family counseling. Fees based on a sliding scale. Outside referral to community services and individual therapists.

Westchester Jewish Community Services
456 North St.
White Plains, NY 10601
(914) 949-1415

Hotlines for help

If you need help immediately, call any of these numbers:

Cocaine Hotline
800-COCAINE
Free referrals to area treatment and counseling centers.

Food and Hunger Hotline
(212) 366-5100

Mental Health Counseling Hotline:
(212) 734-5876

Staten Island Hospital Alcohol Crisis Hotline
(718) 226-9000 ■

What To Do If You Get Fired

Being fired ranks just after the death of someone you love or divorce when it comes to personal traumas. If it should happen to you, take time to evaluate the bad news before accepting a settlement offer. If you quickly accept what your employer has to offer, it will be much more difficult to change your situation later. Tell the boss you want some time to think about a settlement. Then go back in a day or two and negotiate.

Stay on the payroll as long as you can, even if your pride hurts. Find out if you are eligible for part-time work or consulting jobs to tide you over until you find your new job. You may be able to hang on to insurance and other benefits until you've found new employment.

Try to negotiate a generous severance payment. In the last five years, severance agreements have risen dramatically in some industries. What the company offers at first may not be the maximum. Negotiation doesn't always work, but you certainly ought to try to get the most for your years of service.

Check with your personnel office to make sure you're getting all the benefits to which you are entitled, such as vacation pay and profit sharing. Check your eligibility for unemployment compensation before you accept an offer to resign instead of being terminated.

Don't attack management during your termination interview. It may cost you good references and hurt your chances of finding a new job.

Take advantage of any placement assistance that is offered. Don't reject the company's offer to help even if your pride has been stung.

Beating the Job-Hunt Blues

We've mentioned many times that finding a job is hard work and persistence counts, but despite worries about a dwindling bank account, where that right job is or where any job is, even the most dedicated job hunter needs some time off. An afternoon off the beaten job path can help clear your head of the job-hunt blues.

Giving yourself a vacation day in the midst of your job search can revive flagging confidence. A brief selection of free or inexpensive New York area diversions follows.

Remembering that Manhattan is an island can provide several delightful ways to spend a few hours or a day. A **boat trip** around the island can give you a new perspective on the job search while showing you a new perspective of the city. The Circle Line Cruise from Pier 83 in Manhattan costs $18 (212-563-3204). And don't forget the newly refurbished Statue of Liberty and Museums followed up by Ellis Island and its exciting restoration. Not to be missed and all for the cost of a ferry ride—$6 from Battery Park (212-269-5755).

New York is a **walking city** full of interesting neighborhoods. From Chinatown and Little Italy to SoHo to Greenwich Village to Rockefeller Center across from St. Patrick's Cathedral to Central Park. From South Street Seaport to the World Financial and Trade Centers and Wall Street (don't forget the New York Stock Exchange —fascinating and free). Uptown from the United Nations to Carnegie Hall on the upper East Side and Museum Mile on Fifth Avenue...New York is a place to walk and watch.

The warm weather provides many opportunities for **free pleasures**. Both the World Financial Center and World Trade Centers have free open air concerts at noon and late in the day. Lincoln Center has a wealth of free and inexpensive performances throughout the year both inside and on the promenade. Shakespeare in the Park and the Philharmonic provide evenings of entertainment.

And for a night at the theater "on the cheap" there are two TKTS centers available where you can buy **half-price tickets** for Broadway shows on the day of performance: Times Square Center (47th and Broadway), and 2 World Trade Center (Mezzanine level).

Bicycling in Central Park, rowing on the lake, and visiting the Central Park Zoo are all available. There are street fairs throughout the year where you can savor many diverse cultures (and eat to your heart's content).

Both Brooklyn and the Bronx have world famous Botanical Gardens with seasonal displays. After visiting Museum Mile from the Frick to the Museum of the City of New York, there's always the Cloisters—a medieval delight and only a bus or subway ("A" train) ride to a fabulous view of the Palisades.

The winter brings **ice skating** at Rockefeller Center and Central Park and caroling at South Street Seaport. Opportunities for window shopping abound in New York, especially during the holidays when the windows of the department stores show off their finest displays. No matter the season, there's always something to see and do in New York City.

Selecting the Right Job
for You

Welcome to the most pleasant chapter of this book—and the one that's the most fun. You've figured out what you want to do, developed an acceptable resume, and used your network of contacts and other resources to research the job market and generate all sorts of interviews. At this point in the process, you've probably received or are pretty close to landing at least a couple of offers that come fairly close to your objective.

You may have a problem if one of your possibilities becomes a firm offer that demands an immediate response while you're still investigating other promising leads. The employer making this offer is essentially telling you, "We think you have everything we're looking for, and we want you to start as soon as possible." It is difficult to stall or delay your acceptance just because other promising leads still haven't yielded firm offers. You have to use your best judgment in such a case, but try to delay a final decision until all likely offers are in. Unless you're absolutely desperate, there's no reason to jump at the first offer you receive.

You owe it to both yourself and the people who interviewed you to consider all outstanding possibilities and then make your decision. Tell the employer who gave you the offer the truth—that you need more time to review the offer against all the situations that are outstanding and pending—that a decision can't be made for at least two weeks. If the offering company refuses to wait, that tells you a great deal about the atmosphere in which you'd be working. If a company wants you badly enough, they'll wait a reasonable length of time for you to decide.

A job involves much more than a title and base salary. For any firm offer, be sure you understand what your responsibilities will be, what benefits you'll receive besides salary (insurance, vacation, profit sharing, training, tuition reimbursement, and the like), how much overtime is required (and whether you'll be paid for it), how much travel is involved in the job, who your superior will be, how many people you'll be supervising, and where the position might lead. (Is it a dead-end job, or are people in this slot often promoted?) In short, find out anything and everything you need to know to evaluate the offer.

For many positions, especially those requiring several years' experience, it's appropriate to ask for an offer in writing. Such a document would specify the position's title, responsibilities, reporting relationship, compensation, and include a statement of company benefits.

At the very least, before you make a firm decision, be sure to obtain a copy of the company's personnel policy. It will fill you in on such details as the number of paid sick days, overtime and vacation policy, insurance benefits, profit sharing, and the like. These so-called fringe benefits can really add up. It's not a bad idea to try to assign a dollar value to them to help you evaluate the financial pros and cons of each offer.

It seems obvious to us that it's unwise to choose a job exclusively on the basis of salary and benefits. Don't condemn yourself to working with people you can't stand, doing work you find boring, to accomplish goals you don't believe in.

Finding the Right Culture

Career counselors often warn that you ignore a company's "culture" at your own peril. You can find a position that suits you to a "T" but still be unhappy if you don't fit the culture of the company that hires you. It takes some doing to assess an organization's culture, but it's worth your while.

Some signs are fairly obvious: What do people wear? What is the furniture like? Are office doors kept open or closed? Are there any minorities or women in positions of power? How friendly are people to you? To each other? Does anybody laugh? A very important question to ask: Do I feel comfortable here?

There are five aspects of an organization's culture to consider. Try to find out as much as you can about each.

1. What is the relationship between a company and its environment? Does it control its own destiny or must it depend on the mood of an adversarial home office? You probably wouldn't be wise to work for the Department of Defense under a pacifist administration.

2. *How does a company view human nature?* Good or evil? Changeable or immutable? Answers to these questions determine how employees are treated, how much supervision and control is exerted. How openly will employees communicate? Will there be opportunities for training and development?

3. *What are the philosophy and mission* of a company? Printed brochures are often good indicators. A sound company is clear on what business it's in.

4. *How do people relate to each other* in a company? Is there a formal flow chart? Are there many vertical levels (the military)? Or is power more evenly and horizontally spread out (some new high-tech firms)? The more horizontal, the more informal and the easier it is to get things done, generally through relationships.

5. *How are decisions made*, who makes them, and upon what basis? Facts and reason? Politics? Ideology? Good-old-boy or girl network? The whims of an autocrat at the top?

The answers to these questions will determine the working atmosphere for most companies.

Salary Strategy

Before you accept an offer—or bicker about salary—you need to know what other people who fill similar positions are making. The *Occupational Outlook Handbook*, put out by the U.S. Department of Labor every two years, cites salary statistics by field. Probably a better source of information is *The American Almanac of Jobs and Salaries* by John Wright, published by Avon. What you really need to know is what other people with your qualifications and experience are making in the New York area for working the job you're considering. Professional societies and associations frequently provide this sort of information. It's one more good reason to belong to one. Probably the best source of all for salary orientation is—you guessed it—your network of contacts.

For advice on how to get the salary you want, we recommend these books:

BOOKS ON SALARY NEGOTIATION

Chapman, Jack. *How to Make $1000 a Minute*. Berkeley, CA: Ten Speed Press, 1987.
Cohen, Herb. *You Can Negotiate Anything*. New York: Bantam Publishing Co., 1982.
Fisher, Roger, and William Ury. *Getting to Yes*. New York: Penguin Books, 1983.
Kennedy, Marilyn Moats. *Getting the Job You Want and the Money You're Worth*. Piscataway, NJ: American College of Physician Executives, 1987.
Krannich, Ronald, and Rae Krannich. *Salary Success: Know What You're Worth and Get It!* Woodbridge, VA: Impact Publications, 1990.

Compare the Offers on Paper

You've talked with each employer and taken notes about the responsibilities and compensation being offered. Where possible, you've obtained a job offer in writing. You have also read through the company's personnel policy.

Now make yourself a checklist for comparing the relative merits of each offer. We've provided a sample here, but if another format suits your purposes better, use it. The idea is to list the factors that you consider important in any job, and then assign a rating for how well each offer fills the bill in each particular area.

We've listed some of the factors that we think ought to be considered before you accept any offer. Some may not be relevant to your situation. Others that we've left out may be of great importance to you. So feel free to make any additions, deletions, or changes you want.

Once you've listed your factors, make a column for each job offer you're considering. Assign a rating (say, 1 to 5, with 1 the lowest and 5 the highest) for each factor and each offer. Then, total the scores for each offer.

The offer with the most points is not necessarily the one to accept. The chart doesn't take into account the fact that "responsibilities" may be more important to you than "career path," or that you promised yourself you'd never punch a time clock again. Nevertheless, looking at the pros and cons of each offer in black and white should help you make a much more methodical and logical decision.

Factor	Offer A	Offer B	Offer C
Responsibilities	_____	_____	_____
Company reputation	_____	_____	_____
Salary	_____	_____	_____
Insurance	_____	_____	_____
Paid vacation	_____	_____	_____
Pension	_____	_____	_____
Profit sharing	_____	_____	_____
Tuition reimbursement	_____	_____	_____
On-the-job training	_____	_____	_____
Career path (where can you go from this job?)	_____	_____	_____
Company future	_____	_____	_____
Quality of product or service	_____	_____	_____

Location (housing market,　　　 _____　　 _____　　　 _____
　schools, transportation)

Boss(es)　　　　　　　　　 _____　　 _____　　　 _____

Other workers　　　　　　　 _____　　 _____　　　 _____

Travel　　　　　　　　　　 _____　　 _____　　　 _____

Overtime　　　　　　　　　 _____　　 _____　　　 _____

Other　　　　　　　　　　　 _____　　 _____　　　 _____

_____　 _____　　 _____　　　 _____

_____　 _____　　 _____　　　 _____

TOTAL POINTS　　　　　 _____　　 _____　　　 _____

A Final Word

Once you have accepted a job, it's important that you notify each of the people in your network of your new position, company, address, and phone number. Be sure to thank these people; let them know you appreciated their assistance. After all, you never know when you may need to ask them to help you again. *Keep your network alive!*

On each anniversary date of your new job, take the time to run through the self-appraisal process to evaluate your situation and the progress you are making (as measured by increased responsibilities, salary, and abilities). Consider how they compare with the objectives you set at the start of your search. Although you may be completely satisfied in your new assignment, remember that circumstances can change overnight, and you must always be prepared for the unexpected. So make an employment "New Year's Resolution" to weigh every aspect of your job annually and compare the result with what you want and expect from your life's work.

We hope that you have made good use of the job-search techniques outlined in this book. Indeed, we hope that the resulting experiences not only have won you the job you want but—equally important—also have made you a better-informed person. Perhaps the next time you talk to an unemployed person or someone who is employed but seeking a new job, you will look at that person with new insight gained from your own search experiences. We hope you'll gladly share what you've learned about how to get a job in the New York metropolitan area.

Getting a leg up toward that first job

A colleague of ours, a career planning professional at a local college, suggests students begin building the foundation for a successful job search before they finish school. She advises students to seek part-time or summer employment that relates to their chosen field and suggests internships, cooperative education programs (if available), and volunteer work as good ways to gain experience.

In fact, she says, "Any job that strengthens managerial, organizational, and communications skills can be an asset. But keep in mind the importance of gaining experience in your field.

"Getting work is much easier than most students realize. First, try the on-campus job postings. Most universities have bulletin boards listing available work, both on and off campus.

"Next, check the career services office for information on internships and volunteer work. Also, ask about getting in touch with other alumni. At our school, our alumni/mentor program puts undergrads and grad students in touch with alumni who work in various fields. Most often, student and mentor meet, talk over the job picture in their field, and go over job strategies. Getting the inside story can make a big difference when interview time rolls around.

"Finally, find out if any major corporations will be recruiting on campus. I firmly believe that laying the groundwork for a successful career begins with the proper education and the proper work experience." ■

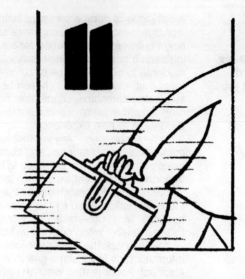

Employers in the New York Metropolitan Area

This chapter contains the names, addresses, and phone numbers of the New York area's top 1,500 employers of white-collar workers. The companies are arranged in categories according to the major products and services they manufacture or provide.

Where appropriate, entries contain a brief description of the company's business and the name of the human resources director or other contact

This listing is intended to help you survey the major potential employers in fields that interest you. It is selective, not exhaustive. We have not, for example, listed all the advertising agencies in the area as you can find that information in the *Yellow Pages*. We have simply listed the top twenty-five or so, that is, the ones with the most jobs.

**Most big firms
have offices in
the suburbs, too**

Most of the corporations listed in this chapter have offices in the suburbs as well as Manhattan. Because of space limitations, we have sometimes listed only the Manhattan location. If you'd like to work in the suburbs, check with the personnel departments in Manhattan about additional offices. They are usually located in new industrial parks in Long Island and Westchester County as well as northern New Jersey and southern Connecticut.

In addition, we've included many firms whose corporate headquarters are in the Tri-State area outside of Manhattan just in case commuting is not a factor in your job search. ■

The purpose of this chapter is to get you started, both looking and thinking. This is the kickoff, not the final gun. Browse through the whole chapter, and take some time to check out areas that are unfamiliar to you. Many white-collar skills are transferable. People with marketing, management, data processing, accounting, administrative, secretarial, and other talents are needed in a huge variety of businesses.

Ask yourself in what area your skills could be marketed. Use your imagination, especially if you're in a so-called specialized field. A dietician, for instance, might look first under Health Care, or maybe Hotels/Motels. But what about Insurance companies, Museums, Banks, or the scores of other places that run their own dining rooms for employees or the public? What about food and consumer magazines? Who invents all those recipes and tests those products?

The tips and insider interviews that are scattered throughout this chapter are designed to nudge your creativity and suggest additional ideas for your job search. Much more detailed information on the area's top employers and other, smaller companies can be found in the directories and other resources suggested in Chapter 4. We can't stress strongly enough that you have to do your homework when you're looking for a job, both to unearth places that might need a person with your particular talents and to succeed in the interview once you've lined up a meeting with the hiring authority.

A word about hiring authorities: if you've read Chapter 5, you know that the name of the game is to meet the person with the power to hire you, or get as close to that person as you can.

You don't want to go to the chairman or the personnel director if the person who actually makes the decision is the marketing manager or customer service director.

Just where are those employers located, anyway?

New York's system of street addresses is very confusing to newcomers. Numbers on the north-south streets, such as Fifth Avenue, do not correspond to the numbers of the cross streets. An out-of-towner would expect a building at Fifth and 53rd Street to have an address such as "5300" or "5301." Not so! Nor do the numbers on the north-south Avenues follow any pattern. A good map or pocket guide is essential if you are new to New York.

To help you become more familiar with the various business districts and industry locations in the New York area, we've described some of the most important ones below.

The Garment District: Most apparel retailers and wholesalers are located in this district, from 30th to 40th Streets between Seventh Avenue and Broadway. Apparel wholesalers maintain offices in the 1300s and 1400s on Broadway. There are also many apparel retailers and wholesalers scattered throughout Brooklyn and Queens.

Publisher's Row: Many publishing houses are located on either Avenue of the Americas or Lexington Avenue. You'll find a few on Madison Avenue and Fifth Avenue and others in lower Manhattan. When people refer to Publisher's Row, they are talking about a section of the Midtown area from 40th Street to 50th Street on Avenue of the Americas.

Madison Avenue: The advertising business is to Madison Avenue what the apparel business is to Seventh Avenue. Many of New York's most prestigious advertising firms can be found on or near Madison Avenue in the Midtown area.

Broadcasting: The main offices of the three major television networks are located on or near Avenue of the Americas in the 50s. NBC has studios in its corporate headquarters. Other television studios and production facilities are located in the 60s, on or near Broadway. There is now a large cable production facility in Astoria, Queens. The Astoria Studios house several radio and TV channels, among them WFAN Radio and The Lifetime TV Channel.

Electronic, Telecommunications, and Office Automations Systems: Most of these companies have offices in Long Island and Westchester. Virtually every one of the leaders in the industry has office space outside of New York City as well as recruiting offices in Manhattan. Usually, recruiting for the suburban jobs is done separately from recruiting in New York. Use a suburban directory if you wish to work in a particular suburb, or call the numbers we've provided to ask about suburban recruiting.

Federal Plaza: You'll find most U.S. government offices in lower Manhattan's Federal Plaza, which is near City Hall Park. You'll find most of the buildings between Broadway and Lafayette Streets, two main avenues that run north and south and are easy to locate.

Hotels: Central Park South is the address of some of New York's grandest hotels that overlook Central Park from the south side of the park. You can stroll along the park and pass such fine hotels as the St. Moritz and the Plaza. You'll find four- and five-star hotels on Fifth, Madison, and Park Avenues.

Insurance: A large number of the insurance firms in New York are located in a small area in lower Manhattan. If you're looking for a job in the insurance business, you will be spending time in this small area in the vicinity of William Street, John Street, Maiden Lane, and Nassau Street. These are small, winding streets that can confuse even the most experienced New Yorker. Try to find an address on a map, or get explicit directions from the company by phone.

Wall Street: New York's financial district, home to the New York Stock Exchange and the nation's largest investment firms, banks, brokerage houses, and financial advisors, is located on the southern tip of Manhattan Island. Also in the neighborhood are the World Trade Center and the World Financial Center complexes. The towers are bordered by West Street and Vesey Street and are a main tourist attraction as well as a financial and cultural center.

Manufacturing: Queens County is just over the 59th Street bridge, a short trip from the east side of Manhattan. Here you will find Long Island City, where hundreds of general manufacturers and production plants are located. If we have not listed a manufacturing company you'd like to work for, check the local Queens *Yellow Pages*. You may find the company in or near Long Island City.

Museums and Galleries: New York's museums are numerous, and they are located all over the city rather than in one area or district. But most galleries are concentrated in one of two locations: 57th Street in the Midtown area, or SoHo and TriBeCa below Greenwich Village in lower Manhattan. ■

Obviously, we can't list every possible hiring authority in the New York area's "Top 1,500." If we tried, you'd need a wagon to haul this book around. Besides, printed directories go out of date—even those that are regularly and conscientiously revised. So always *double-check* a contact whose name you get from a book or magazine, including this one. If necessary, call the company's switchboard to confirm who heads a particular department or division.

Here, then, are the New York area's greatest opportunities. Note that in most cases, nearby New Jersey and Connecticut employers are listed after the New York employers.

The New York area's top 1,500 employers are arranged in the following categories:

Accounting/Auditing Firms and Services
Advertising Agencies
Aerospace Manufacturers, Services, Sales
Apparel/Textile Manufacturers
Architectural Firms
Automobile/Truck/Transportation Equipment Manufacturers
Banks: Commercial and Savings
Book Publishers/Literary Agents
Broadcasting
Chemicals
Computers/Hardware
Computers/Software
Construction
Cosmetics/Perfume/Toiletries
Drugs and Pharmaceuticals
Educational Institutions
Electronics/Telecommunications/Office Automation
Engineering
Entertainment and Recreation
Environmental Services
Food/Beverage Producers and Distributors
Foundations
Government
Health Care
Hospitality: Hotels and Restaurants
Human Services
Insurance
Law Firms
Management Consultants
Market Research Firms
Media, Print

Museums/Art Galleries
Oil and Gas
Paper and Allied Products
Printing
Public Relations
Real Estate Developers and Brokers
Retailers/Wholesalers
Stock Brokers/Financial Services/Investment Banking
Travel/Shipping/Transportation
Utilities

Accounting/Auditing Firms and Services

For networking in accounting and related fields, check out these professional organizations listed in Chapter 5. Also see **"Banks"** and **"Stock Brokers/Financial Services."**

PROFESSIONAL ORGANIZATIONS:

American Institute of Certified Public Accountants
American Society of Women Accountants
CPA Associates International
New York State Society of Certified Public
Accountants Foundation for Accounting Education
New York Society of Independent Accountants

For additional information, you can contact:

American Institute of CPAs
1211 Avenue of the Americas
New York, NY 10036
(212) 575-6200

American Society of Women Accountants
35 E. Wacker Drive
Chicago, IL 60601
(312) 726-9030

Institute of Management Accountants
10 Paragon Drive
Montvale, NJ 07645
(201) 573-9000

National Association of Black Accountants
220 I St., NE, Suite 150

Washington, DC 20002
(202) 546-6222

National Society of Public Accountants
1010 N. Fairfax St.
Alexandria, VA 22314
(703) 549-6400

PROFESSIONAL PUBLICATIONS:

Accounting News
Cash Flow
The CPA Journal
D & B Reports
Journal of Accountancy
Management Accounting
National Public Accountant
The Tax Advisor
The Woman CPA

DIRECTORIES:

Accountants Directory (American Business Directories, Inc.,
    Omaha, NE)
Accounting Firms and Practitioners (American Institute of
    Certified Public Accountants, New York, NY)
Career Opportunities Handbook (New York State Local Public
    Accounting Firms, New York, NY)
Emerson's Directory of Leading U.S. Accounting Firms
    (Emerson's, Seattle, WA)
International Guide to Accounting Journals (Weiner Publications,
    Inc., New York NY)
National Directory of Certified Public Accountants (Peter Norback
    Publishing Co., Princeton, NJ)
Who Audits America (Data Financial Press, Menlo Park, CA)

NEW YORK EMPLOYERS:

Anchin, Block & Anchin
1375 Broadway
New York, NY 10018
(212) 840-3456

Anderson, Arthur, and Company
1345 Avenue of the Americas
New York, NY 10105
(212) 708-4000
Director of Recruiting: Michael Denkensohn

Balaban, Sigmund, and Company
40 Broad St.

New York, NY 10004
(212) 227-8700
Partner: Sigmund Balaban

BDO Seidman
15 Columbus Circle
New York, NY 10023
(212) 765-7500
Director of Recruiting: Jayme Gewing

Berdon, David, and Company
415 Madison Ave.
New York, NY 10017
(212) 832-0400
Contact: Judy Goldberg

Borek, Stockel & Marden
1 Gateway Plaza
Port Chester, NY 10573
(914) 934-2400

Buchbinder Tunick and Company
1 Pennsylvania Plaza
New York, NY 10119
(212) 695-5003
Managing Partner: Frederik Kahn

Cohn, J.H., & Co.
400 Park Ave.
New York, NY 10022
(212) 563-4200
Director of Human Resources: Howard Fishman
Corporate Headquarters in Roseland, NJ

Coopers and Lybrand
1301 Avenue of the Americas
New York, NY 10020
(212) 536-2000
Regional Director of Recruiting: Joseph S. Rorro

Deloitte & Touche
1633 Broadway
New York, NY 10019
(212) 489-1600
Director of Recruiting: John Barch
Corporate Headquarters in Connecticut

Eisner, Richard A., & Co.
575 Madison Ave.
New York, NY 10022
(212) 355-1700
Director of Recruiting: Wendy Weinbach

Ernst and Young
277 Park Ave.
New York, NY 10172
(212) 830-6000
Director of Personnel: Cindy Hirsch

Goldstein Golub Kessler & Co.
1185 Avenue of the Americas
New York, NY 10036
(212) 523-1200

Grant Thornton
605 3rd Ave.
New York, NY 10058
(212) 599-0100
Personnel Manager: Tom Madera

Isaacs, Edward, & Co.
380 Madison Ave.
New York, NY 10022
(212) 297-4800

Israeloff, Trattner & Co.
4 E. 34th St.
New York, NY 10016
(212) 685-1400

KPMG Peat Marwick
345 Park Ave.
New York, NY 10154
(212) 758-9700
Director of Recruitment: Robert J. Zibelli

Leventhal, Kenneth, & Co
805 3rd Ave.
New York, NY 10022
(212) 983-4100
Personnel Director: Al Frazia

Loeb & Troper
270 Madison Ave.
New York, NY 10016
(212) 889-7880
Partner: Allen Fetterman

Lopez, Edwards, Frank & Co.
One Penn Plaza
New York, NY 10119
(212) 685-7000

Mahoney Cohen & Co.
111 W. 40th St.

New York, NY 10018
(212) 490-8000

Margolin, Winer & Evens
600 Old Country Road
Garden City, NY 11530
(516) 228-8600
Director of Human Resources: Stanley Stempler

McGladrey Hendrickson & Pullen
1133 6th Ave.
New York, NY 10036
(212) 382-0024

Mitchell/Titus & Co.
1 Battery Park Plaza
New York, NY 10004
(212) 709-4500

Pannell Kerr Forster and Company
420 Lexington Ave.
New York, NY 10170
(212) 867-8000
Personnel Director: Richard Stewart

Prager and Fenton
675 3rd Ave.
New York, NY 10017
(212) 972-7555
Partner: Jeremy Steinberg

Price Waterhouse and Company
153 E. 53 St.
New York, NY 10022
(212) 371-2000
Director of Recruiting: Steve Butterfield

Weber, Lipshie & Co.
1430 Broadway
New York, NY 10018
(212) 382-3400

Weiser, M.R., & Co.
135 W. 50th St.
New York, NY 10020-1299
(212) 972-2500
Administrator of Personnel: Gail Hoffman

CONNECTICUT EMPLOYERS:

Coopers & Lybrand
One Canterbury Green

P.O. Box 10108
Stamford, CT 06904
Recruiting Manager: Laura Fox

Deloitte & Touche
10 Westport Road
Wilton, CT 06897
(203) 761-3000
Corporate Headquarters

Grant Thornton
One Canterbury Green
Stamford, CT 06904
(203) 353-9700

KPMG Peat Marwick
3001 Summer St., Stamford Square
Stamford, CT 06905
Professional Recruiting: Kathy Padgett

Price Waterhouse
300 Atlantic St.
P.O. Box 9316
Stamford, CT 06904-9316
(203) 358-0001
Recruiting Manager: Patrick Lalor

NEW JERSEY EMPLOYERS:

Amper, Politziner and Mattia
2015 Lincoln Highway
Edison, NJ 08818-0988
(908) 287-1000
Firm Administrator: Carl Conway

Rothstein Kass & Company
280 Corporate Center
85 Livingston Ave.
Roseland, NJ 07068
(201) 994-6666
Partners: Steven Kass and Gary Berger

Wiss and Company
54 Eisenhower Parkway
Livingston, NJ 07039-1086
(201) 994-9400
H.R. Director: Leonard Michielli

Accounting firms big and small

We talked with Richard Craig, a Certified Public Accountant, now a Senior Vice President in finance at a leading data processing firm. We asked how he began his career in accounting and about the advantages and disadvantages associated with the size of the firm you work for.

Said Craig, "I started at Touche Ross(now Deloitte & Touche), one of New York's big eight(now the big six) accounting firms. Usually, working for a larger firm means learning a specific task. Staffs are larger, so each job is more specialized. You don't usually handle as many components of a job as you would in a smaller firm. You sometimes have more opportunity for hands-on experience in a smaller firm and gain more general management experience," Craig advised.

"But regardless of the size of the firm where you begin your career, if you wish to advance you should remain flexible through the first five years. If your job is not what you expected, be willing to make a change.

"Also, if you want a manager's position, you may have to move around to gain general managerial experience. Sometimes, that will mean a transfer to a department that would not necessarily be your first choice. But if the position rounds out your background, it is usually worth at least a temporary stay." ∎

Advertising Agencies

For networking in advertising and related fields, check out the following professional organizations listed in Chapter 5. Also see "**Market Research**" and "**Public Relations.**"

PROFESSIONAL ORGANIZATIONS:

Advertising Club of New York
Advertising Council
Advertising Women of New York
American Association of Advertising Agencies

For additional information, you can contact:

The Advertising Council
261 Madison Ave.
New York, NY 10016
(212) 922-1500

Advertising Women of New York
153 E. 57th St.
New York, NY 10017
(212) 593-1950

American Advertising Federation
1400 K St., NW
Washignton, DC 20005
(202) 898-0089

American Association of Advertising Agencies
666 3rd Ave.
New York, NY 10021
(212) 682-2500

American Marketing Association
250 S. Wacker Dr.
Chicago, ILL 60606
(312) 648-0536

Direct Marketing Association
11 W. 42nd St.
New York, NY 10036
(212) 768-7277

Promotion Marketing Association of America
322 8th Ave.
New York, NY 10001
(212) 206-1100

PROFESSIONAL PUBLICATIONS:

Advertising Age
Adweek
Direct Marketing Magazine
Journal of Advertising Research
Madison Avenue
Marketing Communications Magazine
Marketing News
Potentials in Marketing

DIRECTORIES:

Advertising Career Directory (Career Press, Inc., Hawthorne, NJ)
Standard Directory of Advertising Agencies (National Register
    Publishing Co., Skokie, IL)
For those interested in the advertising field, the industry's *Red Book*,
or *Standard Directory of Advertising Agencies*, is useful in finding a
specific contact in your area of interest. For example, an artist would
contact the agency's Art Director or Creative Director. The directory
is available at most libraries.

NEW YORK EMPLOYERS:

Backer Spielvogel Bates
405 Lexington Ave.
New York, NY 10174
(212) 297-7000
Exec. Vice President, Director of Human Resources: Anne
Melanson

BBDO International
1285 Avenue of the Americas
New York, NY 10019
(212) 909-9226
Director of Personnel: Ron Mason

Bozell Inc.
40 W. 23rd St.
New York, NY 10010
(212) 727-5000
Personnel Director: Joanne Conforti

Carrafielo-Diehl Assoc.
90 N. Broadway
Irvington-on-Hudson, NY 10533
(914) 591-9191
Personnel Director: Elizabeth Cox

D'Arcy, Masius, Benton, and Bowles
1675 Broadway

New York, NY 10019
(212) 468-3622
Personnel: Judith Kemp

DDB Needham
437 Madison Ave.
New York, NY 10022
(212) 415-2000
Personnel Director: Judson Saviskas

Della Femina, McNamee
350 Hudson St.
New York, NY 10014
(212) 886-4100
Personnel Director: Susan Cohen

Doremus and Company
200 Varick St.
New York, NY 10014
(212) 366-3000
Personnel Director: Patricia Cremin

FCB/Leber Katz Partners
767 5th Ave.
New York, NY 10153
(212) 705-1000
Director of Personnel: Sherry McGann

Grey Advertising
777 3rd Ave.
New York, NY 10017
(212) 546-2000
Personnel Director: Janine Walter

Lintas, NY
One Dag Hammarskjold Plaza
New York, NY 10017
(212) 605-8000
Director of Personnel: Patricia Ransom

Lord Bowes Dentsu & Partners
810 7th Ave.
New York, NY 10019
(212) 408-2100
Human Resources Manager: Nedenia West

McCaffrey and McCall
575 Lexington Ave.
New York, NY 10022

McCann Erickson International Advertising
750 3rd Ave.

New York, NY 10017
(212) 697-6000
Personnel Director: Sharon Glynn

NW Ayer
825 8th Ave.
New York, NY 10019
(212) 708-5000
Personnel Director: Joseph Harte

Oglivy and Mather
309 W. 49th St.
New York, NY 10019
(212) 237-4000
Personnel Director: Elizabeth Punkiar

Saatchi & Saatchi Advertising
375 Hudson St.
New York, NY 10014
(212) 463-2000
Personnel Director: Joseph Sansaverino

Thompson, J. Walter
466 Lexington Ave.
New York, NY 10017
(212) 210-7000
Personnel Manager: Ronnie Elson

Wells, Rich, Greene BDDP
1740 Broadway
New York, NY 10019
(212) 303-5000
Personnel Director: Valerie Church

Young and Rubicam
285 Madison Ave.
New York, NY 10017
(212) 210-3000
Human Resources: Carla Wagner

NEW JERSEY EMPLOYERS:

Carlino Barisch
101 Wall St.
Princeton, NJ 08540
(609) 924-7500
Contact: Molly Bograd, Vice President Finance

CONNECTICUT EMPLOYERS:

Blau, Barry, & Partners
1960 Bronson Road

Fairfield, CT 06430
(203) 254-3700

CDHM Advertising
750 E. Main St.
Stamford, CT 06901
(203) 967-7800

Clarion Marketing and Communications
340 Pemberwick Road
Greenwich, CT 06831
(203) 531-3600

Dickison & Hendee
205 Main St.
Westport, CT 06880
(203) 221-1033

The Direct Marketing Agency
One Stamford Landing
Stamford, CT 06902
(203) 325-2800

Marquardt & Roche
600 Summer St.
Stamford, CT 06901
(203)327-0890

Posey Quest Genova
6 Glenville St.
Greenwich, CT 06831
(203) 531-4900

STG Marketing Communications
883 Black Rock Turnpike
Fairfield, CT 06430
(203) 579-1640

Aerospace Manufacturers, Services, Sales

For networking in aerospace and related fields, check out the following professional organization listed in Chapter 5:

PROFESSIONAL ORGANIZATIONS:

Wings Club

For additional information, you can contact:

Aerospace Education Foundation
1501 Lee Highway
Arlington, VA 22209

Aerospace Electrical Society
700 E. South St.
Anaheim, CA 92805
(714) 778-1840

Aerospace Industries Association of America
1250 I St., NW
Washington, DC 20005
(202) 371-8400

American Institute of Aeronautics and Astronautics
370 L'Enfant Promenade, SW
Washington, DC 20024
(202) 646-7400

Int'l. Association of Machinists & Aerospace Workers
9000 Machinists Pl.
Upper Marlboro, MD 20772
(301) 967-4500

PROFESSIONAL PUBLICATIONS:

Aerospace Daily
Aerospace Engineering
Air Cargo Magazine
Aviation Week and Space Technology
Business and Commercial Aviation

DIRECTORIES:

Aviation Week & Space Technology, Marketing Directory Issue
(McGraw-Hill Publishing Co., New York, NY)

NEW YORK EMPLOYERS:

BH Aircraft Company
441 Eastern Parkway
Farmingdale, NY 11735
(516) 249-5000
Personnel Director: Nancy Crimmins
Airplane/aerospace systems and equipment.

Bulova Systems and Instruments Corp.
26-15 Brooklyn-Queens Expressway
Woodside, NY 11377
(718) 204-3384
Personnel Director: Eleanor Smith

Coltec Industries
430 Park Ave.
New York, NY 10022
(212) 940-0400

Grumman Aerospace Corporation
111 Stewart Ave.
Bethpage, NY 11714
(516) 575-8591
Personnel: Angela Traversa
Military parts, services, and systems for the aerospace and
aircraft industries. Also develops and manufactures energy
conservation devices.

Harris Corporation/GSSD
6801 Jericho Turnpike
Syosset, NY 11791
(516) 677-2278
Human Resources Manager: Chuck Gemuendt

Hughes-Treitler Manufacturing Corporation
300 Endo Blvd.
Garden City, NY 11530
(516) 832-8811
Personnel: Joseph Cannova
Heat exchangers used in airplanes and spacecraft.

International Telephone and Telegraph
1330 Avenue of the Americas
New York, NY 10019-5490
(212) 258-1000
Manufactures and develops UHF,VHF radio transmission equipment, ground-to-air tactical radio equipment, air traffic control
radio equipment. The defense-space arm of the technology group
is located in Nutley, NJ, (201) 284-0123.

Lawrence Aviation Industries
Sheep Pasture Road
Port Jefferson, NY 11776
(516) 473-1800

Metro Machine Products Corporation
2362 Westchester Ave.
Bronx, NY 10462
(212) 892-6768
Contact: Personnel Department
Precision components for the aerospace industry.

Sequa Corporation
200 Park Ave.
New York, NY 10166
(212) 986-5500
Personnel Director: Jerry Skoll, location: 3 University Plaza,
Hackensack, NJ 07601, (201) 343-1122
Aerospace systems.

CONNECTICUT EMPLOYERS:

Analysis and Technology
P.O. Box 220
North Stonington, CT 06359
(203) 599-3910
Employment Coordinator: Cheryl Kay

Colt Industries
P.O. Box 1868
Hartford, CT 06101
(203) 236-6311
Labor Relations: Linda Alva
Aerospace systems.

Norden Systems
P.O. Box 5300
Norwalk, CT 06856
(203) 852-5000
Manager—Employment: T. Simpson, Jr.

United Technologies Corporation
United Technologies Building
Hartford, CT 06101
(203) 728-7000
Personnel Manager: Ellen McGroary

NEW JERSEY EMPLOYERS:

Allied Signal
101 Columbia Turnpike
Morristown, NJ 07962

(201) 455-2000
Administration Director: Daniel Geist
Airplane/aerospace systems.

Allied-Signal Corporation
Route 46
Teterboro, NJ 07608
(201) 288-2000
Administrative Employment Recruiter: Richard Feldman

Apparel/Textile Manufacturers

For networking in apparel and textile industries and related fields, check out the following professional organizations listed in Chapter 5:

PROFESSIONAL ORGANIZATIONS:

American Cloak and Suit Manufacturers Association
American Fur Industry
American Fur Merchants' Association
Apparel Guild
Associated Fur Manufacturers
Ladies Apparel Contractors Association
Men's Fashion Association
Metropolitan Area Apparel Association
National Association of Milliners, Dressmakers and Tailors
Textile Distributors Association
Young Mens Wear Association

For additional information, you can contact:

American Apparel Manufacturers Association
2500 Wilson Blvd., Suite 301
Arlington, VA 22201
(703) 524-1864

Association of Bridal Consultants
200 Chestnutland Rd.
New Milford, CT 06776
(203) 355-0464

Council of Fashion Designers of America
1412 Broadway
New York, NY 10018
(212) 302-1821

International Association of Clothing Designers
475 Park Ave. S.

New York, NY 10016
(212) 685-6602

Sportswear Apparel Association
450 7th Ave.
New York, NY 10123
(212) 564-6161

Textile Distributers Association
45 W. 36th St.
New York, NY 10018
(212) 563-0400

Textile Research Institute
Box 625
Princeton, NJ 08540
(609) 924-3150

PROFESSIONAL PUBLICATIONS:

Fabricnews
Fashion Newsletter
Homesewing Trade News
Knitting Times
New York Apparel News
Textile Products
Textile Research Journal
Textile World
Women's Wear Daily

DIRECTORIES:

Apparel Industry Sourcebook (Denyse & Co., Inc., North
    Hollywood, CA)
Apparel Trades Book (Dun & Bradstreet, Inc., New York, NY)
Fairchild's Textile & Apparel Financial Directory (Fairchild
    Publications, New York, NY)
Membership Directory (American Apparel Manufacturers Associa-
    tion, Arlington, VA)
Models Mart Directory (Peter Glenn Publications, New York, NY)
Textile Blue Book (Davison Publishing Co., Glen Rock, NJ)
Wholesale/Manufacturers Apparel Directory (American Business
    Lists, Omaha, NE)

NEW YORK EMPLOYERS:

Aileen, Inc.
1411 Broadway
New York, NY 10018
(212) 398-9770
Women's and children's apparel.

Beacon Looms
295 5th Ave.
New York, NY 10016
(212) 685-5800
Personnel Director: Irma Farnsworth
Produces a wide range of textiles for sale to retailers nationwide.

Belding Hemingway
1430 Broadway
New York, NY 10018
(212) 944-6040
Personnel Director: Susan Brofsky
One of the largest textile and home sewing manufacturers in the country. Manufactures industrial yarns and threads, notions, zippers, buttons, and threads for home sewing.

Beldoch Industries
44 Cherry Valley Ave.
West Hempstead, NY 11552
(516) 485-4400
Personnel Director: Vicki Cogliano

Blass, Bill, Ltd.
550 7th Ave.
New York, NY 10018
(212) 221-6660
Personnel Director: Jackie Damon
Women's apparel wholesaler.

Bonjour International Ltd.
1411 Broadway
New York, NY 10018
(212) 398-1000

Brittania Sportswear
1411 Broadway
New York, NY 10018
(212) 921-0060
Personnel: San Francisco (Division of Levi Strauss)
Apparel manufacturer and wholesaler.

Burlington Industries
1345 Avenue of the Americas
New York, NY 10105
(212) 621-3000
Personnel Director: Janice Jarsky
Textiles and home apparel fabrics; draperies, upholstery, carpets. New York office includes marketing, advertising, sales, and support services.

Butterick Company
161 6th Ave.

New York, NY 10013
(212) 620-2500
Personnel Manager: Rosalynd Gardner

Carnivale Bag Company
544 Park Ave.
Brooklyn, NY 11205
(718) 855-0613

Celanese Corporation
3 Park Ave.
New York, NY 10016
(212) 251-8000
Personnel Manager: Al Reed
Fibers, chemicals, and specialty products.

CHF Industries
1 Park Ave.
New York, NY 10016
(212) 951-7800
Personnel Director: Sarah Abramson
Curtains, home furnishings, and foam products.

Claiborne (Liz)
1441 Broadway
New York, NY 10018
(212) 354-4900
Personnel Director: Kathy Conners
Women's apparel.

Cluett Peabody & Co.
530 5th Ave.
New York, NY 10036
(212) 930-3000
Attention: Charles Ferguson
Leading apparel manufacturer. Labels include Arrowshirts,Ron
Chereskin menswear, Saturdays in California, Duofold Donmoor,
and Dolie Originals.

Collins and Aikman
210 Madison Ave.
New York, NY 10016
(212) 578-1200
Personnel Director: Marie Dendrinos
Specialty fabrics, including fabricated and non-fabricated textile
products and wall coverings.

Concord Fabrics
1359 Broadway
New York, NY 10018
(212) 760-0300
Personnel Director: Leslie Spitzer

Designer of woven and knitted fabrics for sale to manufacturers and retailers. New York office includes administration, design, merchandising, and marketing.

Cone Mills Marketing Company
1440 Broadway
New York, NY 10018
(212) 391-1300
Personnel: Pamela Maxell
Marketing and sales headquarters for this manufacturer.

Damon Creations
1370 6th Ave.
New York, NY 10016
(212) 399-3500
Personnel: Diane Williams

Dan River
111 W. 40th St.
New York, NY 10018
(212) 554-5531
Personnel Manager: Otis A. Braithwaite

Dothon Manufacturing Company
1359 Broadway, Room 612
New York, NY 10018
(212) 564-6450
Director of Personnel: Jim Rolek

Eccobay Sportswear
1411 Broadway
New York, NY 10018
(212) 354-8000
Personnel Director: Herb Chestler
Women's sportwear.

Ellis, Perry
1114 6th Ave.
New York, NY 10018
(212) 221-6795
Personnel: Chris Cicallo
Apparel wholesaler.

Evan-Picone
1411 Broadway
New York, NY 10018
(212) 536-9500
Women's and men's apparel.

Ex-Cell Home Fashions
295 5th Ave.
New York, NY 10016

(212) 213-8000
Personnel Director: Dottie Angerman
Home furnishing products.

Exquisite Form Industries
3010 Westchester Ave.
Purchase, NY 10577
(914) 251-1001
Contact Office Manager

Fine, M., and Sons
350 5th Ave.
New York, NY 10118
(212) 239-1111
Men's work clothes and leisure apparel.

Fownes Brothers and Company
411 5th Ave.
New York, NY 10016
(212) 683-0150
Controller: Howard Chaiet

Goldberg, Dave, Inc.
29-10 Thompson Ave.
Long Island City, NY 11101
(718) 786-7477
Personnel Director: Annie Santiago

Harwood Companies
1350 Avenue of the Americas
New York, NY 10019
(212) 397-6500
Men's & boys' sleepwear/underwear.

Hertling Manufacturing Company
500 Driggs Ave.
Brooklyn, NY 11211
(718) 782-7059

Home Curtain Corporation
295 5th Ave.
New York, NY 10016
(212) 686-2080
Home curtains, drapes, and related products.

Irwin, Harry, Inc.
116 W. 23rd St.
New York, NY 10011
(212) 741-9898

Izod
11 Penn Plaza

New York, NY 10001
(212) 502-3000
Apparel wholesaler and manufacturer.

Jordache Enterprises
498 7th Ave.
New York, NY 10018
(212) 279-7343

Karan, Donna, Co.
770 7th Ave.
New York, NY 10018
(212) 398-0616

Kinney Shoe Corporation
233 Broadway
New York, NY 10279
(212) 720-3700
Personnel Director: Philip Cease

Klein, Anne, & Co.
205 W. 39th St.
New York, NY 10018
(212) 221-7880

Klein, Calvin
205 W. 39th St.,14th Floor
New York, NY 10018
(212) 719-2600
Personnel Director: Tina Olson
Women's and men's apparel.

Lauren, Ralph
550 7th Ave.
New York, NY 10019
(212) 212-0675

Lehigh Valley Industries
345 Hudson St.
New York, NY 10014
Personnel Director: Rich Joline
Textiles and women's footwear.

Liberty Fabrics of New York
295 5th Ave.
New York, NY 10016
(212) 684-3100
Personnel Director: Allen Jammer
Knitted lace and elastic fabrics.

Maidenform, Inc.
90 Park Ave.

New York, NY 10016
(212) 953-1400
Office Manager: Geri Bull
Women's apparel, including undergarments, swimwear, and
sleepwear.

Master Trouser
350 5th Ave.
New York, NY 10001
(212) 760-9200
Personnel Director: Don Eisenberg
Men's and boys' pants.

Melville Corporation
1 Theall Road
Rye, NY 10580
(914) 925-4000

Milliken and Company Apparel/Fabric Sales
1045 Avenue of the Americas
New York, NY 10018
(212) 819-4200
Personnel Director: William Gaffney
Textile yarns and fabrics, apparel, and related chemical and
packaging products.

Movie Star
Subsidiary of Sanmark-Stardust
136 Madison Ave.
New York, NY 10016
(212) 684-3400
Personnel Director: Yolaine Goldberg
Brand names: Movie Star, Movie Star Loungewear, Cinema
Etoile. Also produces men's work and leisure clothes.

Nantucket Hosiery
Division Nantucket Industries
105 Madison Ave.
New York, NY 10016
(212) 889-5656
Personnel Director: Cecila Root
Men's and women's undergarments and hosiery.

National Spinning Company
183 Madison Ave.
New York, NY 10016
(212) 889-3800

Phillips-Van Heusen Corporation
1290 Avenue of the Americas
New York, NY 10104
(212) 541-5200

Men's apparel. Brand names: Van Heusen, Hennessy, Cricketeer, Crestmark, Halston, Geoffrey Beene, and Cacharel.

Rossini Footwear
1795 Express Drive N.
Smithtown, NY 11787
(516) 582-3230

Russ Toggs
1450 Broadway
New York, NY 10018
(212) 626-5800
Personnel Director: Zoita Comboianu
Sportswear, dresses, and separates. Subsidiary of Liz Claiborne

Salant Company
1114 Avenue of the Americas
New York, NY 10036
(212) 221-7500
Personnel Manager: Gloria Adams

Schumacher, F., and Company
79 Madison Ave.
New York, NY 10016
(212) 213-7900
Vice President, Personnel: Jim Hinthorn

Stuffed Shirt
1407 Broadway
New York, NY 10018
(212) 997-1000
Contact: Annemarie Feron

Warnaco Inc.
90 Park Ave.
New York, NY 10016
(212) 661-1300
Men's and women's shirts and sportswear.

West-Point Pepperell
1185 Avenue of the Americas
New York, NY 10036
(212) 930-2050
Director of Human Resources: Linda Harris

CONNECTICUT EMPLOYERS:

Brownell and Company
P.O. Box 362
Moodus, CT 06149
(203) 873-8625
Personnel Director: Cindy Stackowitz

Playtex Apparel
700 Fairfield Ave. P.O. Box 10064
Stamford, CT 06904
(203) 356-8000
Manager of Human Resources: Angela Gizinski

NEW JERSEY EMPLOYERS:

Cooper Sportswear Manufacturing
720 Frelinghuysen Ave.
Newark, NJ 07114
(201) 824-3400

Fabrican
375 Diamond Bridge Ave.
Hawthorne, NJ 07506
(201) 423-4800
Personnel Director: Josie Giovinazzo

Goldberg, S., and Company
20 E. Broadway
Hackensack, NJ 07601
(201) 342-1200
Personnel Manager

Levolor Lorentzen
25 Green Pond Road
Rockaway, NJ 07866
(201) 627-2200

Maidenform—Bayonne
154 Avenue E
Bayonne, NJ 07002
(201) 436-9200

Old Deerfield Fabrics
134 Sand Park Road
Cedar Grove, NJ 07009
(201) 239-6600

Phillips-VanHeusen Croporation
281 Centennial Ave.
Piscataway, NJ 08854
(201) 885-5000
Many divisions and designer names.

United Merchants and Manufacturers
1630 Palisades Ave.
Teaneck, NJ 07666
(201) 837-1700
Personnel Director: Stanley Siegel
Apparel fabrics, home furnishings, yarns, and chemicals.

**Contracting for
a career on 7th
Avenue**

We asked Gary Randazzo, president of Geeankay Dress Company, a mid-sized contractor of women's apparel, to explain the lines of distribution in the apparel, or garment, industry.

"Contractors are the first step in a long and often confusing line of distribution for a garment," says Randazzo. "Contractors put the goods together for manufacturers who do not have their own shops. This is what is known as piece work, assembling garments that have been cut and need only to be sewn together. Some contractors do the actual cutting of the material and construct the garment from the pattern to finished product. The public is generally not aware that contractors even exist, but they are a very important part of the chain.

"Once a garment has been finished, it is usually sent back to the manufacturer for sale to a wholesaler. It is then sold to the retail market. In some instances, large apparel companies can be considered wholesalers and manufacturers. They may also operate retail arms."

We asked if working for a contractor can help round out your experience in the garment industry. "Absolutely. After working for even a small contractor you can move to quality control, product management, and even inventory control for manufacturers or wholesalers. Also, you learn the business from the ground up: working on the shop floor examining dresses, dealing with employees, making contacts with wholesalers and manufacturers. That experience is invaluable in any part of the industry." ■

Architectural Firms

For networking in architecture and related fields, check out the
following professional organizations listed in Chapter 5. Also see
"Construction" and "Engineering."

PROFESSIONAL ORGANIZATIONS:

American Institute of Architects, NY Chapter
American Society of Civil Engineers
Architectural League of New York

For additional information, you can contact:

American Institute of Architects
1735 New York Ave., NW
Washington, DC 20006
(202) 626-7300

National Organization of Minority Architects
101 W. Broad St.
Richmond, VA 23220
(804) 788-0338

Society of American Registered Architects
1245 S. Highland Ave.
Lombard, IL 60148
(708) 932-4622

PROFESSIONAL PUBLICATIONS:

AIA Journal
Architectural Forum
Architectural Record
Building Design & Construction
Progressive Architecture

DIRECTORIES:

AIA Membership Directory (American Institute of Architects,
   Washington, DC)
Architects Directory (American Business Directories,Inc., Omaha,
   NE)
Society of American Registered Architects *National Membership
   Directory* (Society of American Registered Architects,
   Lombard,IL)

NEW YORK EMPLOYERS:

Beyer Blinder Belle
41 E. 11th St.
New York, NY 10017
(212) 777-7800
Personnel Director: Jennie Pococh

Brennan Beer Gorman Architects
515 Madison Ave.
New York, NY 10022
(212) 888-7663

Edward Larrabee Barnes Associates
320 W. 13th St.
New York, NY 10014
(212) 929-3131
Personnel Director: John Lee

Eggers Group, The
440 9th Ave.
New York, NY 10019
(212) 629-4100
Managing Director: Peter Halfon

Ellerbe Becket Architects and Engineers
636 Broadway
New York, NY 10012
(212) 685-9191

Gibbs and Hill
11 Penn Plaza
New York, NY 10001
(212) 216-6000
Personnel Director: Barbara Schiola

Gonchor & Sput Architects and Planners
192 Lexington Avenue
New York, NY 10016
(212) 685-2883

Greenman-Pedersen
325 W. Main St.
Babylon, NY 11702
(516) 587-5060
Personnel Director: Lillian Brueckner

Haines Lundberg Waehler
115 5th St.
New York, NY 10003
(212) 353-4600
Contact: Mary Jane Beatty

Kassner, John J., and Company
6 Ohio Drive
Lake Success, NY 11042
(516) 328-3600
Senior Vice President: Lawrence Lane

Kohn Pedersen Fox Associates
111 W. 57th St.
New York, NY 10019
(212) 977-6500
Administrative Partner: Robert Cioppa

Parsons Brinckerhoff
1 Penn Plaza
New York, NY 10019
(212) 465-5000
Corporate Employment Manager: Ed Schwartz

Pei Cobb Freed & Partners
600 Madison Ave.
New York, NY 10022
(212) 751-3122
Director of Personnel: Susan Appel

Perkins & Will
One Park Ave.
New York, NY 10016
(212) 251-7000
Personnel Director: Mitzi Bollinger

Rose, Beaton and Rose
81 Main St.
White Plains, NY 10601
(914) 682-4850

Roth, Emery, and Sons
560 Lexington Ave.
New York, NY 10022
(212) 753-1733
Office Manager: Robin Moise

Silver and Zikind Architects
233 Park Ave. S.
New York, NY 10003
(212) 477-1900
Contact Office Manager

Skidmore, Owings & Merrill
220 E. 42nd St.
New York, NY 10017
(212) 309-9500

Swanke Hayden Connell Architects
4 Columbus Circle
New York, NY 10019
(212) 977-9696
Personnel Director

Taylor Clark Architects
149 5th Ave.
New York, NY 10010
(212) 460-8840
Personnel Director: Mike Dimare

Tippetts-Abbett-McCarthy-Stratton
655 3rd Ave.
New York, NY 10017
(212) 867-1777
Office Manager: Joseph Scarin

Urbahn Associates
1250 Broadway
New York, NY 10001
(212) 239-0220

Vollmer Associates
50 W. 23rd St.
New York, NY 10010
(212) 366-5600
Personnel Director

Zetlin, Lev, Associates
641 Avenue of the Americas
New York, NY 10011
(212) 741-1300
Personnel Director: J. Prasad

CONNECTICUT EMPLOYERS:

Comstock Group
38 Old Ridgebury Road
Danbury, CT 06810
(203) 792-9800
Vice President, Human Resources: Walter Cheney

NEW JERSEY EMPLOYERS:

Airco Glass
575 Mountain Ave.
Murray Hill, NJ 07974
(908) 464-8100
Director of Recruiting

184

Berger, Louis, International
100 Halsted St.
P.O. Box 270
East Orange, NJ 07019
Correspondence only to Personnel Director

Edwards and Kelcey Organization
70 S. Orange Ave.
Livingston, NJ 07039
(201) 994-4520
Vice President, Human Resources: George Steidle

EMR Photoelectric/Schlumberger, Ltd.
P.O. Box 44
Princeton, NJ 08540
Personnel Manager: Dexter Nash
Correspondence only

Grad Associates
One Gateway Center
Newark, NJ 07102
(201) 621-1700

Automobile/Truck/Transportation Equipment Manufacturers

For information on the automotive industry, you can contact:

PROFESSIONAL ORGANIZATIONS:

American International Automobile Dealers Association
99 Canal Center Plaza
Alexandria, VA 22313
(703) 519-7810

ASIA (Automotive Service Industry Assoc.)
25 NW Point Blvd.
Elk Grove Village, IL 60007
(708) 228-1310

National Independent Automobile Dealers Association
2521 Brown Blvd.
Arlington, TX 76006
(817) 640-3838

Society of Automotive Engineers
400 Commonwealth Drive
Warrendale, PA 15096
(412) 776-4841

PROFESSIONAL PUBLICATIONS:

Automotive News
Motor
Motor Age

DIRECTORIES:

ASIA Membership Directory (Automotive Service Industry Assoc.,
   Elk Grove Village, IL)
Automotive Age, Buyers Guide Issue (Freed-Crown Publishing Co.,
   Van Nuys, CA)
Automotive News, Market Data Book Issue (Crain Automotive
   Group, Detroit, MI)
Jobber Topics, Annual Marketing Directory Issue (Irving-Cloud
   Publishing Co., Chicago IL)
Ward's Automotive Yearbook (Ward's Communications, Inc.,
   Detroit, MI)

NEW YORK EMPLOYERS:

Allomatic Industries
114 Jericho Turnpike
Floral Park, NY 11001
(516) 775-0330
Manufacturer of automotive parts and accessories.

Coltec Industries
430 Park Ave.
New York, NY 10022
(212) 940-0400
Major manufacturer of transportation parts and accessories.

General Motors Corporation
767 5th Ave.
New York, NY 10153
(212) 418-6100
Personnel Director: R.J.Kraus

Grumman Allied Industries
111 Stewart Ave.
Bethpage, NY 11714
(516) 575-8591
Major government contractor for aerospace and aircraft parts and
bodies, as well as a manufacturer of automobile and truck bodies.

Standard Motor Products
37-18 Northern Blvd.
Long Island City, NY 11101
(718) 392-0200
Personnel Director: Roy Rosner

NEW JERSEY EMPLOYERS:

Allied-Signal
Columbia Road 101
Morristown, NJ 07962
(201) 455-2000
Administration Director: Daniel Geist
Manufacturer of electronic diagnostic equipment and automotive
and aerospace parts.

General Automotive Specialty Co.
P.O. Box 3042
N. Brunswick, NJ 08902
(908) 545-7000
Personnel Director: Joseph Hammerman

Ingersoll-Rand Co.
200 Chestnut Ridge Road
Woodcliff Lake, NJ 07675

(201) 573-0123
Mgr. Personnel: Paula Prusko

Jaguar Cars
555 MacArthur Blvd.
Mahwah, NJ 07430
(201) 818-8500

Kem Manufacturing Co.
River Road
Fair Lawn, NJ 07410
(201) 427-2800
Personnel Administrator: Lois Blockburger

Mercedes-Benz of North America
One Mercedes Drive
Montvale, NJ 07645-0350
(201) 573-0600

Rolls-Royce Motor Cars
120 Chubb Ave.
P.O. Box 476
Lyndhurst, NJ 07071
(201) 460-9600

Volvo Cars of North America
One Volvo Drive
Rockleigh, NJ 07647
(201) 768-7300

Banks: Commercial and Savings

For networking in the banking industry and related fields, check out the following professional organizations listed in Chapter 5. Also see **"Stock Brokers/Financial Services/Investment Banking."**

PROFESSIONAL ORGANIZATIONS:

American Finance Association
American Management Association
Financial Women's Association of New York
New York Credit and Financial Management Association
New York Financial Writers' Association
New York Society of Security Analysts
Public Securities Association
Securities Industry Association

For additional information, you can contact:

American Bankers Association
1120 Connecticut Ave., NW
Washington, DC 20036
(202) 663-5000

Bank Marketing Association
1120 Connecticut Ave.
Washington, D.C. 20036
(202) 663-5089

Mortgage Bankers Association of America
1125 15th St., NW
Washington, DC 20005
(202) 861-6500

National Bankers Association
1802 T Street, NW
Washington, DC 20000
(202) 588-5432

New York State Bankers Association
485 Lexington Ave.
New York, NY 10017
(212) 949-1155

Savings and Community Bankers of America
1709 New York Ave., NW
Washington, D.C. 20006
(202) 637-8900

PROFESSIONAL PUBLICATIONS:

ABA Banking Journal
American Banker
American Business
Bank Marketing Magazine
Bankers Magazine
Bankers Monthly
Barron's National Business and Financial Weekly
Boardroom Reports
Business and Society Review
D & B Reports

DIRECTORIES:

American Bank Directory (McFadden Business Publications,
    Norcross, GA)
American Banker's Guide to the First 5,000 U.S. Banks (American
    Banker, New York, NY)
Callahan's Credit Union Directory (Callahan and Associates,
    Washington, DC)
Money Market Directory (Money Market Directories,
    Charlottesville, VA)
Moody's Bank and Finance Manual (Moody's Investor Service,
    New York, NY)
Polk's Bank Directory (R.L. Polk, Nashville, TN)
Rand McNally Bankers Directory (Rand McNally,
    Chicago, IL)
U.S. Savings and Loan Directory (Rand McNally, Chicago, IL)

NEW YORK EMPLOYERS:

Apple Savings Bank
205 E. 42nd St.
New York, NY 10017
(212) 573-8000
Personnel Director: Mr. Dario Rizzi

Bank of America
335 Madison Ave.
New York, 10017
(212) 503-7498

Bank Leumi Trust Company of New York
139 Center St.
New York, NY 10013
(212) 382-4000
Manager of Employment: Herbert Small

Bank of Montreal
430 Park Ave.

New York, NY 10022
(212) 758-6300
Manager: Recruitment Office

Bank of New York
48 Wall St.
New York, NY 10286
(212) 495-1784
Personnel Director: Frank Peterson

Bank of Tokyo Trust
100 Broadway
New York, NY 10005
(212) 766-3400
Recruiting: Ms. Amaura Abad

Banker's Trust Company
280 Park Ave.
New York, NY 10017
(212) 250-2500

Barclays Bank of New York
300 Park Ave.
New York, NY 10017
212) 333-2136
Personnel Director: Sivberto Zoccarras

Barclays International
75 Wall St.
New York, NY 10265
(212) 412-3948
Vice President: Pam Boyle

Bowery Savings Bank
110 E. 42nd St.
New York, NY 10017
(212) 953-8000
Manager of Personnel: Gail Anderson

Chase Manhattan Bank
1 Chase Manhattan Plaza, 27th Floor
New York, NY 10081
(212) 552-2222
Vice-President Professional Recruitment: Christine Hanfman
One of the largest commercial banks in the United States.

Chemical Bank
277 Park Ave.
New York, NY 10172
(212) 310-6161
Personnel Director

One of the largest commercial banks in the United States.
Executive offices.

Citicorp
One Court Square
Long Island City, NY 11120
(718) 248-4800
Personnel Director: Pamela Flaherty
Largest commercial bank in the United States.

Columbia Federal Savings Bank
80-31 Jamaice Ave.
Woodhaven, NY 11421
(718) 296-2927
Vice President Personnel: Eleanor Reed

Crossland Federal
211 Montague St.
Brooklyn, NY 11201
(718) 780-0400
Personnel Director: Paul LaRosa

Daiwa Bank Trust Co.
75 Rockefeller Plaza
New York, NY 10019
(212) 554-7300
Vice President and Personnel Director: Richard DiPiazza

Dime Savings Bank, The
EAB Plaza–E. Tower, 10th Floor
Uniondale, NY 11556
(516) 745-2400
Sr.Vice President Human Resources: Robert DelGuidice

East New York Savings Bank
41 W. 42nd St.
New York, NY 10036
(212) 382-4700
Banking Officer: David Palmer

East River Savings Bank
145 Huguenot St.
New Rochelle, NY 10801
(914) 654-4500
Director of Human Resources: Christopher Cosgrove

Emigrant Savings Bank
5 E. 42nd St.
New York, NY 10017
(212) 850-4000
Senior Vice President: Edward Tully

European American Bank
EAB Plaza
Uniondale, NY 11555
(516) 296-5555
Personnel Director: Raul Cruz

Fidelity New York
1000 Franklin Ave.
Garden City, NY 11530
(516) 746-8500
Vice President, Personnel: Joanne Cordano

First National Bank of Long Island
30 Glen Head Road
Glen Head, NY 11545
(516) 671-4900
Personnel Director: Barbara Shapiro

Greater New York Savings Bank
1 Penn Plaza
New York, NY 10019
(212) 613-4000
Human Resources: John Dresch

Independence Savings Bank
130 Court St.
Brooklyn, NY 11201
(718) 624-6620
Personnel Director: Nancy Pacione

Jamaica Savings Bank
303 Merrick Road
Lynbrook, NY 11564
(516) 887-7000
Sr. Vice President, Personnel: John Conroy

Long Island Savings Bank
201 Old Country Road
Melville, NY 11747
(516) 547-2000
Vice President and Director of Personnel: Donna Kelly

Manhattan Savings Bank
415 Madison Ave.
New York, NY 10017
(212) 688-3000

Marine Midland Bank
140 Broadway, 9th Floor
New York, NY 10015
(212) 658-1000
Adm. Vice President, Personnel: Barbara Schaefer

Morgan Guaranty Trust Company
23 Wall St.
New York, NY 10015
(212) 483-2323
Personnel Representative: David Fagan

National Westminster Bank
175 Water St.
New York, NY 10038
(212) 602-1000
Personnel: Jean Piatowski

Norstar Bank
300 Broad Hollow Road
Melville, NY 11747
(516) 547-7430
Personnel Officer: Molly Horowitz
Corporate Headquarters: Garden City, NY

Queen's County Savings Bank
38-25 Main St.
Flushing, NY 11354
(718) 359-6400
Vice President Personnel: Jeanenne Garman

Republic National Bank of New York
452 5th Ave.
New York, NY 10018
(212) 525-6120

Ridgewood Savings Bank
7102 Forest Ave.
Ridgewood, NY 11385
(718) 240-4800
Personnel Director: Norman McNamee

Roosevelt Savings Bank
1122 Franklin Ave.
Garden City, NY 11530
(516) 742-9300
Sr. Vice President, Personnel: Aileen Cordiello

Royal Bank of Canada
Financial Square
New York, NY 10005
(212) 428-6200
Personnel Director: Richard Clark

Sterling National Bank and Trust Company
355 Lexington Ave.
New York, NY 10017

(212) 490-9809
Personnel Director: Roger Maglio

United States Trust Company of New York
114 W. 47th St.
New York, NY 10036
(212) 852-1000
Director of Personnel: Patricia McGuire

CONNECTICUT EMPLOYERS:

Centerbank
36 N. Main St.
Waterbury, CT 06720
(203) 573-7861
Employment Manager: Whit Knapp

Fleet/Norstar Bank
1 Constitution Plaza
Hartford, CT 06115
(203) 244-4903
Director of Human Resources: Anne Nolan
Corporate Headquarters in Providence, RI, (401) 278-5800

NorthEast Bancorp
300 Main St.
Stamford, CT 06901
(203) 348-6211

Putnam Trust Company
10 Mason St.
Greenwich, CT 06830
(203) 869-3000
Vice President: Gregory S. Hannigan

NEW JERSEY EMPLOYERS:

Citizens First National Bank of New Jersey
208 Harristown Road
Glenrock, NJ 07452
(201) 445-3400
Sr. Vice President, Personnel: Peter Beisler

First Fidelity Bank
765 Broad St.
Newark, NJ 07102
(201) 565-3200
Employment Office

Hudson United
100 Hamilton Plaza
Paterson, NJ 07505

(201) 742-6000
Personnel Director: Karen Foley

Midlantic Bank North
499 Thornall St.
Edison, NJ 08818
(908) 321-8000
Corporate Headquarters.

National Community Bank
113 W. Essex St.
Maywood, NJ 07607
(201) 845-1603
Personnel Officer: Michael Bryan

National Westminster Bank New Jersey
10 Exchange Place Center
Jersey City, NJ 07302
(201) 547-7000
Human Resources Group

Summit Trust Company
750 Walnut
Cranford, NJ 07901
(908) 709-6000
Vice President of Human Resources: George Dorsey

United Jersey Bank/Commercial Trust
210 Main St.
Jersey City, NJ 07302
(201) 434-5100
Personnel: Suzanne Depuyt

United National Bank
65 Reddington Road
Branchburg, NJ 08876
(908) 756-5000
Sr. Vice President, Human Resources: Jean Carr

Valley National Bank
615 Main Ave.
Passaic, NJ 07055
(201) 777-1800
Director Human Resources: Peter Verbout

Book Publishers/Literary Agents

For networking in book publishing and related fields, check out the following professional organizations listed in Chapter 5. Also see **"Media, Print."**

PROFESSIONAL ORGANIZATIONS:

American Book Producers Association
American Booksellers Association
American Society of Composers, Authors and Publishers
Association of American Publishers
Association of Business Publishers
Promotion Marketing Association of America
Publishers Publicity Association

For additional information, you can contact:

American Booksellers Association
560 White Plains Road
Tarrytown, NY 10591
(914) 631-7800

Association of American Publishers
220 E. 23rd St.
New York, NY 10010
(212) 689-8920

PROFESSIONAL PUBLICATIONS:

American Bookseller
Editor and Publisher
Library Journal
Publishers Weekly
Small Press

DIRECTORIES:

American Book Trade Directory (R.R. Bowker, New York, NY)
Literary Market Place (R.R. Bowker, New York, NY)

NEW YORK EMPLOYERS, PUBLISHERS:

Abrams, Harry N.
100 5th Ave.
New York, NY 10011
(212) 206-7715
Personnel Director: Ellvira Giannasca
Trade publisher.

American Heritage Publishing
60 5th Ave.
New York, NY 10011
(212) 206-5500

Atheneum Books
Division of Macmilian Publishing Co.
866 3rd Ave.
New York, NY 10022
(212) 702-2000

Avon Books
Division of Hearst Corporation
1350 Avenue of the Americas
New York, NY 10019
(212) 261-6800
Asst. Personnel Director: Cecile Grant
Paperback publisher.

Ballantine Books/Del Rey/Fawcett
Subsidiary of Random House,
201 E. 50th St.
New York, NY 10022
(212) 751-2600
Editor-in-Chief Trade Division: Joelle Delbourgo
Mass market and trade paperback publisher.

Bantam/Doubleday/Dell
666 5th Ave.
New York,NY 10103
(212) 765-6500
Director of Personnel: Robert Defendorf
Trade publisher.

Barrons Educational Series
250 Wireless Blvd.
Happaugue, NY 11788
(516) 434-3311
Personnel Manager: Vera Burkart
Educational and business publisher.

Matthew Bender & Company
11 Pennyslvania Plaza
New York, NY 10001
(212) 967-7707
Publisher law-related titles.

Berkely Publishing Group
200 Madison Ave.
New York, NY 10016
(212) 951-8800

Personnel Recruiter: Grace Schlemm
Trade publisher.

Cambridge University Press
40 W. 20th St.
New York, NY 10011
(212) 924-3900
Editorial Director: Sydney Landau

Columbia University Press
562 W.113th St.
New York, NY 10025
(212) 316-7100
Editor-in-Chief: Kate Wittenberg

Crown Publishers
201 E. 50th St.
New York, NY 10022
(212) 751-2600
Personnel: Michelle Heiman
Trade publisher.

Dekker, Marcel
270 Madison Ave.
New York, NY 10016
(212) 696-9000
Personnel Representative: Jennifer Foo

Dell Publishing
666 5th Ave.
New York, NY 10103
(212) 765-6500
Director Personnel: Robert Defendorf

Doubleday and Company
245 Park Ave.
New York, NY 10167
(212) 984-7561
Personnel: Mr. Pietro
Trade publisher.

Dun & Bradstreet Corporation
299 Park Ave.
New York, NY 10171
(212) 593-6821
Manager Staffing Programs: Mary A. Ecclesine
Business and financial publisher.

Encyclopaedia Britannica USA
One Suffolk Square
Islandia, NY 11722
(516) 232-1260

Facts on File
460 Park Ave.
New York, NY 10010
(212) 683-2244

Farrar, Strauss and Giroux
19 Union Square W.
New York, NY 10003
(212) 741-6900
Personnel Director: Peggy Miller
Trade publisher.

Golden Press
Division of Western Publishing Company
850 3rd Ave.
New York,NY 10022
(212) 753-8500
Personnel Director: Maureen Avon
Juvenile publisher.

Harcourt Brace Jovanovich
111 5th Ave.
New York, NY 10003
(212) 614-3000

Harlequin/Silhouette Books
300 E. 42nd St.
New York, NY 10017
(212) 682-6080
Romance fiction publishers.

Harper Collins Publishers
10 E. 53rd St.
New York, NY 10022
(212) 207-7000
Personnel Director: Joan Maniscalco
Trade publisher.

Hearst Books Group
1350 Avenue of the Americas
New York, NY 10019
(212) 649-2000
Vice President, Human Resources: Kenneth Feldman

Holt, Rinehart, Winston
151 Benigno Blvd.
Bellmawr, NJ 08031
(800) 426-0462
Personnel Director: Joyce Asay
Educational, business, and trade publisher.

Houghton Mifflin Company
215 Park Ave. S.
New York, NY 10003
(212) 420-5800
Personnel Director: Ann Healy
Trade publisher.

Knopf, Alfred A.
Division of Random House
201 E. 50th St.
New York, NY 10023
(212) 751-2600
Editor-in-Chief: Sonny Mehta
Trade publisher.

Macmillan, Inc.
866 3rd Ave.
New York, NY 10022
(212) 702-2000
Editor-in-Chief, Trade Division: William Rosen
Trade publisher.

McGraw Hill Book Company
1221 Avenue of the Americas
New York, NY 10020
(212) 512-2000
Director of Human Resources: Edward Ridolfi
Trade publisher.

Morrow, William
1350 6th Ave.
New York, NY 10019
(212) 261-6500
Personnel Director: Lenore Johnson

New American Library
Division of Penguin USA
375 Hudson St.
New York, NY 10014
(212) 366-2000
Personnel Director: Shelly Sadler
Trade publisher.

Newmarket Press
18 E. 48th St.
New York, NY 10017
(212) 832-3575
Assistant Editor: Grace Farrell
Trade publisher.

Norton Company, W.W.
500 5th Ave.

New York, NY 10110
(212) 354-5500
Personnel Director: Lisa Gaeth
Trade publisher.

Pantheon Books
201 E. 50th St.
New York, NY 10022
(212) 751-2600
Trade publisher.

Penguin USA
375 Hudson St.
New York, NY 10014
(212) 366-2000
Personnel Manager: Shelly Sadler

Pergamon Press
660 White Plains Road
Tarrytown, NY 10591
(914) 524-9200
Personnel Director: Robert Yardis
Technical and scientific books.

Pocket Books
Division of Simon and Schuster
1230 Avenue of the Americas
New York, NY
(212) 698-7000
Assoc. Human Resources Director: Susan Wexler
Paperback publisher.

Prentice Hall
Division of Gulf and Western Industries
Route 9W
Englewood Cliffs, NJ 07632
(201) 592-2000
Human Resources: Sue Fisher

Putnam-Grosset
200 Madison Ave.
New York, NY 10016
(212) 951-8400
Personnel Director: Carol Peterson
Trade publisher.

Random House
201 E. 50th St.
New York, NY 10022
(212) 751-2600
Trade publishers. Subsidiaries include: Alfred A. Knopf,

Ballantine/Del Rey/Fawcett, Vintage Press, Pantheon, Modern
Library, and Viking/Penguin.

Reader's Digest General Books
261 Madison Ave.
New York, NY 10016
(212) 953-0030
Human Resources: Lauren Gillett
Trade publisher. Headquarters location: Pleasantville, NY 10570.

Sadlier, William H.
9 Pine St.
New York, NY 10005
(212) 227-2120
Personnel Director: Frances Marsh
Trade publisher.

St. Martin's Press
175 5th Ave.
New York, NY 10010
(212) 674-5151
Personnel Director: Carolyn Jensen

Schimer, G.S.
866 3rd Ave.
New York, NY 10022
(212) 702-2000
Employment Representative: Abby Miller
Trade publisher.

Scholastic, Inc.
730 Broadway
New York, NY 10003
(212) 505-3000
Counselor Human Resources: Deborah Fuller
Educational publisher.

Scribner's, Charles, Sons
866 3rd Ave.
New York, NY 10022
(212) 702-2000
Trade publisher.

Simon and Schuster
1230 Avenue of the Americas
New York, NY 10020
(212) 698-7000
Assoc. Personnel Director: Susan Wexler
A leading trade publisher. Major trade subsidiaries include
Touchstone Books and Summit Books.

Sterling Publishing Company
387 Park Ave S.
New York, NY 10016
(212) 532-7160
Controller: Clyde Braunstein

Times Mirror
780 3rd Ave.
New York, NY 10017
(212) 418-9600
Office Manager: Susan Knight
Trade publisher.

Touchstone Books
Division of Simon and Schuster
1230 Avenue of the Americas
New York, NY 10020
(212) 698-7000
Assoc. Personnel Director: Susan Wexler
Trade paperback publisher.

Van Nostrand Reinhold Company
115 5th Ave.
New York, NY 10003
(212) 254-3232
Personnel Manager: Linda Watson
Trade publisher.

Vintage Books
Division of Random House
201 E. 50th St.
New York, NY
(212) 751-2600
Editor-in-Chief: Morty Asher
Trade paperback publisher.

Wallaby Books
Division of Simon and Schuster
1230 Avenue of the Americas
New York, NY 10020
(212) 698-7000
Assoc. Personnel Director: Susan Wexler
Juvenile publisher.

Wanderer Books
Division of Simon and Schuster
1230 Avenue of the Americas
New York, NY 10020
(212) 698-7000
Assoc. Personnel Director: Susan Wexler
Juvenile publisher.

Warren, Gorham's, Lamont
1 Penn Plaza
New York, NY 10119
(212) 971-5000
Human Resources Associate: Jeanette Diaz

Wiley, John, and Sons
605 3rd Ave.
New York,NY 10158
(212) 850-6000
Vice President of Human Resources: Bill Arlington
Trade and educational publisher.

Windmill Publishing Company
Division of Simon and Schuster
1230 Avenue of the Americas
New York, NY 10020
(212) 698-7000
Assoc. Personnel Director: Susan Wexler
Juvenile publisher.

CONNECTICUT EMPLOYERS:

Grolier, Inc.
Sherman Turnpike
Danbury, CT 06816
(203) 796-2560
Director of Employee Relations: Anne Graves

NEW JERSEY EMPLOYERS:

Globe Book Company
190 Sylvan Ave.
Englewood Cliffs, NJ 07632
(201) 592-3342
Secretary to Business Manager: Marta Bemanani
Textbook publisher. Subsidiary of Simon and Schuster.

Reed Reference Publishing
121 Shanlon Road
New Providence, NJ 07974
(908) 464 6800
Personnel Specialist: Eileen Purelis
Several divisions.

Scott, Foresman & Co.
99 Bauer Drive
Oakland, NJ 07436
(201) 337-5861
Office Manager: Sally Memmelaar
International textbook publisher.

EMPLOYERS, LITERARY AGENTS:

Also see "Artists' Representatives" under **Entertainment and Recreation**.

Acton and Dystel
928 Broadway, Suite 301
New York, NY 10010
(212) 473-1700
Contact: Edward J. Acton

Bach, Julian
747 3rd Ave.
New York, NY 10017
(212) 772-8900
Contact: Julian Bach

Borchardt, Georges
136 E. 57th St.
New York, NY 10022
(212) 753-5785
Contact: George Borchardt

Brandt and Brandt Literary Agents
1501 Broadway
New York, NY 10036
(212) 840-5760
Personnel: Carl Younger

Brockman, John, Associates
307 Broadway
New York, NY 10024
(212) 874-0500

Brown, Curtis, Ltd.
10 Aster Place
New York, NY 10106
(212) 473-5400
Literary and dramatic agents.

Donadio, Candida, and Ashworth
231 W. 22nd St.
New York, NY 10011
(212) 691-8077
Contact: Eric Ashworth
Literary and dramatic agents.

International Creative Management
40 W. 57th St.
New York, NY 10019
(212) 556-5600

Director of Operations/Personnel: Andrew Suss
Literary and dramatic agents.

Janklow, Nesbit Associates
598 Madison Ave.
New York, NY 10022
(212) 421-1700
Office Manager: Alice Drucker
Literary and dramatic agents.

Leigh Bureau, The
50 Division St. Suite 200
Summerville, NJ 08876-2955
(609) 921-6141
Manager: Maryellen Mizov
Lecture and literary agency.

Levine, Ellen, Literary Agency
15 E. 26th St., Suite 1801
New York, NY 10010
(212) 889-0620
President: Ellen Levine

Markson, Elaine, Literary Agency
44 Greenwich Ave.
New York, NY 10011
(212) 243-8480
Contact: Geri Thoma
Literary and dramatic agents.

Miller, Peter, Agency
Subsidiary of Lion Entertainment
220 W. 19th St., Suite 501
New York, NY 10011
(212) 929-1222
Contact: Peter Miller
Literary and dramatic agents.

Morris, William, Agency
1350 Avenue of the Americas
New York, NY 10019
(212) 586-5100
Literary and dramatic agents.

Priest, Aaron M., Literary Agency
122 E. 42nd St., Suite 3902
New York, NY 10168
(212) 818-0344
Contact: Aaron Priest
Literary and dramatic agents.

Sobel, Weber, Associates
146 E. 19th St.
New York, NY 10003
(212) 420-8585

Sterling Lord Agency
1 Madison Ave.
New York, NY 10021
(212) 696-2800
Contact: Sterling Lord
Literary and dramatic agents.

Writer's Alliance
127 E. 59th St., Suite 201
New York, NY 10022
(212) 732-2580

Writer's and Artist's Agency
19 W. 44th St., Suite 1000
New York, NY 10036
(212) 391-1112
Literary and dramatic agents.

Broadcasting

For networking in radio, television, and related fields, check out the
following professional organizations listed in Chapter 5:

PROFESSIONAL ORGANIZATIONS:

AFTRA
American Sportscasters Association
American Women in Radio and Television
Association of Independent Commercial Producers
Cabletelevision Advertising Bureau
National Association of Broadcasters
National Association of Media Women
Newswomen's Club of New York
New York Women in Communications
Radio Advertising Bureau
Women's Media Group

For additional information, you can contact:

American Federation of Television and Radio Artists
260 Madison Ave.
New York, NY 10016
(212) 532-0800

Broadcast Promotion and Marketing Executives
62555 Sunset Blvd.
Los Angeles, CA 90028
(213) 465-3777

Corporation for Public Broadcasting
901 E. St., NW
Washington DC 20004
(202) 879-9600

National Academy of Television Arts and Sciences
111 W. 57th St.
New York, NY 10019
(212) 586-8424

National Association of Broadcasters
1771 N St., NW
Washington, DC 20036
(202) 429-5300

National Association of Television Program Executives
2425 Olympic Blvd.
Santa Monica, CA 90404
(310) 453-4440

National Cable Television Association
1724 Massachusetts Ave., NW
Washington DC 20036
(202) 775-3550

National Radio Broadcasters Association
2033 M St., NW
Washington, DC 20036

Radio-Television News Directors Association
1717 K St., NW
Washington, DC 20006
(202) 659-6510

PROFESSIONAL PUBLICATIONS:

Billboard
Broadcast Communications
Broadcasting Magazine
Communications News
International Television Almanac
New York Publicity Outlets
Television Broadcast
Video Week
Variety

DIRECTORIES:

Broadcasting Cable Source Book (Broadcasting Publishing Co., Washington, DC)
Broadcasting Yearbook (Broadcasting Publishing Co., Washington, DC)
Cable Programming Resource Directory: A Guide to Community TV Production Facilities and Programming Services and Outlets (Broadcasting Publications, Washington, DC)
Television and Cable Fact Book (Television Digest, Washington, DC)
TV/Radio Age Ten-City Directory (TV Editorial Corp., New York, NY)

TELEVISION EMPLOYERS:

Television is a huge business with a wide variety of jobs. We've decided to list the personnel people and others as contacts to focus your search. But it would be more helpful to contact the business manager of a particular show. They are the people on the staff of network-produced shows that oversee budgets and allocation of funds. It's a more direct way to find out if positions exist and if you're qualified.

American Broadcasting Company—Capitol Cities
77 W. 66th St.
New York, NY 10023
(212) 456-7777
Major commercial television network.

Australian Broadcasting Company
635 5th Ave., Suite 2260
New York, NY 10111
(212) 757-1177
Australian television network.

British Broadcasting Corporation
630 5th Ave., Suite 2153
New York, NY 10111
(212) 581-7100
Business Manager: Robert Easter
British television network.

Canadian Broadcasting Corporation
350 5th Ave., Room 5507
New York, NY 10118
(212) 760-1500
Canadian television network.

CBS Television Network
51 W. 52nd St.
New York, NY 10019
(212) 975-4321
Major television network.

Fox Broadcasting Company
205 E. 67th St.
New York, NY 10021
(212) 452-5555

King World Productions
1700 Broadway
New York, NY 10019
(212) 315-4000
Personnel Manager: Margie Tortoriello

National Broadcasting Company
30 Rockefeller Plaza
New York, NY 10112
(212) 664-4444
Major commercial television and radio network.

Times Broadcast TV Group
Subsidiary of Times Mirror Co.
780 3rd Ave.

New York, NY 10017
(212) 418-9600

Univision Station Group
330 Madison Ave., 26th Floor
New York, NY 10017
(212) 983-8500

USA Network
1230 Avenue of the Americas
New York, NY 10020
(212) 408-9100
Manager, Human Resources: Jeffrey Kudak

Viacom International
1515 Broadway
New York, NY 10036
(212) 418-9600
Director of Personnel: Collette Gambino
Video/communications company.

Westinghouse Broadcasting Company
888 7th Ave.
New York, NY 10106
(212) 307-3000
Employee Representative: Jody Woods

WABC-TV
77 W. 66th St.
New York, NY 10023
(212) 456-7777
ABC-owned and operated TV station.

WCBS-TV
51 W. 52nd St.
New York, NY 10112
(212) 975-4321
Vice President, General Manager: Roger Coloff
CBS-owned and operated TV station.

WNBC-TV
30 Rockefeller Plaza
New York, NY 10020
(212) 664-4444
NBC-owned and operated TV station.

WNET-TV
Channel 13
356 W. 58th St.
New York, NY 10019
(212) 560-2000

Employment Manager: Leon Goodman
Public broadcasting station.

WNYE FM/Television
112 Tillary St.
Brooklyn, NY 11201
(718) 935-4480
Director of Broadcasting: Terence O'Driscoll

WOR-TV
9 Broadcast Plaza
Secaucus, NJ 07094
(201) 348-0009
Human Resources Director: Michael DiLaura
Independently-owned television station.

WPIX-TV
220 E. 42nd St.
New York, NY 10017
(212) 949-1100
Personnel Director: Donna Coles
Independent television broadcaster.

CABLE-TV EMPLOYERS:

A&E Arts and Entertainment Cable Network
555 5th Ave.
New York, NY 10017
(212) 661-4500

Cable News Network
5 Penn Plaza
New York, NY 10001
(212) 714-7800
Bureau Chief: Ken Chamberlain

CNBC Consumer News and Business Control
2200 Fletcher Ave.
Ft. Lee, NJ 07024
(201) 585-2622

ESPN
ESPN Plaza
Bristol, CT 06010
(203) 585-2000
Cable channel that primarily covers sporting events.

Paragon Cable
5120 Broadway
New York,NY 10034
(212) 304-3000

Home Box Office
Division of Time, Inc.
1100 Avenue of the Americas
New York, NY 10036
Employment Office: (212) 512-1000
Cable broadcasting service.

Lifetime Television
36-12 35th Ave.
Astoria, NY 11106
(718) 482-4000
Personnel Director: Deborah Henderson

Madison Square Garden Cablevision
3 Pennsylvania Plaza
New York, NY 10001
(212) 465-6000
Human Resources Coordinator: Marilyn Housner
The sports arena's in-house cable channel.

MTV Networks
1515 Broadway
New York, NY 10038
(212) 258-7800

Nashville Network, The
Group W Satellite Communications
Box 10210
250 Harbor Plaza Drive
Stamford, CT 06904-2210
(202) 965-6000

Showtime/The Movie Channel
1622 Broadway, 37th Floor
New York, NY 10019
(212) 708-1600

SportsChannel America
3 Crossways Park
Woodbury, NY 11797
(516) 921-3764

Time Warner Cable
120 E. 23rd St.
New York, NY 10010
(212) 598-7200
Personnel Director: Ann Caruso

USA Network
1230 Avenue of the Americas
New York, NY 10020
(212) 408-9100

214

RADIO EMPLOYERS:

ABC Radio Networks
125 West End Ave.
New York, NY 10023
(212) 887-5200

CBS Radio Network-AM
51 W. 52nd St.
New York, NY 10019
(212) 975-4321
Assignment Editor, News Desk

National Broadcasting Company
30 Rockefeller Plaza
New York, NY 10020
(212) 664-4444

Breaking into broadcasting

Susan Symington is an executive at a New York radio station. We asked her how to get started in broadcasting.

"Persevere," she says. "One of my first interviews was with the personnel director of a television station in Albany. 'Do you realize,' he said, 'that SUNY graduated 800 communications majors last year alone? There aren't that many jobs in the whole state.'

"That was a sobering thought. It discourages a lot of people. But you have to keep in there. Send out resumes, read the trades, see who's switching formats, and all that. Do anything on the side that might result in a good lead. The year after I graduated from college, I took a news writing course taught at the New School. In New York there are a lot of broadcasting professionals teaching all over the city; taking a course from a working professional can lead to valuable contacts.

"Another important point is to treat your contacts with respect. Broadcasting is a volatile business. You can't afford to burn a lot of bridges or alienate a lot of people. Somebody can be your assistant one day and your boss the next."

Sheridan Broadcasting Networks
One Times Square Plaza, 18th Floor
New York, NY 10036
(212) 575-0099

Unity Broadcasting Network
505 8th Ave.
New York, NY
(212) 316-6991
Personnel Director: Donna Collier
Mid-size radio broadcasting company.

Wall Street Journal Radio Network
200 Liberty St., 14th Floor
New York, NY 10281
(212) 416-2381

Westwood One
1700 Broadway
New York, NY 10019
(212) 237-2500

WABC Radio
2 Penn Plaza
New York, NY 10121
(212) 613-3800

WBAI Radio
505 8th Ave.
New York, NY 10018
(212) 279-0707
Program Director: Andrew Phillips

WBLS WLIB/Radio
801 2nd Ave.
New York, NY 10016
(212) 661-3344
Program Director: Mike Love

WCBS Radio AM
51 W. 52nd St.
New York, NY 10019
(212) 975-2127
Asst. News Director: Bernard Gershon

WEVD Radio
770 Broadway
New York, NY 10003
(212) 777-7900
Program Director: Bob August

WFAN Radio
34-12 36th St.
Long Island City, NY 11101
(718) 706-7690
Program Director: Mark Chernoff

WHLI Radio
1055 Franklin Ave.
Garden City, NY 11530
(516) 294-8400
News Director: Janell Tuebner

WINS Radio
888 7th Ave.
New York, NY 10106
(212) 397-1010
Program Director: Steve Swenson

WLTW Radio
1515 Broadway
New York, NY 10036
(212) 258-7000
Program Director: Dale Parsons

WMCA Radio
201 Rte. 17 N., Suite 601
Rutherford, NJ 07070
(201) 507-5700
Program Director: Carl Miller

WNEW-FM
655 3rd Ave.
New York, NY 10017
(212) 286-1027
Program Director: Pat St.John, FM Stations

WNYC Radio
Municipal Building
New York, NY 10007
(212) 669-7800

WPIX-FM Radio
220 E. 42nd St.
New York, NY 10017
(212) 949-1100
Program Director: Julie Nunnari

WQXR Radio
122 5th Ave.
New York, NY 10011
(212) 633-7600
Program Director: Tom Bartunek

Chemicals

For networking in the chemical industry and related fields, check out the following professional organizations listed in Chapter 5:

PROFESSIONAL ORGANIZATIONS:

American Institute of Chemical Engineers
Association of Consulting Chemists and Chemical Engineers
Chemists' Club of New York
Drug, Chemical and Allied Trades Association

For additional information, you can contact:

American Chemical Society
1155 16th St., NW
Washington, DC 20036
(202) 872-4600

Chemical Manufacturers Association
2501 N St., NW
Washington, DC 20037
(202) 887-1100

Chemical Specialities Manufacturers Association
1913 I St., NW
Washington, DC 20006
(202) 872-8110

PROFESSIONAL PUBLICATIONS:

Chemical and Engineering News
Chemical Marketing Reporter
Chemical Week

DIRECTORIES:

Chem Sources-U.S.A. (Chemical Sources International, Clemson, SC)
Chemclopedia (American Chemical Society, Washington, DC)
Chemical and Engineering News, Career Opportunities Issue (American Chemical Society, Washington, DC)
Chemical Week , Buyer's Guide Issue (McGraw-Hill, New York, NY)
Chemical Week: Financial Survey of the 300 Largest Companies (McGraw-Hill, New York, NY)

NEW YORK EMPLOYERS:

Aceto Chemical Company
1 Hollow Lane
Lake Success, NY 11042
(516) 627-6000
Director of Personnel: Patricia Miller
Industrial, organic, and inorganic chemicals.

Affrimet-Indussa
1212 Avenue of the Americas
New York, NY 10036
(212) 764-0880
Personnel Director: Maria Macchiarulo
Allied chemicals and metals manufacturers.

Bamberger Polymers
1983 Marcus Ave.
Lake Success, NY 11042
(516) 328-2772
Personnel: Andrea Lickman
A major distributor of plastics and resins.

Ciba Corporation
444 Saw Mill River Road
Ardsley, NY 10502
(914) 479-5000
Human Resources Director: Loretta Czernecki
Pharmaceutical, specialty and agricultural chemicals, resins and plastics manufacturers. Company headquarters.

Diversitron Corp.
61-37 Fresh Meadow Lane
Fresh Meadows, NY 11365
(718) 939-6600
Manufacturer of organic and inorganic chemicals.

ELM Coated Fabrics Division/Kalex Chemical Products
235 Gardner Ave.
Brooklyn, NY 11211
(718) 417-8282

Fehr Brothers
895 Kings Highway
Saugerties, NY 12477
(914) 246-9525
Exporter/importer of chemicals and allied products.

Fritzsche Dodge and Olcott
76 9th Ave.
New York, NY 10011

(212) 929-4000
Manager Corporate Human Resources: Maria Rangos

Grace, W.R., and Company
Grace Plaza
1114 Avenue of the Americas
New York, NY 10036
(212) 819-5500
Manager of Personnel: Christine Hilker
Executive offices in Boca Raton, FL.
Manufacturer of industrial, pharmaceutical and laboratory
chemicals, polyfibers, plastics, petroleums, and rare earth
chemicals.

Grow Group
200 Park Ave.
New York, NY 10166
(212) 599-4400
Asst. Director of Human Resources: Judith Krupka
Company headquarters.

Hoechst-Celanese
1211 Avenue of the Americas
New York, NY 10036
(212) 251-8000
Human Resources: Jane McBunch
Company headquarters.

ICC Industries
720 5th Ave.
New York, NY 10019
(212) 903-1700
Director of Personnel: Ms. Frances Foti
Exporter/importer of industrial and pharmaceutical chemicals.
Company headquarters.

Manheimer, J.
47-22 Pearson Place
Long Island City, NY 11101
(718) 392-7800
Personnel Manager: Lynn Mallon
Marketer of raw materials for food products, flavors, and fra-
grances.
Company headquarters.

Monsanto
1460 Broadway
New York, NY 10036
(212) 382-9600
Office Administrator: Rita Wellstood
Chemical and textile manufacturer.

North American Phillips Corporation
100 E. 42nd St.
New York, NY 10017
(212) 850-5000
Vice President, Director of Personnel: James Miller

Quantum Chemicals
99 Park Ave.
New York, NY 10016
(212) 949-5000
Human Resources Representative: Eileen Delaney
Producer of industrial chemicals and plastics. Company headquarters.

Schwartz Chemical Corporation
104 Rockaway Parkway
Valley Stream, NY 11580
(516) 899-0777

Stinnes Corp.
750 3rd Ave.
New York, NY 10017
(212) 986-1515
Distributor of industrial chemicals. Company headquarters.

Transammonia, Inc.
350 Park Ave.
New York, NY 10022
(212) 223-3200
Personnel Manager: Marguerite Harrington
Exporter/importer of industrial chemicals. Company headquarters.

Witco Chemical Corp.
520 Madison Ave.
New York, NY 10022
(212) 605-3800
Director of Personnel: Jane White
Manufacturer of mineral oil and petroleum. Company headquarters.

CONNECTICUT EMPLOYERS:

Coutinho Caro and Company
300 First Stamford Place
Stamford, CT 06902
(203) 356-4840

Crompton and Knowles Corporation
1 Station Place Metro Center
Stamford, CT 06902
(203) 353-5400

Personnel Director: Esther Mattson
Manufacturer of specialty chemicals, plastics, and related products.

Olin Corporation
120 Long Ridge Road
Stamford, CT 06902
(203) 356-2000
Manager Professional Staffing: V. E. Martin
Chemicals, metals, applied physics.

Union Carbide
39 Old Ridgebury Road
Danbury, CT 06817
(203) 794-2000
Manager of Professional Placement: T.J. Neelan

NEW JERSEY EMPLOYERS:

Allied Signal
10 N. Ave. E
Elizabeth, NJ 07201
(908) 354-3215
Personnel Director: Maritza Perez

American Cyanamid Co
One Cyanamid Plaza
Wayne, NJ 07470
(201) 831-2000
Manufacturers of pharmaceuticals, chemicals, fibers, and consumer health products. Executive headquarters.

American Gas and Chemical Co. Ltd.
220A Pegasus Ave.
Northvale, NJ 07647
(201) 767-7300
Personnel Director: Melanie Kershaw
Manufactures chemical and electronic leak detectors.

BASF Corporation/Chemicals Division
100 Cherry Hill Road
Parsippany, NJ 07054
(201) 316-3000
Human Resources Manager: Robert Stein

Drew Chemical Corporation
1 Drew Plaza
Boonton, NJ 07005
(201) 263-7602
Leading supplier of specialty chemicals and services to the international maritime industry and other industrial markets worldwide.

Engelhard Corporation
101 Wood Ave.
Iselin, NJ 08830
(908) 205-6000
Vice Pres., Human Resources: William Dugle
Manufacturer of specialty metals and chemicals.

Faber-Castell Corp.
4 Century Drive
Parsippany, NJ 07054
(201) 539-4111
Personnel department in Louisburg, TN.
Graphics products and pencils.

GAF Corporation
1361 Alps Road
Wayne, NJ 07470
(201) 628-3000
Personnel Director: James Strupp
Manufacturer of specialty chemicals and building materials.

Hartz Mountain Corp.
700 Rodgers Blvd. S.
Harrison, NJ 07029
(201) 481-4800

Henley and Company
50 Chestnut Ridge Road
Montvale, NJ 07645
(201) 307-0422
Director of Personnel: Michelle Gola
Manufacturer of industrial and pharmaceutical chemicals.

Huls America
Turner Place
Piscataway, NJ 08855
(908) 981-5000
Recruitment/EEO Specialist: James Ryan
Manufacturer of coating chemicals and colorants.

Merck and Company
126 E. Lincoln Ave.
Rahway, NJ 07065
(908) 574-4000
Manager of Corporate Personnel and Relations: E. Jeffrey Stoll
A major pharmaceutical and chemical company.

NAPP Chemicals
199 Main St.
P.O. Box 900
Lodi, NJ 07644
(201) 773-3900

Personnel Director: Marie Galdo
Medical chemicals and bulk pharmaceuticals.

National Starch and Chemical Corporation
10 Finderne Ave.
Bridgewater, NJ 08807
(908) 685-5033
Manager of College Relations: Carol Dedrick
Industrial chemical manufacturer, producing adhesives, resins,
starches, and specialty chemicals.

Oakite Products
50 Valley Road
Berkeley Heights, NJ 07922
(908) 464-6900
Corporate Compensation Manager: Juergen H. Schmeirer
Manufacturer of chemicals used for industrial and institutional
cleaning and metal conditioning.

Penick Corporation
158 Mt. Olivet Ave.
Newark, NJ 0711
(201) 621-2822
Director of Human Resources: Robert Nilsen
Producer of fine chemicals and pesticides.

Rhone Poulenc
CN 5266
Princeton, NJ 08543
(908) 297-0100
Producer of fine chemicals and related products.

Sequa Corporation
3 University Plaza
Hackensack, NJ 07061
(201) 343-1122
Personnel Director: Jerry Skoll

Sun Chemical Corporation
222 Ridge Plaza
Fort Lee, NJ 07022
(212) 695-1076
Personnel Director: Thomas Witkowski

United Mineral and Chemical Corp.
1100 Valley Brook Ave.
Lyndhurst, NJ 07071
(201) 507-3300
Vice President and Director of Personnel: Nurham Becidyan
Manufacturer of high-purity metals and industrial chemicals for use
in water treatment and rubber curing. Corporate headquarters.

Computers/Hardware

For networking in the computer industry, check out the following professional organizations listed in Chapter 5. See also **"Computers/Software"** and **"Electronics."**

PROFESSIONAL ORGANIZATIONS:

Association for Computing Machinery
Special Interest Group for System Documentation

For additional information, contact:

Computer and Business Equipment Manfuacturers Association
1250 I St., NW
Washington, DC 20005
(202) 737-8888

Computer and Communications Industry Association
666 11th St., NW
Washington DC 20001
(202) 783-0070

Institute of Electrical & Electronics Engineers (IEEE)
345 E. 47th St.
New York, NY 10017
(212) 705-7900

Semiconductor Equipment and Materials International
805 E. Middlefield Road
Mountain View, CA 94043
(415) 964-5111

PROFESSIONAL PUBLICATIONS:

Byte
Computer World
Design News
Electronic Products
Electronics Distributor
Electronics News
InfoWorld
PC Computing
PC Magazine
PC World
Semiconductors International

DIRECTORIES:

Data Sources: Hardware-Data Communications Directory (Ziff-Davis, New York, NY)
Electronic News Financial Fact Book and Directory (Fairchild Publications, New York, NY)
EIA Trade Directory (Electronic Industries Association, Washington, DC)
SIA Yearbook (Semiconductor Industry Association, Cupertino, CA)
Who's Who in Electronics (Harris Publishing Co., Twinsburg, OH)

NEW YORK EMPLOYERS:

American Telephone and Telegraph (AT&T)
550 Madison Ave.
New York, NY 10022
(212) 605-5500

Apple Computer
135 E. 57th St.
New York, NY 10022
(212) 339-3700
Contact: Department of Human Resources, Apple Computer, 379 Thornhall St., P.O. Box 2912, Edison, NJ 08818.
Computers for office and home use.

Applied Digital Data Systems
100 Marcus Blvd.
Hauppague, NY 11788
(516) 342-7400
Personnel Director: Steve Green
Cathode ray terminals and data display equipment.

Astrosystems, Inc.
6 Nevada Drive
Lake Success, NY 11042
(516) 328-1600
Director of Personnel: Ann Mulvey
Conversion equipment and computer peripherals.

Canon USA Corporation
One Canon Plaza
Lake Success, NY 11042
(516)488 6700
Personnel Director: Bill Liggan
Photographic and copier equipment. United States company headquarters.

Concurrent Computer Corporation
2 Crescent Place
Oceanport, NJ 07757

(908) 870-4500
Computer systems equipment manufacturer.

Digital Equipment Corporation
2 Penn Plaza
New York, NY 10121
(212) 856-2000
One of the world's largest manufacturers of minicomputers, microcomputers, mainframe computer systems, terminals, word processors, small business computers, networks, and complete office information systems. The company maintains sales, service, and support offices in New York, Long Island, and northern New Jersey.

Hewlett-Packard
2975 Westchester Ave.
Purchase, NY 10577
(914) 935-6300
One of the world's largest manufacturers of information processing systems.

International Business Machines
Old Orchard Road
Armonk, NY 10504
(914) 765-1900
World's largest manufacturer of data processing machines, telecommunications systems, and information processing systems.

Megadata TSD
35 Orville Drive
Bohemia, NY 11716
(516) 589-6800
Personnel Director: Richard DeCosta
Application-oriented computer terminals.

NCR Corporation
2950 Express Drive So.
Ilandia, NY 11722
(516) 232-4200
Write to: NCR Corporation, 17-22 Whitestone Expressway, Whitestone, NY 11357, Attention: Paul Buscemi.
A leading manufacturer of computers for home and office.

North Atlantic Industries
60 Plant Ave.
Hauppage, NY 11788
(516) 582-6500
Personnel Department: Len Stanton
Computer peripherals, including printers and display terminals.

Booting up big $$$ in computer sales

Philip Daniels competes in the fast lane as a computer sales engineer. His clients are Fortune 500 companies, and his products are communications boards, controllers, and disk and tape subsystems manufactured by a relatively new specialty company. "It's an emotionally and physically stressful environment where I constantly have to prove myself," says Philip.

We asked how he got there and what keeps him successful.

"I use every skill and all the experience I've ever had," said the former teacher and editorial assistant for a steel company's community relations department. "When I decided to go back to school for an associate's degree in computers, I needed a job as well. So I sold cars, and that provided invaluable marketing and people experience, plus communications skills that are absolutely essential in my present business.

"Once I got into computer courses, I realized I couldn't settle for a $25,000 programming job and began laying more plans. And, incidentally, you must prepare yourself for the entry position in this field. My first job—strictly commission—was with a small systems house, and within a year I was director of marketing with a sales staff of six. I got a total overview of the business so that I could talk from that perspective on my next round of interviews.

"I used an employment agent who specializes in computer sales to get this position and was very specific with him about my requirements."

Asked to explain his current success, Philip responds: "I'd have to say the number one factor is technical expertise—with sales ability second. I read, listen, and pick brains to stay on top of the products and a changing market place so that my company provides a service to the client by sending me. By the way, with little more education than a $25,000 programmer, I'll make at least three times that this year. And the perks are great, too." ∎

Periphonics Corporation
4000 Veterans Memorial Highway
Bohemia, NY 11716
(516) 467-0500
Personnel Director: Janet Anderson
Voice-controlled computer systems.

Pitney Bowes
1 Penn Plaza
New York, NY 10119
(212) 239-6900
Operations Manager: Ann Tagliareni
Telecopiers and computers.

Unisys Corporation
155 E. 55th St., Room 203
New York, NY 10022
(212) 484-4444
Personnel: Warren Cohen
Formed from the merger of Burroughs Corporation and Sperry
Corporation. A leading producer of information processing systems and services, as well as electronic systems for defense and
aerospace.

CONNECTICUT EMPLOYERS:

Executive Business Machines
2 Post Road
Fairfield, CT 06430
800-533-5326

Perkin-Elmer
761 Main Ave.
Norwalk, CT 06859
(203) 762-4210

XEROX
P.O. Box 1600
800 Long Ridge Road
Stamford, CT 06904
(203) 329-8700

NEW JERSEY EMPLOYERS:

Global Turnkey Systems
4 N St.
Waldwick, NJ 07463
(201) 445-5050
Personnel Director: Barbara Cullen
Sales and service of computer software and hardware.

Hewlett Packard/New Jersey Division
150 Green Pond Road
Rockaway, NJ 07866
(201) 627-6400
Produces computer-controlled data acquisition, test, and control
systems and system components and DC systems and laboratory
power supplies.

Kulite Semiconductor Products
1 Willow Tree Road
Leonia, NJ 07605
(201) 461-0900
Produces computerized metering systems for medical applications
and for use in aircraft.

Science Management Corporation
140 Allen Road
Liberty Corner, NJ 07938
(908) 647-7000
Director of Human Resources: Virginia Brandt
Professional services and computer systems.

Computers/Software

For networking in computer programming, software, and related
fields, check out the following professional organizations listed in
Chapter 5. Also see **"Computers/Hardware" and "Electronics."**

PROFESSIONAL ORGANIZATIONS:

**Data Processing Management Association, NY Chapter
Women in Data Processing**

For additional information you can contact:

Association for Women in Computing
6421 N. 24th St.
Arlington, VA 22207
(703) 536-2088

Data Processing Management Association
505 Busse Highway
Park Ridge, IL 60068
(708) 825-8124

Information Industry Association
555 New Jersey Ave., NW
Washington, DC 20001
(202) 639-8262

Information Technology Association of America
1616 N. Ft. Myer Drive
Arlington, VA 22209
(703) 522-5055

National Computer Graphics Association
2722 Merrilee Drive
Fairfax, VA 22031
(703) 698-9600

Software Publishers Association
1730 M St. NW
Washington, DC 20036
(202) 452-1600

PROFESSIONAL PUBLICATIONS:

Byte
Computer World
Datamation
Design News
PC Computing
PC Magazine

DIRECTORIES:

Data Sources: Software Directory (Ziff-Davis, New York, NY)
Design News Electronic Directory (Cahners Publishing Co.,
   Boston, MA)
Engineering, Science and Computer Jobs (Peterson's Guides,
   Princeton, NJ)
ICP Software Directory (International Computer Programs,
   Indianapolis, IN)
Membership Directory (Information Technology Assoc. of America,
   Arlington, VA)
Yearbook/Directory (Semiconductor Industry Association, San
   Jose, CA)

EMPLOYERS:

ADP (Automatic Data Processing)
2 Journal Square Plaza
Jersey City, NJ 07306
(201) 714-3000
Human Rersources: (201) 714-3000
Computer services company.

Advanced Computer Techniques Corporation
24 E. 38th St., Suite 5A
New York, NY 10016
(212) 679-4040
Personnel Department: Gary Epstein, 146 Nassau Ave, Islip,
NY 11751
Software consultants.

Computer Assistance
A division of Coopers & Lybrand
200 Park Road
W. Hartford, CT 06119
(203) 233-9848
Personnel Manager: Michael Bianca
Consulting firm.

Computer Associates
One Computer Associates Plaza
Ilandia, NY 11788
(516) 342-5224
Software development for personal computers and microcomputers. Best known for the WANG office system.

Computer Horizons Corporation
747 3rd Ave.
New York, NY 10017
(212) 371-9600
Vice President, Director of Personnel: Janet Toscano
Software consultants.

Datalogix
100 Summit Lake Drive
Valhalla, NY 10595
(914) 747-2900

Grumman Corporation
111 Stewart Ave., C07-GHQ
Bethpage, NY 11714
(516) 575-0574
Contact: Employment Office
Software development, largely for government contracts.

Information Builders
1250 Broadway
New York, NY 10001
(212) 736-4433
Director of Personnel: Lila Goldberg
Software development.

International Business Machines
44 S. Broadway
White Plains, NY 10601
(914) 288-3000
Contact: Westchester Personnel
Software development branch of IBM.

Microsoft
825 8th Ave.
New York, NY 10019
(212) 245-2100

Personnel: 9 Hillside Ave., Waltham, MA 02154
A leading software development company.

Prodigy Services Company
445 Hamilton Ave.
White Plains, NY 10601
(914) 993-8000
Software development and interactive video services.

Securities Industry Automation Corp.
55 Water St.
New York, NY 10041
(212) 383-4800
Personnel Director: Jack Shein, 2 Metrotech Center, Brooklyn,
NY 11201
Data processing company.

Standard and Poor's Corporation
25 Broadway
New York, NY 10004
(212) 208-8000
Personnel Manager: Bob Gemignani
Data processing and software information services.

Volt Information Sciences
1133 Avenue of the Americas, 19th Floor
New York, NY 10036
(212) 704-2400
Personnel Recruiter: Dorothy Ellison
Software development.

Construction

For networking in the construction industry and related fields, check out the following professional organization listed in Chapter 5. Also see **"Engineering."**

PROFESSIONAL ORGANIZATIONS:

American Society of Civil Engineers

For additional information, you can contact:

American Society of Civil Engineers
347 E. 47 St.
New York, NY 10017
(212) 705-7496

Associated Builders and Contractors
729 15th St., NW
Washington, DC 20005
(202) 637-8800

National Asphalt Pavement Association
5100 Forbes Blvd.
Lanham, MD 20706
(301) 731-4748

National Association of Home Builders of the U.S.
1201 15th St., NW
Washington, DC 20005
(202) 822-0200

National Association of Minority Contractors
1333 F St., NW, Suite 500
Washington, DC 20004
(202) 347-8259

National Association of Women in Construction
327 S. Adams St.
Fort Worth, TX 76104
(817) 877-5551

PROFESSIONAL PUBLICATIONS:

Building Design & Construction
Engineering News-Record
Glass Industry
New York Construction News
Pit and Quarry

DIRECTORIES:

Associated Builders & Contractors Membership Directory (Associated Builders & Contractors, Washington, DC)
Blue Book of Major Homebuilders (LSI Systems, Inc., Crofton, MD)
Construction Equipment Buyers Guide (Cahners Publishing, Des Plaines, IL)
Construction Equipment: Construction Giants (Cahners Publishing, Des Plaines, IL)
Constructor, Directory issue (Associated General Contractors of America, Washington, DC)
Directory of Construction Associations (Metadata, Inc., New York, NY)
ENR Directory of Contractors (McGraw-Hill, New York, NY)
Guide to Information Sources in the Construction Industry (Construction Products Manufacturers Council, Arlington, VA)

NEW YORK EMPLOYERS:

American Standard
1114 Avenue of the Americas
New York, NY 10036
(212) 840-5100
Personnel Director: Sofia Stratis

Charan Industries
370 Old Country Road
Garden City, NY 11530
(516) 747-6500

Dover Corporation
280 Park Ave.
New York, NY 10017
(212) 922-1640

EBASCO Services
2 World Trade Center
New York, NY 10048
(212) 839-1000
Engineering and construction

Fischbach Corporation
7 Hanover Square, 10th Floor
New York, NY 10004
(212) 440-2100
Chief Administrative Officer: Patricia Moore

Fuller, George A., Company
919 3rd Ave.
New York, NY 10022

(212) 355-2700
Contractor.

Moore, Benjamin, & Company
51 Chestnut Ridge Road
Montvale, NJ 07645
(201) 573-9600
Corp. Personnel: Phillip D. Shalett

Morse/Diesel
1515 Broadway
New York, NY 10036
(212) 730-4000
Director of Human Resources: Irwin Wecker

Posillico, J.D., Inc.
1610 New Highway
Farmingdale, NY 11735
(516) 249-1872
Exec. Secretary: Anne M. Seeley

Slattery Associates
16-16 Whitestone Expressway
Whitestone, NY 11357
(718) 392-2400
Director of Employee Benefits: Timothy J. Klein

Starrett Housing Corporation
909 3rd Ave.
New York, NY 10022
(212) 751-3100

Turner Construction Company
375 Hudson St.
New York, NY 10014
(212) 229-6000

Universal Builders Supply
216 S. Terrace Ave.
Mt. Vernon, NY 10550
(914) 699-2400

CONNECTICUT EMPLOYERS:

Lone Star Industries
300 Stamford Place
Stamford, CT 06912
(203) 661-3100
Corporate Personnel Representative: Tom Curtin

NEW JERSEY EMPLOYERS:

Arvey Corporation
20 Sand Park Road
Cedar Grove, NJ 07009
(201) 239-8100
Human Resources Department

Concrete Plank P.J.R. Industries
P.O. Box 183
Bayone, NJ 07002
(201) 998-7600

Ingersoll-Rand Co.
200 Chestnut Ridge Road
Woodcliff Lake, NJ 07675
(201) 573-0123
Personnel Recruiter: Paula Prusko

Schiavone Construction Company
1600 Paterson Plank Road
Secaucus, NJ 07096
(201) 867-5070
Contact Personnel Department

Cosmetics/Perfume/Toiletries

For networking in cosmetics and related fields, check out the following professional organizations listed in Chapter 5:

PROFESSIONAL ORGANIZATIONS:

Cosmetic Executive Women
Cosmetic Industry Buyers and Suppliers
Drug, Chemical and Allied Trades Association

For more information you can contact:

Cosmetic, Toiletry and Fragrance Association
1101 17th St. NW
Washington, DC 20036
(202) 331-1770

Society of Cosmetic Chemists
1995 Broadway, 17th Floor
New York, NY 10023
(212) 874-0600

PROFESSIONAL PUBLICATIONS:

Beauty Fashion
Cosmetic Technology
Cosmetic World
Soaps/Cosmetics/Chemical Specialties

DIRECTORIES:

Beauty Fashion—Fragrance Directory Issue (Beauty Fashion, Inc., New York, NY)

NEW YORK EMPLOYERS:

Almay, Inc.
Division of Revlon
625 Madison Ave.
New York, NY 10022
(212) 527-4700
Personnel Director: Sally Dickinson

American Home Products Corp.
685 3rd Ave.
New York, NY 10017
(212) 986-1000

Contact: Personnel
Company headquarters.

Arden, Elizabeth
1345 Avenue of the Americas, 35th Floor
New York, NY 10105
(212) 261-1000

Avon Products
9 W. 57th St.
New York, NY 10019
(212) 546-6015
Director of Personnel: Angelica Cantlon
Company headquarters.

Bristol-Myers
345 Park Ave.
New York, NY 10154
(212) 546-4000
Contact: Personnel
Company headquarters.

Carter-Wallace
1345 Avenue of the Americas
New York, NY 10105
(212) 339-5000
Personnel Manager: Denise Duka

Chanel, Inc.
9 W. 57th St.
New York, NY 10019
(212) 688-5055

Clairol, Inc.
Division Bristol-Myers
345 Park Ave.
New York, NY 10154
(212) 546-5000
Contact: Employment services for Bristol-Myers
Company headquarters.

Clarins USA
135 E. 57th St., 15th Floor
New York, NY 10022
(212) 980-1800

Clinique Laboratories
Division of Estee Lauder
767 5th Ave.
New York, NY 10153
(212) 572-3800
Human Resources: Judy Gostenberg

Colgate-Palmolive
300 Park Ave.
New York, NY 10022
(212) 310-2000
Personnel Director: Ms. Lee Boyd
Manufacturer of soaps and cosmetics.

Cosmair, Inc.
575 5th Ave.
New York, NY 10017
(212) 818-1500

Coty Division
237 Park Ave.
New York, NY 10017
(212) 850-2300
Director of Personnel: Eileen Harris

Del Laboratories
565 Broad Hollow Road
Farmingdale, NY 11735
(516) 293-7070
Personnel Director: Charles Schneck

Estee Lauder
767 5th Ave.
New York, NY 10153
(212) 572-4200
Diversified manufacturer and marketer of cosmetics under the
Lauder and Clinique names.

Florasynth, Inc.
300 North St.
Teeterboro, NJ 07608
(212) 371-7700
Personnel Manager: Gary Weldstein

International Flavors and Fragrances
521 W. 57th St.
New York, NY 10019
(212) 765-5500
Manager Employer Relations: Sheila A. Darken

Lever Brothers Company
390 Park Ave.
New York, NY 10022
(212) 688-6000
Employment Manager: Jim McGrath
Company headquarters.

Manheimer, J.
47-22 Pearson Place

Long Island City, NY 11101
(718) 392-7800
Personnel Director: Lynne Mallon
Company headquarters.

Matney, Arthur, Company
4014 1st Ave.
Brooklyn, NY 11232
(718) 788-3200

McGregor Corp.
600 Madison Ave.
New York, NY 10022
(212) 307-8100
Formerly Faberge (cosmetics, toiletries)

Pfizer, Inc.
235 E. 42nd St.
New York, NY 10017
(212) 573-2323
Company headquarters.

Revlon, Inc.
625 Madison Ave.
New York, NY 10022
(212) 572-5000
Personnel Director: Janet DeBlasio
Company headquarters.

St. Laurent, Yves
40 W. 57th St.
New York, NY 10019
(212) 621-7300
Director of Personnel: Trudy Trier
Company headquarters.

Sterling Drug
90 Park Ave.
New York, NY 10016
(212) 907-2000
Personnel Director: Macklin Rothenbuhler
Company headquarters.

Whitehall Laboratories
Division American Home Products
685 3rd Ave.
New York, NY 10017
(212) 986-1000
Company headquarters.
Corporate Personnel Manager: Edward Behrendt

CONNECTICUT EMPLOYERS:

Bristol-Myers Squibb Co
1 Blachley Road
Stamford, CT 06992
(203) 357-5839

Chesebrough-Pond's USA
33 Benedict Place
Greenwich, CT 06830
(203) 661-2000
Vice President Personnel: James W. McCall
Cosmetics, pharmaceuticals

Conair Corporation
1 Cummingspoint Road
Stamford, CT 06904
(203) 351-9000
Corporate Director of Human Resources: Anne Marie Cioffi

Drugs and Pharmaceuticals

For networking in the drug industry and related fields, check out the following professional organizations listed in Chapter 5:

PROFESSIONAL ORGANIZATIONS:

Chemists' Club of New York
Drug, Chemical and Allied Trades Association

For additional information you can contact:

American Pharmaceutical Association
2215 Constitution Ave., NW
Washington, DC 20037
(202) 628-4410

Association of Biotechnology Companies
1666 Connecticut Ave., NW
Washington, DC 20009
(202) 234-3330

National Association of Chain Drugstores
413 N. Lee St.
Arlington, VA 22313
(703) 549-3001

National Association of Pharmaceutical Manufacturers
747 3rd Ave.
New York, NY 10017
(212) 838-3720

National Wholesale Druggists Association
1821 Michael Faraday Drive
Reston, VA 22090
(703) 787-0000

Pharmaceutical Manufacturers Association
1155 15th St., NW
Washington, DC 20005
(202) 835-3400

PROFESSIONAL PUBLICATIONS:

American Druggist
Cosmetic Technology
DrugStore News
Drug Topics

PMA Newsletter
Soap/Cosmetics/Chemical Specialties

DIRECTORIES:

Biotechnology Directory (Stockton Press, New York, NY)
Blue Book American Druggist (Hearst Corp,
  New York, NY)
Drug Topics Red Book (Litton Publications, Oradell, NJ)
Health Care Directory (Litton Publications, Oradell, NJ)
NACDS Membership Directory (National Association of Chain
  Drugstores, Arlington, VA)
NWDA Membership Directory (National Wholesale Druggists
  Association, Scarsdale, NY)
Pharmaceutical Manufacturers of the U.S. (Noyes Data Corp.,
  Park Ridge, NJ)

NEW YORK EMPLOYERS:

American Home Products
685 3rd Ave.
New York, NY 10017
(212) 878-5000
Company headquarters.

American White Cross Laboratories
40 Nardozi Place
New Rochelle, NY 10802
(914) 632-3045
Personnel Director: Diane Cannistraro

Bolar Pharmaceutical
33 Ralph Ave.
Copiague, NY 11726
(516) 842-8383
Personnel Director: Fran Herman

Bristol-Myers Company
345 Park Ave.
New York, NY 10154
(212) 546-4000
Company headquarters.

Carter-Wallace
1345 Avenue of the Americas
New York, NY 10105
(212) 758-4500
Personnel Manager: Denise Duka
Company headquarters.

Ciba Corporation
444 Saw Mill River Road

Ardsley, NY 10502
(914) 479-5000
Human Resources Director: Loretta Czernecki

Darby Drugs Co.
100 Banks Ave.
Rockville Centre, NY 11570
(516) 536-3000
Personnel Director: Diane Weinstein

Del Laboratories
565 Broadhollow Road
Farmingdale, NY 11735
(516) 293-7070
Personnel Director: Charles Schenk

Dupont Pharmaceuticals
1000 Stewart Ave.
Garden City, NY 11530
(516) 832-2210
Personnel Director: Laura Steinke

Forest Labs
150 E. 58th St.
New York, NY 10155
(212) 421-7850
Contact: Personnel

Freeman Industries
100 Marbledale Road
Tuckahoe, NY 10707-0415
(914) 961-2100

Lederle Labs
Division of American Cyanamid
401 N. Middletown Road
Pearl River, NY 10965
(914) 732-5000
Personnel Manager: Dave Barnhill

Marlop Pharmaceuticals
5704 Mosholu Ave.
Bronx, NY 10471
(212) 796-1570
President: Rubin Delgado

Pfizer, Inc.
235 E. 42nd St.
New York, NY 10017
(212) 573-2323
Company headquarters.

Sterling Drug
90 Park Ave.
New York, NY 10016
(212) 907-2000
Personnel Manager: Macklin Rothenbuhler
Company headquarters.

Taro Pharmaceuticals USA
Six Skyline Drive
Hawthorne, NY 10532
(914) 345-9001

Whitehall Laboratories
Division of American Home Products
685 3rd Ave.
New York, NY 10017
(212) 878-5500
Corporate Personnel Manager: Edward Behrendt

CONNECTICUT EMPLOYERS:

Bristol-Myers Squibb Co
One Blachley Road
Stamford, CT 06992
(203) 357-5839

NEW JERSEY EMPLOYERS:

Becton, Dickinson
1 Becton Drive
Franklin Lakes, NJ 07417
(201) 847-6800
Vice President of Human Resources: James Fink

Block Drug Company
257 Cornelison Ave.
Jersey City, NY 07302
(201) 434-3000, ext. 224
Personnel Director: J.H. McCormick

Bard, C.R., Inc.
730 Central Ave.
Murray Hill, NJ 07974
(908) 277-8000

Hausmann Industries
130 Union St.
Northvale, NJ 07647
(201) 767-0255

Hoffman-La Roche
340 Kingsland St.

Nutley, NJ 07110
(201) 235-4201
Asst. Vice President, Director of Staffing and Employee Services:
A.L. Vinson

Johnson and Johnson
1 J&J Plaza
New Brunswick, NJ 08933
(201) 524-0400

Mada Medical Products
60 Commerce Road
Carlstadt, NJ 07072
(201) 460-0454
Comptroller: Bob Chasmar

Merck and Company
P.O. Box 2000
Rahway, NJ 07065
(908) 594-4000

Organon, Inc.
374 Mt. Pleasant Ave.
W. Orange, NJ 07052
(201) 325-4546

Pharacia Eni Diagnostics
368 Passaic Ave.
Fairfield, NJ 07007
(201) 227-6700
Manager of Human Resources: Carol Newman

Precision Technology
50 Maple St.
Norwood, NJ 07648
(201) 767-1600
Director of Personnel: Delia Levero

Sandoz Pharmacueticals
59 Route 10
E. Hanover, NJ 07936
(201) 503-7500

Schering-Plough Corporation
2000 Galloping Hill Road
Kenilworth, NJ 07033
(908) 298-4373
Director of Personnel: Richard Happel

Warner-Lambert
201 Taybor Road
Morris Plains, NJ 07950

(201) 540-2000
Corporate headquarters.
Several Human Resources Departments within company.

Zenith Laboratories
140 LeGrand Ave.
Northvale, NJ 07647
(201) 767-1700
Personnel Director: Winifred Stavros

Educational Institutions

For networking in education and related fields, check out the following professional organizations listed in Chapter 5:

PROFESSIONAL ORGANIZATIONS:

American Association of University Women
American Federation of School Administrators

For additional information, you can contact:

American Association of School Administrators
1801 N. Moore St.
Arlington, VA 22209
(703) 528-0700

American Association of University Professors
1012 14th St., NW
Washington, DC 20005
(202) 737-5900

Association of School Business Officials
11401 N. Shore Drive
Reston, VA 22090
(703) 478-0405

Career College Association
750 1st St., NE
Washington, DC 20002
(202) 336-6700

Council for Educational Development and Research
2000 L St.
Washington, DC 20036
(202) 223-1593

National Education Association of the U.S.
1201 16th St., NW

Washington, DC 20036
(202) 833-4000

PROFESSIONAL PUBLICATIONS:

Chronicle of Higher Education
Education Week
Instructor
School Administrator
Teaching Pre-K-8
Technology & Learning
Today's Catholic Teacher

DIRECTORIES:

Bricker's International Directory of University Executive Programs
    (Peterson's Guides, Princeton, NJ)
Directory of Education Associations (Marquis Publishing Co.,
    Chicago, IL)
Peterson's Guide to Four Year Colleges (Marquis Publishing Co.,
    Chicago, IL)
Peterson's Guide to Independent Secondary Schools (Peterson's
    Guides, Princeton, NJ)
Private Schools of the United States. Council for American Private
    Education Schools (CAPE). (Market Data Retrieval, Inc.,
    Shelton, CT)
QED's School Guide (Quality Education Data, Denver, CO)
Yearbook of Higher Education (Marquis Publishing Co., Chicago,
    IL)

A quick tip   If you are interested in an academic position
with a college or university, it sometimes helps
to contact the Dean of your discipline as well as
the personnel office. Contact local boards of
education for information on local schools. ■

COLLEGES AND UNIVERSITIES, NEW YORK
EMPLOYERS:

Adelphi University-Main Campus
South Ave.
Garden City, NY 11530
(516) 877-3000
Assoc. Vice Pres. of Human Resources and Labor Relations:
Donald H. Flanders

Adelphi University-Urban Center
75 Vanick St.
New York, NY 10013
(212) 941-9332

Bank Street College of Education
610 W. 112th St.
New York, NY 10025
(212) 222-6700
Director of Personnel: Janet Koztowski

Baruch, Bernard M., College
17 Lexington Ave.
New York, NY 10010
(212) 387-1060
Personnel Director: Ronny Widener

Bronx Community College
181st and University Ave.
Bronx, NY 10453
(212) 220-6450
Personnel: Shelly Levey

City College, The
Convent Ave. and 138th St.
New York, NY 10031
(212) 650-7000
Personnel Director: Steven Nisbett

City University of New York
535 E. 80th St.
New York, NY 10021
(212) 794-5555
 Contact: Esmeralds Reyes, Central Personnel Office

College of Staten Island
130 Stuyvesant Place
Staten Island, NY 10301
(718) 390-7733

Columbia University
116th St. and Broadway
New York, NY 10027
(212) 854-1754

Cornell University
1300 York Ave.
New York, NY 10021
(212) 746-5454

Fashion Institute of Technology (SUNY)
227 W. 27th St.

New York, NY 10001
(212) 760-7654
Personnel Director: Rosalyn Dover

Fordham University
E. Fordham Road
Bronx, NY 10458
(212) 841-5100
Personnel: Frank Cella

Hofstra University
1000 Fulton Ave.
Hempstead, NY 11550
(516) 463-6600
Asst. Vice Pres. Personnel: Irmgard Pfennig

Hunter College
695 Park Ave.
New York, NY 10021
(212) 772-4000
Personnel Director: William Carrozza

Iona College
715 North Ave.
New Rochelle, NY 10801
(914) 633-2000
Associate Academic Dean: Brian Monahan

Jay, John, College of Criminal Justice
445 W. 59th St.
New York, NY 10019
(212) 237-8000
Personnel Director: Margaret Schultz

Kingsborough Community College
2001 Oriental Blvd.
Brooklyn, NY 11235
(718) 368-5000
Dean of Faculty: Provost Zivrin

La Guardia Community College
31-10 Thomson Ave.
Long Island City, NY 11101
(718) 857-3580

Lawrence, Sarah, College
1 Meadway
Bronxville, NY 10708
(914) 395-2510

Long Island University
University Center, Northern Blvd.

Greenvale, NY 11548
(516) 299-0200
University Director of Personnel: Howard White

Manhattan Community College
199 Chambers St.
New York, NY 10007
(212) 618-1000
Personnel Director: Alyne Holmes Coy

Manhattanville College
Purchase St.
Purchase, NY 10577
(914) 694-2200
Personnel: Carol Tirado

Mercy College
555 Broadway
Dobbs Ferry, NY 10522
(914) 693-4500
Administration: Mary Jane Chase

Molloy College
1000 Hempstead Ave.
Rockville Center, NY 11570
(516) 678-5000
Academic Dean: Patricia Morris

Nassau Community College (SUNY)
Stewart Ave.
Garden City, NY 11530
(516) 222-7501

New School for Social Research
66 W. 12th St.
New York, NY 10011
(212) 229-5600

New York Institute of Technology
Wheatley Road
Old Westbury, NY 11568
(516) 686-7516
Faculty Positions: Herbert Fox

New York University
246 Green St.
Washington Square
New York, NY 10003
(212) 998-1250
Academic Dean: Richard West

252

Pace University
1 Pace Plaza
New York, NY 10038
(212) 346-1200
Personnel: Yvonne Ramierez-Lesce

Pace University
Westchester Campus
Bedford Road
Pleasantville, NY 10570
(914) 773-3200
Personnel: Kathy Paribello

Pace University
Westchester Campus
78 N. Broadway
White Plains, NY 10603
(914) 422-4000

Polytechnic Institute of New York
333 Jay St.
Brooklyn, NY 11123
(718) 260-3600
Director Human Resources: Steve Nowaski

Pratt Institute
200 Willoughby Ave.
Brooklyn, NY 11205
(718) 636-3600
Personnel: Lynn Plavnick

Queens College
65-30 Kissena Blvd.
Flushing, NY 11367
(718) 520-7000

Queensborough Community College
222-05 56th Ave.
Bayside, NY 11364
(718) 631-6262
Personnel Director: Edward Haran

St. John's University
Grand Central and Utopia Parkways
Jamaica, NY 11439
(718) 990-6161

St. John's University
Staten Island Campus
300 Howard Ave.
Staten Island, NY 10301
(718) 447-4343

State University at Farmingdale/Architectural and Technical College (SUNY)
Melville Road
Farmingdale, NY 11735
(516) 420-2000
President of College: Frank A. Cipriani

State University at Purchase (SUNY)
735 Anderson Hill Road
Purchase, NY 10577
(914) 251-6000
Personnel Director: Peter Brown

State University at Stony Brook (SUNY)
Nicolls Road
Stonybrook, NY 11794
(516) 689-6000
Director Personnel: Dianne Rulnic

Westchester Community College
75 Grasslands Road
Valhalla, NY
(914) 285-6900

CONNECTICUT, EMPLOYERS:

Fairfield University
North Benson Road
Fairfield, CT 06430
(203) 254-4100

Sacred Heart University
5151 Park Ave.
Fairfield, CT 06432
(203)371-7880

Western Connecticut State University
181 White St.
Danbury, CT 06810
(203) 797-4298

NEW JERSEY, EMPLOYERS:

Drew University
Madison Ave.
Madison, NJ 07940
(201) 408-3739

Fairleigh Dickinson University
270 Montross Ave.
Rutherford, NJ 07070
(201) 460-5267

Jersey City State College
2039 Kennedy Blvd.
Jersey City, NJ 07305
(201) 547-3234

Keon College of New Jersey
Lenon, NJ 07083
(203) 527-2196

Mont Clair State College
Valley Road and Normal Ave.
Upper Mont Clair, NJ 07043
(201) 893-4444

New Jersey Institute of Technology
University Heights
Newark, NJ 07102
(201) 596-3300

Ramapo College of New Jersey
505 Ramapo Valley Road
Mahwah, NJ 07430
(201) 529-7600

Saint Peter's College
2641 Kennedy Blvd.
Jersey City, NJ 07306
(201) 915-9213

Seton Hall University
400 South Orange Ave.
South Orange, NJ 07079
(201) 761-9332

Stevens Institute of Technology
Costle Point
Hoboken, NJ 07030
(201) 420-5194

William Paterson College of New Jersey
300 Pompton Road
Wayne, NJ 07470
(201) 596-2125

LOCAL BOARDS OF EDUCATION

Information on individual schools in an area can be obtained by
contacting Boards of Education which often have listings of
current openings in their systems. Also available are directories
for all *Non-Public Schools and Administrators* and *Public Schools
and Administrators* published annually by the New York State
Education Department, Information on Education, Albany, NY.

Archdiocese of New York
1011 First Ave.
New York, NY 10022
(212) 371-1000, ext. 2876
Recruitment Center for 312 elementary and high schools in NYC
and neighboring counties.

Board of Cooperative Educational Services, Nassau
Westbury, NY 11590
(516) 997-8700

**Board of Cooperative Educational Services, Northern
Westchester and Putnam**
Pinesbridge Road
Yorktown Heights, NY 10598
(914) 245-2700

**Board of Cooperative Educational Services, Southern
Westchester No. 2**
17 Berkley Drive
Rye Brook, NY 10580
(914) 937-3820

Connecticut State Board of Education
165 Capital Ave., Room 322
Hartford, CT 06106-1630
(203) 566-7822

New Jersey State Board of Education
225 E. State St.
CN500
Trenton, NJ 08625
(609) 292-4444

New York City Board of Education
210 Livingston St.
Brooklyn, NY 11201
(718) 935-2000

PRIVATE SCHOOLS:

New York:

Brearley School
610 E. 83 St.
New York, NY 10028
(212) 744-8582

Calhoun School
433 W. End Ave.
New York, NY 10024
(212) 877-1700

Collegiate School
214 W. 71 St.
New York, NY 10024
(212) 769-6500

Dalton School
108 E. 89 St.
New York, NY 10128
(212) 722-5160

Fieldston School
39 Fieldston Road
Bronx, NY 10471
(718) 543-5000

Friends Academy
2 DuckPond Road
Locust Valley, NY 11560
(516) 676-0393

Hackley School
293 Benedict Ave.
Tarrytown, NY 10591
(914) 631-0128

Horace Mann-Barnard School
231 W. 246 St.
Bronx, NY 10471
(718) 548-4000

Nightingale-Bamford School
20 E. 92 St.
New York, NY 10128
(212) 289-5020

Packer Collegiate Institute
170 Joralemon St.
Brooklyn, NY 11201
(718) 875-6644

PolyTechnic Prep. Country Day School
92nd St. and 7th Ave.
Brooklyn, NY 11228
(718) 836-9800

Riverdale Country Day School
5250 Fieldston Road
Bronx, NY 10471
(718) 549-8810

Trinity School
139 W. 91 St.

New York, NY 10024
(212) 873-1650

Connecticut:

Greenwich Academy
200 N. Maple Ave.
Greenwich, CT 06830
(203) 869-4020

Greenwich Country Day School
Old Church Road
Greenwich, CT 06830
(203) 622-8500

King And Low-Heywood Thomas School
1450 Newfield Ave.
Stamford, CT 06905
(203) 322-3496

New Jersey:

Dwight-Englewood School
315 E. Palisade Ave.
Englewood, NJ 07631
(201) 569-9502

Montclair Kimberly Academy
201 Valley Road
Montclair, NJ 07042
(201) 746-9800

Newark Academy
915 Orange Ave.
Livingston, NJ 07039
(201) 992-7000

Electronics/Telecommunications/Office Automation

For networking in electronics, telecommunications, and the office automation systems field, you can contact the following organization listed in Chapter 5. Also see **"Computers."**

PROFESSIONAL ORGANIZATIONS:

Association for Computing Machinery

For more information you can contact:

Electronics Industries Association
2001 Pennsylvania Ave., NW
Washington, DC 20006
(202) 457-4900

Institute of Electrical and Electronics Engineers (IEEE)
345 E. 47th St.
New York, NY 10017
(212) 705-7900

North American Telecommunications Assoc.
2000 M St., NW
Washington, DC 20036
(202) 296-9800

PROFESSIONAL PUBLICATIONS:

Communication Week
Design News
Electronic Business
Electronic News
Electrical World
Electronics
Technology News of America
Telecommunications
Telephony

DIRECTORIES:

Corporate Technology Directory (Corporate Technology Information Services, Wellesley Hills, MA)
Directory & Buyers Guide (Telephony, Chicago, IL)
EIA Trade Directory & Membership List (Electronics Industries Assoc., Washington, DC)

Electronic News Financial Fact Book and Directory (Fairchild
 Publications, New York, NY)
IWP Word Processing Directory (International Word Processng
 Association, Willow Grove, PA)
NOMDA Who's Who (National Office Machine Dealers Associa-
 tion, Elk Grove Village, IL)
NOPA Directory (National Office Products Association, Alexan-
 dria, VA)
Who's Who in Electronics (Harris Publications, Twinsburg, OH)
Who's Who in Technology (Gale Research, Detroit, MI)

NEW YORK EMPLOYERS:

American Telephone and Telegraph
32 Avenue of the Americas
New York, NY
(212) 644-1000
Personnel Office:
100 Southgate Parkway
Morristown, NJ 07960
(201) 898-3918
Telephone, telegraph, satellite communications, and computer
systems. One of the largest long-distance carriers in the world.

Capcon, Inc.
147 W. 25th St.
New York, NY 10001
(212) 243-6275
Personnel Department: Dennis Henderson

Circuit Technology
100 Smith St.
Farmingdale, NY 11735
(516) 293-8686
Vice President Human Resources: Dennis J. McGuire
Manufacturer of custom-designed hybrid microcircuits, including
electrical systems used in aircraft maintenance, etc.

Concord Electronics Corporation
30 Great Jones St.
New York, NY 10012
(212) 777-6571
Personnel Director: Josie Wheaton
Electronics manufacturing firm.

Contel Information Systems
130 Steamboat Road
Great Neck, NY 11024
(516) 829-5900
A subsidiary of Continental Telecom

Continental Connector Corporation
34-63 56th St.
Woodside, NY 11377
(718) 899-4422
Manufactures and sells multi-precision rack and panel circuit connectors.

Digital Equipment Corporation
2 Penn Plaza
New York, NY 10121
(212) 856-2000
One of the largest manufacturers of office automation systems equipment and computer equipment.

Eagle Electric Manufacturing Company
45-31 Court Square
Long Island City, NY 11101
(718) 937-8000
Personnel Director: Jerry Rocker
Manufactures electrical wiring devices.

Eaton Corporation/AIL Division
Commack Road
Deer Park, NY 11729
(516) 595-5000
Director of Personnel: Pat Cominskey
Engineers and manufactures electronic systems, including defensive avionics, etc.

Executone Information Systems
3 Expressway Plaza
Roslyn Heights, NY 11577
(516) 625-9100
Telecommunications systems.

Gem Electric Manufacturing Company
390 Vanderbilt Motor Parkway
Hauppauge, NY 11788
(516) 273-2230
Plant Manager: Bob Becker
Manufactures electrical wiring devices.

Gull Electronic Systems
300 Marcus Blvd.
Smithtown, NY 11787
(516) 231-3737
Personnel Director: Thomas Castoro
Digital electronic conversion devices.

Hazeltine, Inc.
450 E. Pulaski Road, M S I-54
Greenlawn, NY 11740

How to Get a Job

(516) 261-7000
Personnel Administrator: Roger Grinstead
Electronics and commercial equipment for command control
display and computer-based flight instruction.

Hitachi America
50 Prospect Ave.
Tarrytown, NY 10591
(914) 332-5800

International Business Machines Corporation
Employment Solutions
44 S. Broadway
White Plains, NY 10601
(914) 288-3000
Handles IBM employment. The world's largest producer of office
automation systems, telecommunications systems, and computers.

**International Telephone and Telegraph World
Communications**
1330 Avenue of the Americas
New York, NY 10019
(212) 258-1000
Director of Personnel: Linda Sussman
Company headquarters for this worldwide communications firm.
ITT is involved in the development and implementation of long
distance telephone and telegraph lines.

Levitton Manufacturing Company
59-25 Little Neck Parkway
Little Neck, NY 11362
(718) 229-4040
Manufactures electrical wiring devices.

Loral Corporation
600 3rd Ave.
New York, NY 10016
(212) 697-1105
Telecommunications. Company headquarters.

MCI Telecommunications
5 International Drive
White Plains, NY 10560
(914) 251-2056
Recruiting Coordinator: Mary Quinn

Monroe Systems for Business
99 Hudson St.
New York, NY 10013
(212) 431-8500
Office automation systems.

NCR Corporation
1290 Avenue of the Americas
New York, NY 10104
(212) 484-5400
Director of Personnel: Joseph Steward
Information processing systems.

New York Telephone
Division of NYNEX
1095 Avenue of the Americas
New York, NY 10036
(212) 395-2121
Personnel Director: Ben Howard
Executive offices of New York's telephone service.

Closing the deal on sales

Jerry Packer put in a long and successful stint as a salesman for Xerox, then got an MBA and went to work as district manager for a comparatively risky, aggressive new electronics manufacturing company. We asked him about the differences between selling for a giant and taking a risk with a relatively unknown firm.

"Xerox is probably typical of any large corporation," says Jerry, "in that they are very structured. It was a good place to work, but it didn't provide much opportunity for individual decision making. A new company offers a fantastic chance to exercise some entrepreneurial skills. The corporation sets general goals, but it's up to me how I meet them. I can try out different marketing techniques, divide up the territory in new ways, create teams, whatever. It's neat to be able to exercise that kind of flexibility."

We asked Jerry what it takes to be a good salesperson. "A lot of folks think that salespeople are forever buying lunches for clients and playing golf," says Jerry. "But in order to be really successful, you have to work hard. I don't necessarily mean 80 hours a week. But you need to put in sufficient time to do the things that are necessary. A second important requirement is an absolutely thorough understanding of the products you're selling. Not only your own products but also your competitors'.

"In high-level selling, sales people have to be especially sharp in terms of interpersonal skills. There's an old saying, and it's true: people don't buy from companies, they buy from people. When you're selling systems that range upward of $5 million, you're also selling yourself. It's important that your clients feel you'll be around after the sale to handle any problems that might come up. To establish that kind of rapport, you have to act responsibly and be very articulate. It also helps if you have good written communication skills." ■

Northern Telecom
330 Madison Ave.
New York, NY 10017
(212) 856-7300
Director of Personnel: Dick Petree
Telecommunications and telephone service.

NYNEX Corporation
335 Madison Ave.
New York, NY 10017
(212) 370-7400

Pass & Seymour/ Legrand
45 Sea Cliff Ave.
Glen Clove, NY 11542
(516) 671-7000
Personnel Director: John Leto
Manufactures and sells wiring devices.

Pickering and Company
200 Terminal Drive
Plainview, NY 11803
(516) 349-0200
Personnel Manager: Virginia Rumpler
Manufactures a variety of electronics and electro-magnetic products.

Signal Transformer/Division of Insilica
500 Bayview Ave.
Inwood, NY 11696
(516) 239-5777
Engineering Manager: John Bisci
Manufactures and distributes transformers.

Sprint
1 Manhattanville Road
Purchase, NY 10577
(914) 935-7000
Manager Personnel: Joan Field

Syntrex
1 Penn Plaza
New York, NY 10119
(212) 643-1088
Branch Manager: Ron Stella
Manufactures and services office automation systems.

Telephone Support Systems
2224 Hewlett Ave.
Merrick, NY 11566
(516) 867-2500
Personnel: Glen Charles
Automatic call distribution systems and related management
information systems for the telecommunications industry.

Volt Information Sciences
1133 Avenue of the Americas, 19th Floor
New York, NY 10036
(212) 704-2400
Personnel Recruiter: Dorothy Ellison
Computerized typesetting and electronic publishing systems.

Wang Laboratories
780 3rd Ave.
New York, NY 10017
(212) 418-1000
A major manufacturer of office automation systems, data processing, and word processing equipment.

CONNECTICUT EMPLOYERS:

Amphenol/Danbury
One Kennedy Ave.
Danbury, CT 06810
(203) 743-9272
Personnel Director: Vivian Senft
Producer of connectors, microwave coaxial switches, and fiber
optic interconnect devices.

Burndy Corporation
51 Richards Ave.
Norwalk, CT 06856
(203) 838-4444
Designs, manufactures, and sells electrical and electronic connectors and allied products.

General Electric Company
3135 Easton Turnpike—W2L2
Fairfield, CT 06431
(203) 373-2211
Human Resources by division.
Researches, develops, manufactures, and markets electrical,
electronic, chemical, microelectronic products.

General Signal Corporation
High Ridge Park
P.O. Box 10010
Stamford, CT 06904

(203) 357-8800
Personnel Director: Eileen Joyce

Gestetner Corporation
599 W. Putnam Ave.
Greenwich, CT 06836
(203) 625-7600
Vice President, Human Resources: Wayne Muirhead
Leading manufacturer of office computing, accounting, and copier equipment.

GTE Corporation
One Stamford Forum
Stamford, CT 06904
(203) 965-2000
Corporate headquarters.
Manager Human Resources: Nancy Ormsby

New Haven Manufacturing Corporation
446 Blake St.
New Haven, CT 06515
(203) 387-2572
Vice President Human Resources: E.R. Calistro
Electronic hardware.

Rolm Company
P.O. Box 5017
Norwalk, CT 06856-5017
(203) 849-6000
Manager Human Resources: Stanley Brice
Telecommunications systems.

Sealectro Corporation
585 E. Main St.
New Britain, CT 06051
(203) 223-2700
Director Human Resources: John Berry
Manufactures cable assemblies and coaxial connectors.

NEW JERSEY EMPLOYERS:

AT&T Corp.
100 Southgate Plaza
Morristown, NJ 07960
(201) 898-3918

Brown, Boveri and Company
1460 Livingston Ave.
N. Brunswick, NJ 08902
(908) 932-6000
Industrial electric power equipment.

Cap Gemini America
960 Holmdel Road
Holmdel, NJ 07733
(908) 946-8900
Information technology, systems development.

Dewey Electronics Corporation
27 Muller Road
Oakland, NJ 07436
(201) 337-4700
Systems-oriented civilian and military electronics development, design, engineering, and manufacturing firm.

Dialight Corporation
1913 Atlantic Ave.
Manasquan, NJ 08736
(908) 223-9400
Personnel Manager: Tony Cortina
Operations in consumer products and services, electrical/electronic components, and professional equipment.

Dowty Control Technologies
Powerville Road
Boontown, NJ 07005
(201) 334-3100
Personnel Director: Marge Samuelson

Electro-Scan
45 Outwater Lane
Garfield, NJ 07026
(201) 478-6800
Personnel Department: Judy Bowen
Produces electronic scanning products.

Electronic Measurements
425 Essex Road
Neptune, NJ 07753
(908) 922-9300
Personnel Manager: Brenda Murtha
Manufacturer of DC power supplies.

ESC Electronics Corporation
534 Bergen Blvd.
Palisades Park, NJ 07650
(201) 947-0400
Electronics manufacturer.

Federal Electric Corporation
421 Industrial Ave.
Paramus, NJ 07652
Worldwide service subsidiary of ITT Corporation.

Gould, Inc.
405 Murryhill Parkway
E. Rutherford, NJ 07073
(201) 935-1717
Manufactures and develops electronic, electrical, battery, and industrial products.

McGraw-Edison Company
7 Fairfield Crescent
West Caldwell, NJ 07006
(201) 575-0760
Plant Manager: Michael Gerardi
Manufactures and supplies electrical and mechanical products.

MCI Telecommunications
201 Centennial Ave.
Piscataway, NJ 08859
(908) 885-4000
Staff Specialist: Gary Brennan
Long distance telephone service carrier.

Metro Media Communications
1 Meadowlands Plaza
East Rutherford, NJ 07073
(201) 804-6400
Fourth larges long distance carrier in the United States.

Metromedia Company
1 Meadowlands Plaza
East Rutherfoord, NJ 07073
(201) 804-6400
Cellular radio telephone services.

Monroe Systems for Business
1000 The American Road
Morris Plains, NJ 07950
(201) 993-2510
Sr. Human Resources Representative: Kevin Hornish

Sharp Electronics Corp.
Sharp Plaza
P.O. Box 650
Mahwah, NJ 07430
(201) 529-8200
Manufacturer and marketer of electronic products.

Sony Corporation of America
One Sony Drive
Park Ridge, NJ 07656-8003
(201) 930-1000

Thomas and Betts Corporation
36 Butler St.
Elizabeth, NJ 07207
(908) 351-8800
Personnel Director: Jon Schierer
Designs, manufactures, and markets electrical and electronic
components and related systems.

Western Union Corporation
One Lake Street
Upper Saddle River, NJ 07458
(201) 818-5000

Engineering

For networking in engineering and related fields, check out the
following profesional organizations listed in Chapter 5. Also see
"Construction."

PROFESSIONAL ORGANIZATIONS:

American Society of Civil Engineers
American Society of Engineers
American Society of Mechanical Engineers
Institute of Electrical & Electronics Engineers
Society of Women Engineers
United Engineering Trustees

For more information, you can contact:

American Institute of Plant Engineers
3975 Erie Ave.
Cincinnati, OH 45208
(513) 561-6000

American Society of Civil Engineers
203 N. Wabash Ave.
Chicago, IL
(312) 263-1606

Institute of Electrical and Electronics Engineers (IEEE)
345 E. 47th St.
New York, NY 10017
(212) 705-7900

Institute of Industrial Engineers
25 Technology Park
Atlanta, GA 30092

Institute of Mechanical Engineers
345 E. 47th St.
New York, NY 10017
(212) 705-7722

National Society of Professional Engineers
1420 King St.
Alexandria, VA 22314
(703) 684-2800

PROFESSIONAL PUBLICATIONS:

Building Design and Construction
Chemical Engineering Progress
Civil Engineering
Engineering News Record
Journal of Petroleum Technology

DIRECTORIES:

Directory of Contract Service Firms (C.E. Publications, Kenmore, WA)
Who's Who in Engineering (Engineers Joint Council, New York, NY)
Who's Who in Technology Today (Technology Recognition Corp., Pittsburgh, PA)

NEW YORK EMPLOYERS:

Ammann and Whitney
96 Morton St.
New York, NY 10014
(212) 524-7200
Personnel Director: Philip Donato
Civil engineers.

Bettigole Andrews and Clark
49 W. 37th St.
New York, NY 10018
(212) 869-7800
Civil engineers.

Behre Dolbear Riverside
275 Madison Ave.
New York, NY 10017
(212) 684-4150
Mineral and mining engineers.

Bienstock, Lucches and Associates
134 Broadway
Amityville, NY 11701

(516) 691-2020
Sanitary, water, electrical, mechanical.

Blauvelt Engineering Company
1 Park Ave.
New York, NY 10016
(212) 481-1600
Cunsulting engineers.

Bowne,Sidney B., and Son
235 E. Jericho Turnpike
Mineola, NY 11501
(516) 746-2350
Civil engineers.

Edwards and Zuck
330 W. 42nd St.
New York, NY 10036
(212) 736-3400
Personnel Department: Carl Graber
Fire protection.

Elmendorf Environmental
100 Clarbrook Road
Elmsford, NY 10523
(914) 347-5654

Flack and Kurtz Consulting Engineers
475 5th Ave.
New York, NY 10017
(212) 532-9600
Director of Personnel: Elena Capolino
Civil engineers.

Hardesty and Hanover
1501 Broadway
New York, NY 10036
(212) 944-1150
Personnel Administrator: Albert Zarn
Consulting engineers.

Hazen and Sawyer
730 Broadway
New York, NY 10003
(212) 777-8400
Personnel Director: Diane Carcich
Consulting engineers.

Lawler, Matusky and Skelly Engineers
1 Blue Hill Plaza
Pearl River, NY 10965
(914) 735-8300

Personnel Director: Jim O. Gorman
Consulting engineers.

Lehr Associates
130 W. 30th St.
New York, NY 10001
(212) 947-8050
Personnel: Howard Mandell
Civil engineers.

Lockwood, Kessler and Bartlett
1 Ariel Way
Syosset, NY 11791
(516) 938-0600
Contact: Abdo Yazgi
Consulting engineers.

Loring, Joseph R., and Associates
1 Penn Plaza
New York, NY 10119
(212) 563-7400
Personnel: Momi Lani Kau
Electrical/mechanical engineers.

Metcalf and Eddy
60 E. 42nd St.
New York, NY 10017
(212) 867-3076
Sanitary engineers.

Meyer Strong and Jones
11 Penn Plaza
New York, NY 10001
(212) 239-7600
Controller: Guy Dimemmo
Consulting engineers.

Mueser Rutledge Consulting Engineers
708 3rd Ave.
New York, NY 10017
(212) 490-7110
Civil engineers.

Pirnie, Malcolm
2 Corporate Park Drive
White Plains, NY 10602
(914) 694-2100
Personnel: Tony Kusinski
Environmental engineers.

Severud Associates
485 5th Ave.

New York, NY 10017
(212) 986-3700
Contact: Personnel
Structural engineers.

Stone and Webster Engineering Corporation
1 Penn Plaza
New York, NY 10001
(212) 290-6000
Industrial engineers.

Tams Consultant
655 3rd Avenue
New York, NY 10017
(212) 867-1777
Consulting engineers.

Weidlinger Associates
333 7th Ave.
New York, NY 10001
(212) 563-5200
Director of Personnel: Helen Pelekanos
Civil engineers.

Weiskopf and Pickworth
79 Madison Ave.
New York, NY 10016
(212) 683-9696
Personnel: Murray Feldman
Civil engineers.

CONNECTICUT EMPLOYERS:

McDonald & Vander Poll
2 Landmark Sq.
Stamford, CT 06901
(203) 327-0408

Osher Joseph & Associates Structural Mecnanical
250 High Ridge Road
Stamford, CT 06905
(203) 322-6921

Steanns & Wheler
Hazardous Waste Consulting Wetlands
19 Old Kings Highway S.
Darien, CT 06820
(203) 655-7979

NEW JERSEY EMPLOYERS:

Cheshen, Charles S., Associates
395 Franklin
Blommfield, NJ 07657
(201) 429-7220
Structural engineers.

Cushman and Wakefield
10 Exchange Place
Jersey City, 07306
(201)451-9808
Construction engineers.

Factory Mutual Engineering and Research
30 Vreeland Road, Suite 60
Florham Park, NJ 07932-1993
(201) 822-2010
Loss-prevention service.

GPU Nuclear Corp.
1 Upper Pond Road
Parsippany, NJ 07054

Johnson Soils Engineering
752 Grand Ave.
Ridgefield, NJ 07631
(201) 943-1793

Keuffel and Esser Company
Ford Road
P.O. Box 800
Rockaway, NJ 07866
(201) 625-9005

Killman, Elson T., Associates
P.O. Box 1008
Millburn, NJ 07041
(201) 379-3400
Personnel: Phyllis Carroll
Hydraulic and environmental engineering consulting.

Lozano, August, CPE
500 Grand Ave.
Englewood, NJ 07631
(201) 871-7068

Robins Engineers and Constructors
1055 Parsippany Blvd.
Parsippany, NJ 07054
(201) 256-7600
Designs and installs bulk material handling systems.

Entertainment and Recreation

For networking in the entertainment industry, check out the following professional organizations listed in Chapter 5:

PROFESSIONAL ORGANIZATIONS:

AFTRA
American Society of Composers, Authors and Publishers
American Sportscasters Association
Association of Independent Commercial Producers
National Association of Women Artists
Women's Media Group

For more information, you can contact:

Academy of Motion Picture Arts & Sciences
8949 Wilshire Blvd., #800
Beverly Hills, CA 90211
(310) 247-3000

American Film Institute
Kennedy Center for the Performing Arts
Washington, DC 20566

Amusement & Music Operators Association
111 E. Wacker Drive
Chicago, IL 60601
(312) 245-1021

National Recreation & Parks Association
2775 S. Quincy St., Suite 300
Arlington, VA 22206
(703) 820-4940

National Sporting Goods Association
1699 Wall St.
Mt. Prospect, IL 60096-5780
(708) 439-4000

PROFESSIONAL PUBLICATIONS:

American Film
Backstage
Billboard
Film Comment
Parks and Recreation
Show Business
Sporting Goods Trade

Theater Times
TV Radio Age
Variety
Video Retailing

DIRECTORIES:

Back Stage Film / Tape / Syndication Directory (Back Stage
   Publications, New York, NY)
Blue Book (Hollywood Reporter, Hollywood, CA)
Contemporary Music Almanac (Macmillan Publishers, New York, NY)
Film Producers, Studios, and Agents Guide (Lone Eagle, Beverly
   Hills, CA)
Mass Entertainment Buyers Guide (Billboard Publications,
   Nashville, TN)
Music Business Handbook & Career Guide (Sherwood Co., Los
   Angeles, CA)
New American Guide to Athletics, Sports, and Recreation (New
   American Library, New York, NY)
Sporting Goods Directory (Sporting Goods Dealer, St. Louis, MO)
Sports Administration Guide and Directory (National Sports
   Marketing Bureau, New York, NY)
Theatre Directory (Theatre Communications Group, New York, NY)
Who's Who in the Motion Picture Industry (Packard House,
   Beverly Hills, CA)
Who's Who in Television (Packard House, Beverly Hills, CA)

BROADWAY THEATER EMPLOYERS:

Most of New York's Broadway theaters are run by large production
companies or theater chains. Two of the largest are the Nederlander
Theatre Group and the Schubert Organization Corporation. Employment decisions for all the theaters in a chain are made by the
theater group's personnel office. A few Broadway theaters are
independently owned, and the house manager usually makes all
employment decisions.

Nederlander Productions
810 7th Ave.
New York, NY 10019
(212) 262-2400

Brooks-Atkinson
Gershwin
Lunt-Fontanne
Marriott Marquis
Minskoff
Nederlander Theater
Neil Simon
Palace
Richard Rodgers

Shubert Organization Corporation
234 W. 44th St.
New York, NY 10036
(212) 944-3700
Director of Personnel: Elliott Greene

Ambassador	**Imperial**
Barrymore	**Longacre**
Belasco	**Lyceum**
Booth	**Majestic**
Broadhurst	**Plymouth**
Broadway	**Royale**
Cort	**Shubert**
Golden	**Winter Garden Theatre**

INDEPENDENT THEATER EMPLOYERS:

Beck, Martin, Theatre
302 W. 45th St.
New York, NY 10036
(212) 239-6200

Helen Hayes Theatre
240 W. 44th St.
New York, NY 10036
(212) 944-9450

Music Box Theatre
239 W. 45th St.
New York, NY 10036
(212) 239-6200

O'Neill, Eugene, Theatre
230 W. 49th St.
New York, NY 10019
(212) 239-6200

St. James Theatre
246 W. 44th St.
New York, NY 10036
(212) 398-0280

OFF-BROADWAY THEATER EMPLOYERS:

Astor Place Theatre
434 Lafayette St.
New York, NY 10003
(212) 254-4370

Circle in the Square
1633 Broadway

New York, NY 10019
(212) 307-2000

City Center
131 W. 55th St.
New York, NY 10019
(212) 581-7907

Minetta Lane Theatre
18 Minetta Lane
New York, NY 10012
(212) 420-8000

New York Shakespeare Theater
425 Lafayette St.
New York, NY 10003
(212) 598-7100
General Manager: Betsy Gardella

Roundabout Theater Co.
1530 Broadway
New York, NY 10036
(212) 719-9393

Sullivan Street Playhouse
181 Sullivan St.
New York, NY 10012
(212) 674-3838

Theatre East
211 E. 60th St.
New York, NY 10022
(212) 838-0177

Theatre Eighty St. Marks
80 St. Marks Place
New York, NY 10003
(212) 254-7400

MOTION PICTURE COMPANIES:

Columbia Pictures International
711 5th Ave.
New York, NY 10022
(212) 751-4400
Personnel Director: Barbara Lopipero

Disney, Walt
500 Park Ave.
New York, NY 10022
(212) 593-8900
Office Manager: Marion Mazzini

New Line Cinema Corp.
888 7th Ave.
New York, NY 10019
(212) 649-4900

Orion Pictures Corporation
1325 Avenue of the Americas
New York, NY 10019
(212) 505-0051
Personnel: Marsha Hook

Paramount Pictures
Subsidiary of Gulf and Western Industries
1 Gulf and Western Plaza
New York, NY 10023
(212) 373-7000

Thomas, Bob, Productions
60 E. 42nd St.
New York, NY 10165
(212) 883-0887
Contact: Bob Thomas

Twentieth Century Fox
1211 Avenue of the Americas, 3rd Floor
New York, NY 10036
(212) 556-2400

Vestron Inc.
1010 Washington Blvd.
Stamford, CT 06901
(203) 978-5400

Warner Brothers Distributing Corporation
1325 Avenue of the Americas
New York, NY 10019
Manager, Corporate Human Resources: Helen McGuire
(212) 522-1212

Breaking into film production

Tracey Barnett was working in public relations when she decided to break into film production. Although she didn't know anyone in the industry when she began, today she is a successful freelance production manager. We asked her how she did it.

"Most important was my desire to do it," says Tracey, "and I didn't get discouraged. I began by making a few contacts in the industry through people I knew in related fields. Then I set up interviews with these contacts. At the end of each interview, I asked for the names of three to five other contacts. This strategy opened a lot

of doors for me. I followed up each interview
with a phone call. I also kept in touch with my
contacts on a monthly basis."

We asked Tracey what jobs are available for
beginners in the film business and what
qualifications are needed for those jobs.

"Entry-level positions include production
assistant, stylist, assistant wardrobe manager,
and grip," says Tracey. "There are no special
requirements for these jobs. You don't need a
degree in film to work in the business. In fact,
people with film degrees begin at the same level
as everybody else. What does count is intelligence and the ability to get things done quickly
and efficiently. You need to think on your feet
and be able to anticipate what needs to be
done."

According to Tracey, freelance production
assistants begin at about $75-$100 per day.
More experienced production assistants can
make as much as $175 per day. "But keep in
mind that as a freelancer, you don't have the
security of a regular paycheck," says Tracey.
"You may not work every day." She advises
those who need a more reliable income to look
for a staff position in the industry.

Tracey advises those who want to break into
the film business to keep at it: "Don't count your
inexperience as a negative. Tenacity and
enthusiasm will get you the first job. Approach
your contacts and keep approaching them—over
and over and over again." ■

RECORDING COMPANIES:

A&M Records
595 Madison Ave.
New York, NY 10022
(212) 826-0477

Arista Records
6 W. 57th St.
New York, NY 10019
(212) 489-7400

Atlantic Records
75 Rockefeller Plaza
New York, NY 10019
(212) 484-6000
Personnel Director: Linda Wade

BMG Records
1133 Avenue of the Americas
New York, NY 10036
(212) 930-4000

Electra Records
75 Rockefeller Plaza
New York, NY 10019
(212) 275-4570
Vice President Personnel: Mary Ann Mastropaolo

EMI Music Worldwide
1250 Avenue of the Americas
New York, NY 10019
(212) 492-1200
Personnel Director: Ann Yarmouk

Epic Records
A division of Sony Music Entertainment
51 W. 52nd St.
New York, NY 10019
(212) 975-4321

Island Records
14 E. 4th St.
New York, NY 10012
(212) 477-8000

Polygram Record
825 8th Ave.
New York, NY 10019
(212) 333-8000

Servisound, Inc.
35 W. 45th St.
New York, NY 10036
(212) 921-0555
Personnel Director: Chris Nelson
Sound for commercials, television, film, industrial shows, and
multimedia.

Sire Records
A division of Warner Bros.
75 Rockefeller Plaza
New York, NY 10019
(212) 484-6800

Sony Music Entertainment
P.O. Box 4450
New York, NY 10101-4450
Attn: Recruitment
(212) 445-4321

Triton-Sound
123 W. 43rd St.
New York, NY 10036
(212) 575-8055
Recording studios for radio and television commercials.

Vitt Media International
1114 Avenue of the Americas
New York, NY 10036
(212) 921-0500
Office Manager: Gail Sihona
Media buying and planning.

ARTISTS' REPRESENTATIVES:

Also see "Literary Agents" under **Book Publishers/Literary Agents.**

Brown, Curtis, Ltd.
10 Aster Place
New York, NY 10003
(212) 473-5400
Literary and dramatic agents.

Candida Donadio and Ashworth
231 W. 22nd St.
New York, NY 10011
(212) 691-8077
Contact: Eric Ashworth
Literary and dramatic agents.

Carlton, Royce, Inc.
866 UN Plaza
New York, NY 10017
(212) 355-3210
Vice President: Carlton Sedgeley
Agents and managers for lectures, lecture brokerage services, teleconferencing, and performing arts.

Craven Design Studios
234 5th Ave.,4th Floor
New York, NY 10001
(212) 696-4680
Artists' representatives.

Fulton, Richard, Inc.
66 Richfield
Plainview, NY 11803
(516) 349-0407
Vice President: Robert Paul
Represents authors for speaking engagements.

International Creative Management
40 W. 57th St.
New York, NY 10019
(212) 556-5600
Director of Operations/Personnel: Andrew Suss
Literary and dramatic agents.

Janklow Nesbit Associates
598 Madison Ave.
New York, NY 10022
(212) 421-1700
Office Manager: Alice Drucker
Literary and dramatic agents.

Leigh Bureau, The
50 Division St., Suite 200
Somerville, NJ 08876-2955
(609) 921-6141
Manager: Maryellen Mizov
Lecture and literary agents.

Lewis, Norma, Agency
521 5th Ave.
New York, NY 10175
(212) 751-4955
President: Norma Lewis
Represents creative individuals in all media, specializing in children and young adults.

Markson, Elaine, Literary Agency
44 Greenwich Ave.
New York, NY 10011
(212) 243-8480
Contact: Geri Thoma
Literary and dramatic agents.

Miller, Peter, Agency
Subsidiary of Lion Entertainment
220 W. 19th St., Suite 501
New York, NY 10018
(212) 929-1222
Contact: Peter Miller
Literary and dramatic agents.

Morris, William, Agency
1350 Avenue of the Americas
New York, NY 10019
(212) 586-5100
Literary and dramatic agents.

Priest, Aaron M., Literary Agency
122 E. 42nd St., Suite 3902

New York, NY 10016
(212) 818-0344
Contact: Aaron Priest
Literary and dramatic agents.

Sterling Lord Agency
1 Madison Ave.
New York, NY 10010
(212) 696-2800
Contact: Sterling Lord
Literary and dramatic agents.

Writer's and Artist's Agency
19 W. 44th St., Suite 1000
New York, NY 10036
(212) 391-1112
Literary and dramatic agents.

OTHER EMPLOYERS:

Aqueduct Race Track
Rockaway Blvd.
Ozone Park, NY 11417
(718) 641-4700
Personnel Director: Sal Cartaginie

Belmont Race Track
Hempstead Turnpike and Plainfield Ave.
Elmont, NY 10003
(718) 641-4700

Bronx Zoo
Fordham Road at Bronx River Parkway
Bronx, NY 10460
(212) 220-5100
Director: William Conway, c/o The New York Zoological Society,
E. 185th St. and Southern Blvd., Bronx, NY 10460

Carnegie Hall
881 7th Ave.
New York, NY 10019
(212) 903-9601
House Manager: James Gerald

Central Park Conservancy
10 Columbus Circle
New York, NY 10023
(212) 315-0385

Lincoln Center for the Performing Arts
140 W. 65th St.
New York, NY 10023

(212) 875-5000
Director of Personnel: Jay Spivak
Consisting of Alice Tully Hall, the Vivian Beaumont Theatre,
Avery Fisher Hall, the Metropolitan Opera House, and New York
State Theatre.

Madison Square Garden
2 Penn Plaza
New York, NY 10121
(212) 465-6741
Director of Personnel: Ralph Mulhare
Major center for sports events, live concerts, circuses, national
and international sports meets. Home of the New York Nets,
Knicks, and Rangers.

Metropolitan Opera Association
Lincoln Center
New York, NY 10023
(212) 799-3100
Director Personnel: Sean McKillop

**New Jersey Sports and Exposition Authority/
Meadowlands**
50 Route 120
E. Rutherford, NY 07073
(201) 935-8500
Asst. Director Personnel: Gina Klein

New York Botanical Garden
Southern Blvd. at 200th St.
Bronx, NY 10458
(212) 220-8700

New York City Center
131 W. 56th St.
New York, NY 10019
(212) 581-7907
House Manager: Carol Branigan

Radio City Music Hall
1260 Avenue of the Americas
New York, NY 10020
Personnel: Regina Paleau
(212) 632-4000

Shea Stadium
Roosevelt Ave. at 126th St.
Flushing, NY 11368
(718) 507-6387
Personnel: Russ Richardson
Home of the New York Mets.

How to Get a Job

United States Tennis Association
Flushing Meadow Park
Flushing, NY 11368
(718) 592-8000
Facilities Manager: David Meehan
Home of the United States Open Tennis Championship.

Veteran's Memorial Nassau Coliseum
Hempstead Turnpike
Uniondale, NY 11553
(516) 794-9300
Long Island's premier entertainment center. Home of the New York Islanders hockey team.

Westbury Music Fair
960 Brush Hollow Road
Westbury, NY 11590
(516) 333-7228
General Manager: Gloria D'Amico
Major entertainment center and concert hall.

Yankee Stadium
River Ave. at 161st St.
Bronx, NY 10451
(212) 293-4300
Home of the New York Yankees.

286

Environmental Services

For networking in environmental fields, check out the following professional organizations listed in Chapter 5:

PROFESSIONAL ORGANIZATIONS:

Environmental Defense Fund
Greenpeace Action
National Association of Environmental Professionals

For additional information, you can contact:

Air and Waste Management Association
P.O. Box 2861
Pittsburgh, PA 15230
(412) 232-3444

Alliance for Environmental Education
10751 Ambassador Drive, Suite 201
Manassus, VA 22110
(703) 335-1025

American Association for the Advancement of Science
1333 H St., NW
Washington DC 20005
(202) 326-6400

American Wilderness Alliance
7600 E. Arapahoe Road, Suite 114
Englewood, CO 80112
(303) 771-0380

Association of Corporate Environmental Officers
P.O. Box 4117
Timonium, MD 21093
(800) 876-6618

The Conservation Foundation
1250 24th St., NW
Washington DC 20037
(202) 293-4800

Earthwatch
P.O. Box 403N
Watertown, MA 02272
(617) 926-8200

Environmental Careers Organization
286 Congress St., 3rd Floor

Boston, MA 02210-1009
Northeast Regional Office
(617) 426-4783

Greenpeace USA
1436 U St., NW
Washington DC 20009
(202) 462-1177

National Wildlife Federation
1400 16th St., NW
Washington DC 20036-2266
(202) 797-6800

Sierra Club
730 Polk St.
San Francisco, CA 94109
(415) 776-2211

PROFESSIONAL PUBLICATIONS:

Buzzworm, The Environmental Journal
E, The Environmental Magazine
Environmental Business Journal
Environmental Watch
Inside EPA
New Age Journal
Pollution Engineering
Resource Exchange & News
Water Engineering & Management
Water and Wastes Digest

DIRECTORIES:

The Complete Guide to Environmental Careers (The CEIP Fund,
Island Press, Washington, DC)
Conservation Directory (National Wildlife Federation, Washington, DC)
Directory of National Environmental Organizations (U.S. Environmental Directories, St. Paul, MN)
EI Environmental Services (Environmental Information Ltd.,
Bloomington, MN)
The Environmental Career Guide (John Wiley & Sons, New York)
*Green at Work: Finding a Business Career That Works for the
Environment* (Island Press, Washington, DC)

EMPLOYERS, PRIVATE SECTOR:

American Environmental Technologies
3 Towbridge Drive

Bethel, CT 06801
(914) 279-5097

Aquaterra Environmental Co. Services
79 5th Ave.
New York, NY 10003
(212) 675-8200
Consulting firm for control of work environments.

Eldon Environmental Management Corporation
900 Ellison Ave.
Westbury, NY 11590
(516) 683-3330

ESPL Environmental Consultants
110 Greenwich St.
New York, NY 10006
(212) 587-1287

Great Forest
11 Penn Plaza
New York, NY 10001
(212) 967-4757
Environmental consulting firm.

Hoskawa Micron USA
780 3rd Ave.
New York, NY 10017
(212) 826-3830

Pirnie, Malcolm, Inc.
2 Corporate Park Drive
White Plains, NY 10602
(914) 641-2900
Environmental consultants.

Savin Engineers
200 White Plains Road
Tarrytown, NY 10591-5805
(914) 332-4830

Soil Mechanics Environmental Services
3770 Merrick Road
Seaford, NY 11783
(516) 221-7500

EMPLOYERS, GOVERNMENT AGENCIES:

Environmental Protection Agency
401 M St., NW
Washington DC, 20460
Regional office:

26 Federal Plaza, Room 937-C
New York, NY 10278
(212) 264-0016

New York State Department of Environmental Conservation
47-40 21st St.
Long Island City, NY
(718) 482-4990
Albany headquarters (518) 457-3446

U.S. Department of Energy
376 Hudson St.
New York, NY 10014-3621
(212) 620-3607

Westchester County Environmental Facilities
270 North Ave.
New Rochelle, NY
(914) 637-3073

EMPLOYERS, NON-PROFIT ORGANIZATIONS:

Environmental Defense Fund
257 Park Ave. S.
New York, NY 10010
(212) 505-2100

Greenpeace Action
462 Broadway
New York, NY
(212) 941-0994

Greenworking Inc.
115 Tompkins Ave.
Pleasantville, NY 10570
(914) 741-2424
Contact: Tim Boylan

National Audubon Society
950 3rd Ave.
New York, NY 10022
(212) 546-9100

National Resources Defense Council
40 W. 20th St.
New York, NY 10011
(212) 727-2700

A "growth" industry

An environmental consultant friend of ours says the enforcement of federal regulations and emphasis on compliance with hazardous waste removal and clean air and water acts has put increased demands on her office. Opportunities for lawyers, engineers, and environmentalists are growing in large corporations and non-profit organizations. As she says, "It's a growth industry." ■

Food/Beverage Producers and Distributors

For networking in the food industry and related fields, check out the following professional organization listed in Chapter 5. Also see **"Hospitality"** and for grocery chains, **"Retailers."**

PROFESSIONAL ORGANIZATIONS:

National Association for the Specialty Food Trade Sales Executives Club of New York

For more information, you can contact:

American Institute of Food Distribution
28-12 Broadway
Fairlawn, NJ 07410
(201) 791-5570

Association of Food Industries
P.O. Box 776
5 Ravine Drive
Matawan, NJ 07747
(908) 583-8188

Distilled Spirits Council
1250 I St., NW
(Washington, DC 20005
(202) 628-3544

Food Marketing Institute
800 Connecticut Ave., NW
Washington, DC 20006
(202) 452-8444

National Association of Beverage Importers–Wine–Spirits–Beer
1025 Vermont Ave.

Washington, DC 20005
(202) 638-1617

National Association for the Specialty Food Trade
8 W. 40th St.
New York, NY 10018
(212) 921-1690

National Food Brokers Association
1010 Massachusetts Ave., NW
Washington, DC 20001
(202) 789-2844

National Food Distributors Association
401 N. Michigan Ave.
Chicago, IL 60611
(312) 644-6610

National Food Processors Association
1401 New York Ave.
Washington, DC 20005
(202) 639-5900

National Frozen Foods Association
P.O. Box 6069, 4755 Linglestown Road
Harrisburg, PA 17112
(717) 657-8601

National Soft Drink Association
1101 16th St., NW
Washington, DC 20036

Wine & Spirits Wholesalers of America
1025 15th St., NW
Washington, DC 20005

PROFESSIONAL PUBLICATIONS:

Beverage World
Fancy Food
Food and Beverage Marketing
Food Industry Newsletter
Food Management
Food and Wine
Foodservice Product News
Forecast for Home Economics
Grocery Marketing
Institutional Distribution
Progressive Grocer
Quick Frozen Foods
Wines and Vines

DIRECTORIES:

Frozen Food Executive (National Frozen Food Association, Harrisburg, PA)
Frozen Food Fact Book & Directory (National Frozen Food Association, Harrisburg, PA)
Impact Yearbook: A Directory of the Wine and Spirits Industry (M. Shanken Communications, New York, NY)
National Beverage Marketing Directory (Beverage Marketing Corp., New York, NY)
NFBA Directory (National Food Brokers Association, Washington, DC)

NEW YORK EMPLOYERS:

A & W Brands
709 Westchester Ave.
White Plains, NY 10604
(914) 397-1700
Manager Human Resources: Elizabeth Sherwood
Beverages.

American Frozen Foods
Rye Brook, NY
National Recruitment Office:
111 Sibley Ave.
Ardmore, PA 19003
800-241-7187

Boar's Head Provision Co.
24 Rock St.
Brooklyn, NY 11206
(718) 456-3600
Personnel Director: Larry Helfant

Borden
277 Park Ave.
New York, NY 10172
(212) 573-4000
Food products manufacturer.

Business Food Service
117-19 14th Road
College Point, NY 11356
(718) 445-8100
Employee food services.

**Mouth–watering
opportunities in
food service
management**

Kate Williams, manager of the dietary department of a suburban hospital, sees the food
service industry as a growing field with tremendous potential. The many hospitals in the New
York area offer varied opportunities in food
services, according to Kate. Some of the jobs,
such as clinical or administrative dietitian,
require a college degree in nutrition. But many
do not.

"Some employees have experience working at
a fast-food restaurant," says Kate. "Others just
learn on the job. Still others have completed
one–or two-year programs in food service offered
by various colleges."

Besides registered dietitians, Kate's staff
includes food service supervisors, who manage
the personnel who prepare food; diet techni-
cians, who prepare and implement menus based
on information about the patient; diet aides, who
perform such tasks as delivering meals to
patients; a chef and cooking staff; and a food
purchasing agent.

Kate is optimistic about employment prospects in the food service industry as a whole.
"There are tremendous opportunities for those
with culinary arts skills, as well as for hotel or
restaurant food service managers. Opportunities
exist in food equipment companies, public and
private schools, contract food companies, and
food service consulting firms. Right now the
possibilities in food marketing are phenomenal.

"The nutritional needs of the growing elderly
population," Kate adds, "will also create many
new jobs in the food service business as
hospitals and other organizations become
involved in long-term care." ■

Chock Full O'Nuts Corp.
370 Lexington Ave.
New York, NY 10017
(212) 532-0300
Vice President Labor Relations: Peter Baer

Continental Grain Co.
277 Park Ave.
New York, NY 10172
(212) 207-5100
Produces and markets cereal grain foods

CPC International
International Plaza
Route 9W

Englewood Cliffs, NJ 07632
(201) 894-4000
Food products manufacturers, including Hellmann's mayonnaise
and Skippy peanut butter products.

Culbro Corporation
387 Park Ave. S.
New York, NY 10016
(212) 561-8700
Personnel Manager: Robert Grimaldi
Snack foods.

Dannon Company
1111 Westchester Ave.
White Plains, NY 10604
(914) 697-9700
Vice President Human Resources: Rick Corcoran

Domino Sugar Corporation
1114 Avenue of the Americas
New York, NY 10036
(212) 789-9700
Personnel Manager:Rodney Hebert

Entenmann's, Inc.
1724 5th Ave.
Bayshore, NY 11706
(516) 273-6000
Human Resources Manager: Mr. Cordell Price

F & C International
599 Johnson Ave.
Brooklyn, NY 11237
(718) 497-4664
Director of Personnel:
890 Redna Terrace
Cincinnati, OH 45215
(513) 771-5904
Manufacturer of food flavors and fragrances.

Fink Baking Corporation
535 54th Ave.
Long Island City, NY 11101
(718) 392-8300
Controller: Norman Mast

4C Foods Corporation
580 Fountain Ave.
Brooklyn, NY 11208
(718) 272-4242
Personnel Officer: Ron Long

Heinz, H.J., Company
999 Walt Whitman Road
Melville, NY 11747
(516) 385-2343
District Manager: Kenneth Pring
Catsup and relishes.

Kane-Miller
555 White Plains Road
Tarrytown, NY 10591
(914) 631-6900
Food processing plant.

Kraft General Foods Corporation
A division of Phillip Morris
250 North St.
White Plains, NY 10625
(914) 335-2500
One of the world's largest producers of dry and processed foods.

Krasdale Foods
400 Food Center Drive
Bronx, NY 10474
(212) 378-1100
Personnel Manager: Alan Kenduck

Lever Brothers Company
Division of Unilever N.V.
390 Park Ave.
New York, NY 10022
(212) 688-6000
Personnel Manager: Kathy Tsougranis
Food products manufacturer.

Nabisco Brands
Divisional Office
1313 4th Ave.
New Hyde Park, NY 11040
(516) 775-0211
A major producer of dry foods.

Nestle Beverages
250 Fulton Ave.
Garden City Park, NY 11040
(516) 294-8282
Personnel Administrator: Monica Hytner

Ogden/Allied Food Service
2 Penn Plaza
New York, NY 10121
(212) 868-6000
Director of Personnel: Hank Martone

Provides food service to business and industry. Also serves the sports, recreation, travel, and entertainment industries.

Pepcom Industries
867 E. Gate Blvd.
Garden City, NY 11530
(516) 228-8200

Pepsico, Inc.
700 Anderson Hill Road
Purchase, NY 10577
(914) 253-2000
One of the world's largest producers of snacks, soft drinks, and convenience foods.

Pepsicola Company
One Pepsi Way
Somers, NY 10589
(914) 767-7436
Staffing Manager: Cathy Parker

Philip Morris
120 Park Ave.
New York, NY 10017
(212) 880-5000
A major producer of soft drinks, food products, and cigarettes.

Pollio Dairy Products
120 Mineola Blvd.
Mineola, NY 11501
(516) 741-8000
Human Resources Asst.: Eileen A Ferringno

Refined Sugars
1 Federal St.
Yonkers, NY 10705
(914) 963-2400
Personnel Manager: Donald Brainard

Seagram, Joseph E., and Sons
375 Park Ave.
New York, NY 10152
(212) 572-7000
Personnel Recruiter: Jeanette DeCarlo
Alcoholic beverages.

Stella D'Oro Biscuit Co.
184 W. 237th St.
Bronx, NY 10463
(212) 549-3700
Vice President Industrial Relations: James V. Perduto

Tuscan Foods/Dairylea
155-25 Styler Road, Building C
Jamaica, NY 11433
(718) 899-9300
Office Manager: Donna Christina
Dairy.

White Rock Productions Corporation
16-16 Whitestone Expressway
Whitestone, NY 11357
(718) 746-3400
Soft drinks.

CONNECTICUT EMPLOYERS:

American Brands
1700 E. Putnam Ave.
Old Greenwich, CT 06870
(203) 698-5000
Personnel Administrator: Jonathan L. Parker

American Maize Products Co.
250 Harbor Drive
Stamford, CT 06902
(203) 356-9000
Corn products, tobacco.

Best Foods Baking Group
10 Hamilton Ave.
Greenwich, CT 06830
(203) 531-2000
Wholesale baker and food processor.

Cadbury Beverages
P.O. Box 3800
High Ridge Park
Stamford, CT 06905
(203) 968-5600
Soft drinks.

Carvel Corporation
20 Batterson Park Road
Farmington, CT 06032
(203) 677-6811

Coca Cola Bottling Co.
20 Horseneck Lane
Greenwich, CT 06830
(203) 625-4000
Manager of Employment: Linda Campanelli

Pepperidge Farm
595 Westport Ave.
Norwalk, CT 06851
(203) 846-7000
Corporate Manager Human Resources: Thomas Flanagan

Perrier Group of America
777 W. Putnam Ave.
Greenwich, CT 06830
(203) 531-4100

Peter Paul
P.O. Box 310
Naugatuck, CT 06770
(203) 729-0221
Manager Human Resources: Paul M. Russo
Confectionery products.

Tetley, Inc.
100 Commerce Drive
Shelton, CT 06484
(203) 929-9200
Manager Compensation and Staffing: Edward Schuler

NEW JERSEY EMPLOYERS:

Anheuser-Busch
200 US Highway 1
Newark, NJ 07101
(201) 645-7700
Personnel Director: Paul Charrier

Best Foods
180 Baldwin Ave.
Jersey City, NJ 07306
(201) 653-3800
Manager of Human Resources: Tom Martin

Campbell Soup Company
Campbell Place
Camden, NJ 08103
Manager Human Resources: Ann Bollinger
Major food company.

Canteen Corporation
495 River Road
Clifton, NJ 07014
(201) 779-0600
Comptroller: Patricia Allegretto
Food service company.

CPC International
P.O. Box 8000
Englewood Cliffs, NJ 07632
(201) 894-4000
Director of Management and Organizational Development: John
Jordan
Grocery products and corn wet milling.

General Foods/Maxwell House Division
1125 Hudson St.
Hoboken, NJ 07030
(201) 420-3414

Great Bear Spring Company
A division of Perrier.
Great Bear Plaza
Teterboro, NJ 07608
(201) 288-6070
Human Resources through Perrier in Greenwich, CT.

Greenwich Mills
520 Secaucus Road
Secaucus, NJ 07094
(201) 865-0200
Office Manager: Lorraine Sadowski
Produces and distributes coffee for commercial use.

International Proteins Corporation
P.O. Box 1169
Fairfield, NJ 07006
(201) 227-2710
Primarily operates in the fishing industry.

Lipton, Thomas J.
800 Sylvan Ave.
Englewood Cliffs, NJ 07632
(201) 567-8000
Corporate headquarters location.

Marathon Enterprises
66 E. Union Ave.
E. Rutherford, NJ 07073
(201) 935-3330
Manufacturer of provisions and baked goods.

Mars, Inc.
800 High St.
Hackettstown, NJ 07840-1552
(908) 852-1000
International company manufacturing and marketing food
products.

Nabisco Brands
Nabisco Brands Plaza
6 Campus Drive
Parsippany, NJ 07054
(201) 898-7100

Sunshine Biscuits
100 Woodbridge Center
Woodbridge, NJ 07095
(908) 855-4000
Manufacturer of cookies and crackers.

Tuscan Farm Products
750 Union Ave.
Union, NJ 07083
(908) 686-1500
Corporate headquarters location. Contact Human Resources.

Foundations

For additional information on foundations and related fields you can contact:

PROFESSIONAL ORGANIZATIONS:

Council on Foundations
1828 L St., NW
Washington, DC 20036
(202) 466-6512

Foundation Center
79 5th Ave.
New York, NY 10003
(212) 620-4230

Independent Sector
1828 L St., NW
Washington, DC 20036
(202) 223-8100

PROFESSIONAL PUBLICATIONS:

Charities USA
Chronicle of Philanthropy
Foundation News
The Humanist

DIRECTORIES:

Corporate 500: The Directory of Corporate Philanthropy (Public
    Management Institute, San Francisco, CA)
Foundation Center Source Book Profiles (Foundation Center, New
    York, NY)
Foundation Directory (Foundation Center, New York, NY)
National Directory of Corporate Giving (Foundation Center, New
    York, NY)
New York State Foundations (Foundation Center, New York, NY)

NEW YORK EMPLOYERS:

Carnegie Corporation of New York
437 Madison Ave.
New York, NY 10022
(212) 371-3200
Assistant Secretary and Personnel Director: Dee Holden
Philanthropic fund; grants to education projects.

Clark Foundation
30 Wall St.
New York, NY 10005
(212) 269-1833
Secretary: Joe Cruckshank
Support for a hospital and museums in Cooperstown, New York.
Grants for charitable welfare and educational purposes.

Commonwealth Fund
1 E. 75th St.
New York, NY 10021
(212) 535-0400
Contact: Karen O'Brien
Support for research and analysis that will help the nation's
academic health centers.

Ford Foundation
320 E. 43rd St.
New York, NY 10017
(212) 573-5000
Grants primarily to institutions for experience, demonstration,
and development efforts within the foundation's major areas of
interest: urban poverty, improvement of secondary education,
education programs for disadvantaged youth and welfare recipients, child care, health and nutrition services, reduction of street
crime and arson, housing rehabilitation, and research on urban
problems.

Hearst Foundation
888 7th Ave.
New York, NY 10106
(212) 586-5404
Director: Robert Frehse, Jr.
Programs to aid poverty-level and minority groups, education
programs, health delivery systems and medical research, and
cultural programs with records of public support.

Luce, Henry, Foundation
111 W. 50th St., Room 3710
New York, NY 10020
(212) 489-7700
President: John Wesley Cook
Grants for specific projects in public affairs, East/West relations,
and theology.

Mellon, Andrew W., Foundation
140 E. 62nd St.
New York, NY 10021
(212) 838-8400
Assistant to Program Director: Julia Marks
Grants for higher education, medical and public health education
and population research, cultural affairs, and the performing arts.

MS. Foundation for Women
141 5th Ave.
New York, NY 10011
(212) 353-8580

New York Community Trust
2 Park Ave., 24th Floor
New York, NY 10016
(212) 686-0010
Contact: Personnel
Grants to charitable organizations; priority given to projects
having significance for New York City area.

Penney, J.C., Foundation
1633 Broadway, 39th Floor
New York, NY 10019
(212) 830-7490
Grants given primarily for special projects. Emphasis on commu-
nity-based organizations and state or national coalitions.

Reader's Digest Foundation
Pleasantville, NY 10570
(914) 238-1000
President: J. Edward Hall
Particularly interested in journalism and education.

Rockefeller Foundation
1133 Avenue of the Americas
New York, NY 10036
(212) 869-8500
Personnel Manager: Charlotte Church
Active in six fields: agricultural sciences, population sciences,
health sciences, equal opportunity, international relations, and
arts and humanities.

Sloan, Alfred P., Foundation
630 5th Ave.
New York, NY 10111
(212) 649-1649
Personnel: Stuart Campbell
Grants in science, technology, education, economics, management.

Texaco Philanthropic Foundation
2000 Westchester Ave.
White Plains, NY 10650
(914) 253-4000
Contact: Personnel
Supports cultural programs, social welfare and civic organizations, hospitals, and health agencies.

CONNECTICUT EMPLOYERS:

Casey, Annie E., Foundation
1 Lafayette Place
Greenwich, CT 06830
(203) 661-2773

GTE Foundation
1 Stamford Forum
Stamford, CT 06904
(203) 965-3620

Xerox Foundation
P.O. Box 1600
800 Long Ridge Road
Stamford, CT 06904
(203) 968-3000

NEW JERSEY EMPLOYERS:

Exxon Education Foundation
P.O. Box 101
Florham Park, NJ 07932
(201) 765-3004

Johnson, Robert Wood, Foundation
P.O. Box 2316
Princeton, NJ 08543-2316
(609) 452-8701

Nabisco Foundation
Nabisco Brands Plaza
Parsippany, NJ 07054
(908) 682-7098

Prudential Foundation
15 Prudential Plaza
Newark, NJ 07101
(201) 802-7354

Government

For information about jobs in government and related fields, you can contact the following organizations:

PROFESSIONAL ORGANIZATIONS:

American Federation of Government Employees
80 F St., NW
Washington, DC 20001
(202) 737-8700

American Federation of State, County and Municipal Employees
1625 L St., NW
Washington, DC 20036
(202) 452-4800

American Society for Public Administration
1120 G St., NW
Washington, DC 20005
(202) 393-7878

Council of State Governments
P.O. Box 11910
3572 Iron Works Pike
Lexington, KY 40578
(606) 231-1939

Government Finance Officers Association of U.S. and Canada
180 N. Michigan Ave.
Chicago, IL 60601
(312) 977-9700

National Association of Government Employees
159 Thomas Burgin Parkway
Quincy, MA 02169
(617) 376-0220

PROFESSIONAL PUBLICATIONS:

AFSCME Leader
Bureaucrat
The Chief
Federal Times
Government Executive
Public Employee Newsletter
Public Management
Public Works Magazine

DIRECTORIES:

Braddock's Federal-State-Local Government Directory (Braddock
   Communications, Alexandria, VA)
City of New York Official Directory (Citybooks, New York, NY)
The Government Directory of Addresses and Telephone Numbers
   (Omnigraphics, Inc., Detroit, MI)
New York State Directory (Robert M. Walsh, San Mateo, CA)
New York RedBook (New York Legal Publishing Corporation,
   Guilderland, NY)

CITY GOVERNMENT EMPLOYERS:

City Government Phone Directory
(212) 788-4636

Borough President of Bronx
851 Grand Concourse
Bronx, NY 10451
(212) 590-3500
Personnel Director: Barbara Becker

Borough President of Brooklyn
209 Joralemon St.
Brooklyn, NY 11201
(718) 802-3700
Personnel Director: Barry Eagleston

Borough President of Manhattan
1 Center St., 19th Floor South
Municipal Building
New York, NY 10007
(212) 669-8300

Borough President of Queens
120-55 Queens Blvd.
Kew Gardens, NY 11424
(718) 520-3220

Borough President of Staten Island
Borough Hall Room 120
Staten Island, NY 10301
(718) 390-5105
Personnel Director: Irene McKinney

City Planning Department
2 Lafayette St.
New York, NY 10007
(212) 442-4660
Personnel Director: Donald Young

Civil Service Commission
1 Center St.
New York, NY 10007
(212) 669-2609
New York City Department of Personnel: Judith Levitt

Comptroller's Office
1 Centre St.
Municipal Building
New York, NY 10007
(212) 669-7318
Personnel Department: Roberta Rubin

Corporation Counsel
100 Church St.
New York, NY 10007
(212) 788-0303
Director of Personnel: Dawn Besthoff, (212) 788-0319

Fire Department
250 Livingston St.
Brooklyn, NY 11201
(718) 403-1403

Housing Preservation and Development
100 Gold St.
New York, NY 10038
(212) 978-6700

New York City Department of Investigation
80 Maiden Lane
New York, NY 10038
(212) 825-5900

New York City Department of Personnel
49 Thomas St.
New York, NY 10013
(212) 487-6501
All applications must be filled out and presented in person for all
civil service positions.

New York City Department of Personnel: Department of Social Services
250 Church St.
New York, NY 10013
(212) 274-5400

New York City Department of Personnel: Office of Management and Budget
75 Park Place
New York, NY 10007
(212) 788-5800

Parks and Recreation
16 W. 61 St.
New York, NY 10023
Personnel: (212) 830-7851

Police Department
1 Police Plaza
New York, NY 10038
(212) 374-5000

COUNTY GOVERNMENT EMPLOYERS:

Nassau County

Nassau County: Civil Service Commission
140 Old Country Road
Mineola, NY 11501
(516) 535-2511
Contact: Personnel, 140 Old Country Road, Mineola, NY 11501.

Nassau County: Commerce and Industry
1550 Franklin Ave., Room 139
Mineola, NY 11501
(516) 571-4159

Nassau County: County Clerk's Office
240 Old Country Road
Mineola, NY 11501
(516) 535-2663

Nassau County: Department of Health
240 Old Country Road, 5th Floor
Mineola, NY 11501
(516) 535-3410

Nassau County: Department of Labor
1550 Franklin Ave.
New York, NY 11501
(516) 535-3095

Nassau County: Department of Public Works
1 West St.
Mineola, NY 11501
(516) 571-4150

Nassau County: Division of Public Transportation
400 County Seat Road
Mineola, NY 11501
(516) 535-5836

Westchester County

Westchester County: Comptroller's Office
240 Old Country Road
Mineola, NY 11501
(516) 535-2679

Westchester County: County Clerk's Office
110 Grove St.
White Plains, NY 10604
(914) 285-3080

Westchester County: County Executive Office
148 Martine Ave., Building 1
White Plains, NY 10601
(914) 285-2900

Westchester County: District Attorney
111 Grove St.
White Plains, NY 10601
(914) 285-2000

Westchester County: Environmental Facilities
M.O.B. 148 Martine Ave., Room 400
White Plains, NY 10601
(914) 285-2450

Westchester County: Finance Department
720 Michaelian Office Building
White Plains, NY 10601
(914) 285-2756

Westchester County: Health Department
19 Bradhurst Ave.
Hawthorne, NY 10532
(914) 593-5100

Westchester County: Personnel Department
48 Martine Ave.
White Plains, NY 10601
Asst. Director of Employee Selection and Development: Susan
Welling
(914) 285-2103

STATE OF NEW YORK EMPLOYERS:

Attorney General
120 Broadway
New York, NY 10271
(212) 416-8000
Personnel Department: Nancy Kramer, Department of Law

Banking Department
2 Rector St.
New York, NY 10006
(212) 618-6445

Commerce Department
1515 Broadway
New York, NY 10036
(212) 827-6100

Controller
270 Broadway
New York, NY 10017
(212) 417-5003

Court Administration
270 Broadway
New York, NY 10007
(212) 417-5900
Personnel Director: Wayne McGrath

Economic Developement
1515 Broadway
New York, NY 10036
(212) 827-6100

Environmental Conservation
47-40 21st St.
Long Island City, NY 11101
(718) 482-4949

Insurance Department
150 W. Broadway
New York, NY 10013
(212) 602-0203

Labor Department
247 W. 54th St.
New York, NY 10019
(212) 265-2700

Metropolitan Transportation Department
347 Madison Ave.
New York, NY 10019
(212) 878-1000

Parks Recreation and Historic Preservation
New York City Regent Headquarters
915 Broadway
New York, NY 10011
(212) 387-0271

State Department
270 Broadway
New York, NY 10011
(212) 417-5800

Urban Development
151 Broadway
New York, NY 10036
(212) 930-9000

UNITED STATES GOVERNMENT EMPLOYERS:

To apply for a position with the federal government, you must appear
in person at the Office of Personnel Management, 26 Federal Plaza,
New York, NY 10278. Job listings are available at the plaza and the
application process is explained. To give you an idea of the kind of
departments in which you may find positions, we've listed some of
the larger government agencies that maintain offices in the metropolitan area.

Air Force, Department of Office of Public Affairs
133 E. 58th St.
New York, NY 10022
(212) 753-5609

Census Bureau
26 Federal Plaza, Room 37130
New York, NY 10278
(212) 264-3860

Commerce, Department of
26 Federal Plaza
New York, NY 10278
(212) 264-0634

Drug Enforcement Administration
99 10th Ave.
New York, NY
(212) 337-3900

Environmental Protection Agency
26 Federal Plaza
New York, NY 10278
(212) 264-2657

Federal Bureau of Investigation
26 Federal Plaza
New York, NY 10278
(212) 553-2700

Federal Communications Commission
201 Varick St.

New York, NY 10014
(212) 620-3438

Immigration and Naturalization
26 Federal Plaza
New York, NY 10278
(212) 206-6500
Personnel: Floyd Bennett Field, Brooklyn (718) 338-3844

Inspector General, Office of the
26 Federal Plaza
New York, NY 10278
(212) 264-7510

Interior, Department of
26 Federal Plaza
New York, NY 10278
(212) 264-2960

Internal Revenue Service
120 Church St.
New York, NY 10008
(212) 264-2190

Justice, Department of
United States Attorney
1 St. Andrews Plaza
New York, NY 10007
(212) 791-0008

Labor Department
Job Service
1 Main St.
Brooklyn, NY 11201
(718) 797-7933

Marine Corps
133 E. 58th St., Suite 1500
New York, NY 10022
(212) 755-7846

National Weather Service
30 Rockefeller Plaza
New York, NY 10020
(212) 315-2705

Peace Corps
90 Church St.
New York, NY 10007
(212) 264-6981

Personnel Management, Office of
Federal Job Information and Testing Center
26 Federal Plaza
New York, NY 10278
(212) 264-0422

Postal Service
Postmaster and Executive Offices
8th Ave. and 33rd St.
New York, NY 10199
(212) 330-3636

Secret Service
6 World Trade Center, Room 623
New York, NY 10048
(212) 466-4400

Securities and Exchange Commission
75 Park Place
New York, NY
(212) 264-8500(Personnel)

Treasury Department
Bureau of Alcohol, Tobacco and Firearms
6 World Trade Center
New York, NY 10048
(212) 264-2104

US Information Agency
666 5th Ave., 6th Floor
New York, NY 10103
(212) 399-5750

Veterans' Administration
Regional Office
252 7th Ave.
New York, NY 10001
(212) 620-6901

Voice of America Radio
26 Federal Plaza
New York, NY 10278
(212) 399-5954 United Nations Office
(212) 264-2345 New York Bureau

Health Care

For networking in health care and related fields, check out the following professional organizations listed in Chapter 5:

PROFESSIONAL ORGANIZATIONS:

Greater New York Hospital Association
National League for Nursing

For additional information, you can contact:

American Dental Association
211 E. Chicago Ave
Chicago, IL 60611
(312)440-2500

American Dental Hygienists Association
444 N. Michigan Ave., Suite 3400
Chicago IL, 60611
(312)440-8900

American Health Care Association
1201 L St., NW
Washington, DC 20005
(202)842-4444

American Hospital Association
840 N. Lake Shore Drive
Chicago, IL 60611
(312)280-6000

American Medical Association
515 N. State St.
Chicago, IL 60610
(312)464-5000

American Public Health Association
1015 15th St., NW
Washington, DC 20005
(202)789-5600

National Association of Social Workers
750 First St., NE
Washington, DC 20002
(201)408-8600

National Council of Community Mental Health Centers
1200 Twinbrook Pkwy.

Rockville, MD 20852
(301)984-6200

PROFESSIONAL PUBLICATIONS:

ADA News
AHA News
American Journal of Nursing
American Journal of Public Health
Contemporary Administration
HMO Practice
Hospital Practice
Hospital Purchasing News
Hospitals
JAMA (Journal of the American Medical Association)
Modern Healthcare
Nursing Outlook

DIRECTORIES:

Directory of Health Care Coalitions in the U.S. (American Hospital Association, Chicago, IL)
Directory of Hospitals (SMG Marketing Group, Chicago, IL)
Guide to the Health Care Field (American Hospital Association, Chicago, IL)
Saunders Health Care Directory (W.B. Saunders, Philadelphia, PA)

NEW YORK EMPLOYERS:

Aetna Health Plans
2700 Westchester Ave.
Purchase, NY 10577
(914) 251-0600

Bellevue Hospital Center
1st Ave. and 27th St.
New York, NY 10016
(212) 561-4141
Human Resources: Brenda Chapman
City hospital.

Beth Israel Medical Center
215 Park Ave. S.
New York, NY 10003
(212) 387-6900
Assistant Vice Pres. of Human Resources: Fred Graumann

Blythedale Children's Hospital
Bradhust Ave.

Valhalla, NY 10595
(914) 592-7555

Booth Memorial Medical Center
Main St. at Booth Memorial Ave.
Flushing, NY 11355
(718) 670-1231
Director of Personnnel: Linda Isaacs

Brooklyn Hospital Center
121 Dekalb Ave.
Brooklyn, NY 11201
(718) 403-8000

Bronx Children's Psychiatric Center
1000 Waters Place
New York, NY 10461
(212) 892-0808
Personnel Director: Jack Bellephine
City hospital.

Bronx Lebanon Hospital Center
1276 Fulton Ave.
New York, NY 10456
(212) 590-1800
Director of Personnel: Denise Corvino

Catholic Medical Center of Brooklyn and Queens
88-25 153rd St.
Jamaica, NY 11432
(718) 657-6800

Cigna Health Plan of New York
1010 Northern Blvd.
Great Neck, NY 11021
(516)466-1000

City Hospital Center at Elmhurst
79-01 Broadway, Elmurst Station
Flushing, NY 11373
(718) 334-4000
Personnel Director: Herman Smith, 40-20 76th St. office
City hospital.

Columbia Presbyterian Medical Center
622 W. 168th St
New York, NY 10032
(212) 305-2500

Flushing Hospital and Medical Center
4500 Parsons Blvd.
Flushing, NY 11355

(718) 670-5000
Director of Human Resources: Steven November

Health Insurance Plan of Greater New York
7 W. 34th St.
New York, NY 10001
(212) 630-5000

Hospital for Joint Diseases, Orthopedic Institute
1919 Madison Ave.
New York, NY 10035
(212) 423-4000
Personnel Director: Paul Puca

Hospital for Special Surgery
535 E. 70th St.
(212) 606-1000

Kaiser Foundation Health Plan of the Northeast
1103 Central Ave.
Scarsdale, NY 10583
(914) 472-8500

Kings County Hospital Center
451 Clarkson Ave.
Brooklyn, NY 11203
(718) 245-3131
City hospital.

Kingsboro Psychiatric Center
681 Clarkson Ave.
Brooklyn, NY 11203
(718) 245-3131
City hospital.

Lenox Hill Hospital
100 E. 77th St.
New York, NY 10021
(212) 439-2345

Lincoln Medical and Mental Health Center
234 E. 149th St.
Bronx, NY 10451
(212) 579-5000
City hospital.

Long Island Jewish Medical Center
New Hyde Park, NY 11042
(718) 470-7000
Nursing Recruiter: Jane Bailey

Manhattan Psychiatric Center
Ward's Island
600 E. 125th St.
New York, NY 10035
(212) 369-0500
City hospital.

Memorial Sloan-Kettering Cancer Center
1275 York Ave.
New York, NY
(212) 794-7722

Mercy Hospital
1000 N. Village Ave.
Rockville Centre, NY 11570
(516) 255-0111

MetLife Health Care Network
2929 Express Drive, N.
Hauppauge, NY 11787
(516)348-4280
HMO.

Metropolitan Hospital Center
1901 1st Ave.
New York, NY 10029
(212) 230-6262
City hospital.

Montefiore Hospital and Medical Center
111 E. 210th St.
Bronx, NY 10467
(212) 920-4321

Mt. Sinai Medical Center
100th St. at 5th Ave.
New York, NY 10029
(212) 241-6500

Mt. Vernon Hospital
12 N. 7th Ave.
Mt. Vernon, NY 10550
(914) 664-8000

Nassau County Medical Center
2201 Hempstead Turnpike
East Meadow, NY 11554
(516) 542-0123
Personnel Director: David Papalardo

New York Downtown Hospital
170 William St.

New York, NY 10038
(212) 312-5000

New York University Medical Center
550 1st Ave.
New York, NY 10016
(212) 263-5111
Nursing Recruiter

North Shore University Hospital
300 Community Drive
Manhasset, NY 11030
(516) 562-0100

Penninsula Hospital Center
51-15 Beach Channel Drive
Far Rockaway, NY 11691
(718) 945-7100

Phelps Memorial Hospital
North Broadway
N. Tarrytown, NY 10591
(914) 366-3000
Personnel Director: Judy Byrne

Roosevelt, Franklin Delano, Veteran's Administration Hospital
Albany Post Road
Montrose, NY 10548
(914) 737-4400
Personnel Director: Mel Hooker

St. Luke's Roosevelt Hospital Center
428 W. 59th St.
New York, NY 10019
(212) 523-4000

Careers in health care

"If you wish to work in the hospital field, it's important to pick a speciality and pursue it as early as possible," said Carl Martino, director of personnel at Booth Memorial Medical Center, when we asked him about the hospital industry. "Most hospital professions are very specialized and require a great deal of education. Many hospitals recruit right from high school or college if they operate training programs in allied health fields.

"Once you've been working for a while," adds Martino, "I would suggest to anyone, whether in the business or medical end of the hospital industry, that it's a good idea to join an association or society representing your occupation. The industry is known for its networking, and many associations have placement services. I rarely use an employment agency or place an ad in the paper to fill a position. Trade associations have been more helpful and more effective in filling any opening I might have. Also, for the job hunter, their services are confidential and fairly quick." ■

St. Vincent's Hospital and Medical Center of NY
153 W. 11th St.
New York, NY 10011
(212) 790-7000

St. Vincent's Medical Center of Richmond 355 Bard Ave.
Staten Island, NY 10310
(718) 876-1234
Personnel Director: James Duran

South Nassau Communities Hospital
2445 Oceanside Road
Oceanside, NY 11572
(516) 763-2030

State University Hospital, Downstate Medical Center
450 Clarkson Ave.
Brooklyn, NY 11203
(718) 270-2401
Personnel: Joan McCallum

Staten Island University Hospital
475 Seaview Ave.
Staten Island, NY 10305
(718) 226-9000

United Hospital Medical Center
406 Boston Post Road
Port Chester, NY 10573
(914) 939-7000

Veterans' Administration Medical Center
130 W. Kingsbridge Road
Bronx, NY 10408
(212) 584-9000
Personnel Officer: Dan Bisgrove
Federal hospital.

Veterans' Administration Medical Center
423 23rd St.
New York, NY 10010
(212) 686-7500
Federal hospital.

Veterans' Administration Medical Center
79 Middleville Road
Northport, NY 11768
(516) 261-4400
Personnel Director: Donna J. Cardillo
Federal hospital.

Visiting Nursing Service of New York
350 5th Ave.
New York, NY 10118
(212) 560-3370
Contact: Recruitment and Staffing Department

Westchester County Medical Center
Rt. 100
Valhalla, NY 10595
(914) 285-7000

White Plains Hospital Center
Davis Ave. at East Post Road
White Plains, NY 10601
(914) 681-0600

CONNECTICUT EMPLOYERS:

Greenwich Hospital
5 Perryridge Road
Greenwich, CT 06830
(203) 863-3000

Hall-Brooke Hospital
Long Lots Road
Westport, CT 06880
(203) 227-1251

Mt. Sinai Hospital
500 Blue Hills Ave.
Hartford, CT 06112
(203) 242-4431

Norwalk Hospital Association
Maple Ave.
Norwalk, CT 06850
(203) 852-2000

Oxford Health Plans
320 Post Road
Darien, CT 06820
(203) 656-1442
Human Resources Director: Jeanne Wisniewski
Major health maintenance organization.

St. Joseph Medical Center
128 Strawberry Hill Ave.
Stamford, CT 06904
(203) 353-2000

Stamford Hospital
Shelburne Road and W. Broad St.
Stamford, CT 06904
(203) 325-7000

NEW JERSEY EMPLOYERS:

Columbus Hospital
495 N. 13th St.
Newark, NJ 07107
(201) 268-1400

Hackensack Community Medical Center
30 Prospect Ave.
Hackensack, NJ 07601
(201) 288-0800

HMO Blue
3 Penn Plaza, E.
Newark, NJ 07105
(201)466-4000

Meadowlands Hospital Medical Center
Meadowland Parkway
Secaucus, NJ 07096
(201) 392-3100

Medical Center at Princeton
253 Witherspoon St.
Princeton, NJ 08540
(609) 497-4000

Newark Beth Israel Medical Center
201 Lyons Ave.
Newark, NJ 07112
(201) 926-7000

Hospitality: Hotels and Restaurants

For networking in the hospitality industry and related fields, check out the following professional organization listed in Chapter 5:

PROFESSIONAL ORGANIZATIONS:

Hotel Credit Managers Association

For more information, you can contact:

American Hotel and Motel Association
1201 New York Ave., NW, Suite 600
Washington, DC 20005
(202)789-3100

Chefs de Cuisine Association of America
830 8th Ave.
New York, NY 10019
(212) 262-0404

Hospitality Industry Foundation of New York
505 8th Ave.
New York, NY 10001
(212)714-1330

Hotel Sales & Marketing Association International
1300 L St., NW, Suite 800
Washington, DC 20005
(202)789-0089

International Association of Convention and Visitor Bureaus
P.O. Box 758
Champaign, IL 61824-0758
(217) 359-8881

International Special Events Society
46 Turner St.
Boston, MA 02135
(617) 254-2557

National Restaurant Association
1200 17th St., NW
Washington D.C. 20036
(202) 331-5900

New York Hotel and Motels Trade Council
708 8th Ave.

New York, NY 10036
(212) 245-8100

New York State Hospitality and Tourism Association
508 8th Ave.
New York, NY 10018
(212) 564-2300

New York State Restaurant Association
505 8th Ave.
New York, NY 10018
(212) 714-1330

PROFESSIONAL PUBLICATIONS:

Club Management
Hotel and Motel Management
Hotel and Resort Industry
Meetings and Conventions
Nation's Restaurant News
Restaurant Business
Restaurant Hospitality
Restaurants & Institutions
Successful Meetings

DIRECTORIES:

Directory of Hotel and Motel Systems (American Hotel Association
    Directory Corp., New York, NY and Motel Association,
    Washingtion, DC)
Hotel and Motel Redbook (American Hotel and Motel Association,
    Washington, DC)
Meetings and Conventions Magazine, Directory issue (Murdoch
    Magazines, New York, NY)
Restaurant Hospitality–Hospitality 500 Issue (Penton/IPC, Inc.,
    Columbus, OH)
Restaurants and Institutions–Annual 400 Issue
 (Cahners Publishing Co., Des Plaines, IL)

HOTEL EMPLOYERS:

Carlyle Hotel
35 E. 76th St.
New York, NY 10021
(212) 744-1600
General Manager: Dan Camp

Essex House
160 Central Park South
New York, NY 10019

(212) 247-0300
Personnel Director: Ida Alexandrino

Four Seasons Hotels
New York Regional Office
505 Park Ave., 17th Floor
New York, NY 10022
(212) 980-0101

Harley Hotel
212 E. 42nd St.
New York, NY 10017
(212) 490-8900
General Manager: Rafael Juan

Helmsley Palace
455 Madison Ave. (at 50th St.)
New York, NY 10022
(212) 888-1624-reservations desk, ask for information

Helmsley/Parklane Hotel
36 Central Park South
New York, NY 10019
(212) 888-1624

Hotel Intercontinental, NY
111 E. 48th St.
New York, NY 10017
(212) 755-5900

Hyatt Hotels
675 3rd Ave.
New York, NY 10174
(212) 490-6464

Loews Hotels Holding Corp.
1 Park Ave.
New York, NY 10016-5801
(212) 545-3000

Marriott Eastside
525 Lexington Ave.
New York, NY 10017
(212) 755-4000
Also Marriott Marquis (212) 398-1900. Marriott at World Financial Center (212) 385-4900.

New York Hilton Hotel
1335 Avenue of the Americas
New York, NY 10019
(212) 586-7000

Omni Berkshire Hotel
21 E. 52nd St.
New York, NY 10022
(212) 753-5800
Personnel Director: Chuck Wing

Omni Park Central Hotel
870 7th Ave.
New York, NY 10019
(212) 247-8000
Personnel Director: Patty Michuad

Pierre Hotel
A Four Seasons hotel
5th Ave. at 61st St.
New York, NY 10021
(212) 838-8000

Plaza Hotel
5th Ave. at 59th St.
New York, NY 10019
(212) 759-3000

Hotel management: more than puttin' on the Ritz

With a little more than two years' experience in the hotel business, our friend Kirk landed a job as sales manager for a Midtown hotel. We asked him for an overview of the hospitality industry. "If you want to move up quickly," says Kirk, "this industry is the place to be. It's anything but a dead-end business. Some people stay with the same organization for most of their careers. But I'd say the average is probably around five years with any given company. People are constantly calling and making job offers.

"I studied hotel management and general business. But you can't just walk out of college and into a middle-management position. I started as a receptionist at the Plaza. Then I became a secretary. I don't know anyone who hasn't paid dues for a year or two. If you're interested in food or beverages, you might start out as a dining room assistant. Essentially, you'd be doing the same thing as a secretary—typing up contracts or menus, that sort of thing. You really have to learn the business from the bottom up.

"In sales you move from secretarial work to a full-fledged sales position. I was a sales representative, then was promoted to sales manager. The next step might logically be director of sales or marketing, where I'd be responsible for advertising and marketing strategies, developing budgets, and so on. An equivalent position would be director of food and beverages, the person who's responsible for all the food and drink served in the hotel, room service, all the dining rooms, special banquets, everything. After director of sales or food and beverages, you go on to general manager.

"I'd say the competition is about average—not nearly as fierce as the advertising industry, for example. Earning potential is pretty good, too, depending, of course, on the size of the hotel and the city you're in and what kind of company you're working for. You start out pretty low, maybe around $20,000 or $21,000 a year. But each time you move up, you get a hefty raise, or ought to." ■

St. Moritz
50 Central Park South
New York, NY 10019
(212) 755-5800

St. Regis–Sheraton
Two 5th Ave.
New York, NY 10022
(212) 753-4500
Manager: Rick Segal

Trump Park Plaza Hotel
106 Central Park South
New York, NY 10019
(212) 247-7000

Waldorf Astoria
Subsidiary of Hilton Hotels
301 Park Ave.
New York, NY 10022
(212) 355-3000

WESTCHESTER HOTELS:

Doral Arrowwood Conference Center
Anderson Hill Road
Rye Brook, NY 10573
(914) 939-5500

Hilton Inn, Tarrytown
455 South Broadway
Tarrytown, NY 10591
(914) 631-5700

Holiday Inn Crowne Plaza
66 Hale Ave.
White Plains, NY 10601
(914) 682-0050

Stouffer Westchester Hotel
80 W. Red Oak Lane
White Plains, NY 10604
(914) 694-5400

Westchester Marriott
670 White Plains Road
Tarrytown, NY 10591
(914) 631-2200

CONNECTICUT HOTELS:

Ethan Allen Inn
21 Lake Avenue Extension
Danbury, CT 06811
(203) 744-1776

Hilton, Danbury
18 Old Ridgebury Road
Danbury, CT 06810
(203) 794-0600

Marriot, Trumball
180 Hawley Lane
Trumball, CT 08611
(203) 378-1400

Ramada Inn
Exit 8, Interstate 84
Danbury, CT 06810
(203) 792-3800

Sheraton Stamford Hotel & Towers
One First Stamford Place
Stamford, CT 06902
(203) 967-2222

Tara Stamford Hotel
2701 Summer St.
Stamford, CT 06905
(203) 359-1300

NEW JERSEY HOTELS:

Hilton at Short Hills
41 John F. Kennedy Parkway

Short Hills, NJ 07078
(201) 379-0100

Loews Glenpointe Hotel
100 Frank W. Burr Blvd.
Teaneck, NJ 07666
(201) 288-6100

Marriott–Park Ridge
300 Brae Blvd.
Park Ridge, NJ 07656
(201) 307-0800

Sheraton Hasbrouck Heights
650 Terrace Ave.
Hasbrouck Heights, NJ 07604
(201) 288-6100

Sheraton Tara
199 Soneth Road
Parsippany, NJ 07054
(201) 515-2000

RESTAURANTS

There are thousands of restaurants in the New York metropolitan area. We have chosen the cream of the crop. You will find here restaurants rated three and four stars by major restaurant critics, restaurant chains, and some of the most famous of New York's eateries.

Bouley
165 Duane St.
New York, NY 10014
(212) 608-3852

Captain's Table
46th and 2nd Ave
New York, NY 10017
(212) 697-9538

Coach House, The
110 Waverly Place
New York, NY 10011
(212) 777-0303

Elaine's
1703 2nd Ave.
New York, NY 10128
(212) 534-8114

Four Seasons, The
99 E. 52nd St.
New York, NY 10022
(212) 754-9494

Helmsley Enterprises
60 E. 42nd St.
New York, NY 10165
(212) 687-6400
Lodging, restaurant, and food service.

Il Nido
251 E. 53rd St.
New York, NY 10022
(212) 753-8450

Kentucky Fried Chicken
District Headquarters
1 Lefrak Plaza
Flushing, NY 11368
(718) 760-5000

La Grenouille
3 E. 52nd St.
New York, NY 10022
(212) 752-1495

Le Bernardin
155 W. 51st St.
New York, NY 10019
(212) 489-1515

Le Cirque
58 E. 65th St.
New York, NY 10021
(212) 794-9292

Le Cygne
53 E. 54th St.
New York, NY 10022
(212) 759-5941

Lutece
249 E. 50th St.
New York, NY 10022
(212) 752-2225

McDonald's Corp.
Regional Headquarters
One Crossroads Drive, Building A
Bedminster, NJ 07921

(908) 658-4100
V.P., Regional Manager: Annis Alston

Nathan's Famous
1400 Old Country Road
Westbury, NY 11590
(516) 338-8500
Director of Personnel and Training: Karen Brown

National Restaurant Management
162 W. 34th St.
New York, NY 10001
(212) 563-7440
Manages 200 restuarants within metropolitan New York area.

Rainbow Room
30 Rockefeller Plaza
New York, NY 10020
(212) 632-5100

Restaurants Associates Industries
120 W. 45th St.
New York, NY 10036
(212) 789-8100
Restaurants and catering.

Russian Tea Room
150 W. 57th St.
New York, NY 10019
(212) 265-0947

Sardi's
234 W. 44th St.
New York, NY 10036
(212) 221-8440

Tavern On The Green
Central Park West at 67th St.
New York, NY 10023
(212) 873-3200

"21" Club
21 W. 52nd St.
New York, NY 10019
(212) 582-7200

Union Square Cafe
21 E. 16th St.
New York, NY 10011
(212) 243-4020

Windows On The World
One World Trade Center
New York, NY 10048
(212) 938-1111

Human Services

For networking in human services and related fields, check out the following professional organizations listed in Chapter 5. Also see **"Foundations"** and **"Health Care."**

PROFESSIONAL ORGANIZATIONS:

Human Resource Planning Society
National League for Nursing

For more information, you can contact:

National Assoc. of Social Workers
750 1st St., NE
Washington, DC 20002
(202)408-8600

National Federation of Societies for Clinical Social Work
c/o Sidney H. Grossberg
P.O. Box 3740
Arlington, VA 22203
(703)522-3866

Volunteers of America
3813 N. Causeway Blvd.
Metairie, LA 70002
(504)836-5225

PROFESSIONAL PUBLICATIONS:

Children and Youth Services Review
The Nonprofit Times
Society

DIRECTORIES:

Directory of Agencies (National Association of Social Workers, Washington,DC)
Hotline: Crisis Intervention Directory (Facts on File, New York, NY)
National Directory of Children and Youth Services (Marion Peterson Longmont, CO)

How to Get a Job

National Directory of Private Social Agencies (Croner Publications, Queens Village, NY)

EMPLOYERS:

American Bible Society
1865 Broadway
New York, NY 10023
(212) 581-7400
Personnel: Catherine Contessa

American Cancer Society
19 W. 56th St.
New York, NY 10019
(212) 586-8700

American Red Cross
106 N. Broadway
White Plains, NY 10603
(914) 946-6500
Personnel Director: Ann Miller
New York Office (212) 787-1000

American Society for the Prevention of Cruelty to Animals
424 E. 92nd St.
New York, NY 10128
(212) 876-7700
Personnel Director: Brigitte O'Carroll

Association for the Help of Retarded Children
200 Park Ave. S.
New York, NY 10003
(212) 254-8203

Big Brothers, Big Sisters
223 E. 30th St.
New York, NY 10016
(212) 686-2042

Boy Scouts of America
345 Hudson St.
New York, NY 10014
(212) 242-1100
Personnel Director: Violet Schwictenberg

Cancer Care, Inc., and the American Cancer Foundation
1180 Avenue of the Americas
New York, NY 10036
(212) 221-3300
Personnel Director: Loretta Dunn

Girl Scout Council of Greater New York
43 W. 23rd St.
New York, NY 10010
(212) 645-4000

Girl Scouts of the USA
420 5th Ave.
New York, NY 10016
(212) 852-8000

Girls, Inc.
30 E. 33rd St., 7th Floor
New York, NY 10016
(212) 689-3700
Personnel Director: Winifred Zubin

Jewish Child Care Association
575 Lexington Ave.
New York, NY 10022
(212) 371-1313
Personnel Director: Sandy Shapiro

Jewish Community Center Association
15 E. 26th St.
New York, NY 10010
(212) 532-4949
Assistant Director of Personnel Services: Bessie Pine

Lighthouse Industries
36-20 Northern Blvd.
Long Island City, NY 11101
(718) 937-9338
Personnel Director: Zabel Stein
There is also an office in Manhattan: (212) 808-0077.

National Council on Alcoholism
National Headquarters
12 W. 21st St.
New York, NY 10010
(212) 206-6770

National Urban League
500 E. 62nd St.
New York, NY 10021
(212) 310-9000

Planned Parenthood Federation of America
810 7th Ave.
New York, NY 10019
(212) 541-7800
Personnel Director: Larry Beers

Police Athletic League
34 1/2 E. 12th St.
New York, NY 10003
(212) 477-9450 Ext. 310
Recreational and educational programs for disadvantaged children.

Salvation Army, The
132 W. 14th St.
New York, NY 10011
(212) 807-6100
Personnel Director: Susan Tow

United Cerebral Palsy Association
330 W. 34th St.
New York, NY 10001
(212) 947-5770
Personnel Coordinator: Joy Gasper

United Cerebal Palsy Association
King St.
Purchase, NY 10577
(914) 937-3800

United Way-Greater New York Fund
99 Park Ave.
New York, NY 10016
(212) 973-3800

United Way of Westchester and Putnam
336 Central Ave.
White Plains, NY 10606
(914) 997-6700

Westchester Association for Retarded Citizens
39 Westmoreland Ave.
White Plains, NY 10606
(914) 681-0650

Young Adult Institute
460 W. 34 St.
New York, NY 10001
(212) 563-7474

Young Men's Christian Association
333 7th Ave., 15th Floor
New York, NY 10001
(212) 630-9600
Personnel: Lauri Dorf

Young Women's Christian Association
610 Lexington Ave.

New York, NY 10022
(212) 755-4500

Insurance

For networking in insurance and related fields, check out the following professional organizations listed in Chapter 5:

PROFESSIONAL ORGANIZATIONS:

American Insurance Association
Insurance Information Institute
Insurance Society of New York

For more information, you can contact:

American Council of Life Insurance
1001 Pennsylvania Ave., NW
Washington, DC 20004
(202) 624-2000

American Insurance Association
1130 Connecticut Ave., NW
Washington, DC 20036
(202) 828-7100

National Association of Independent Insurers
2600 River Road
Des Plaines, IL 60018
(708) 297-7800

National Association of Life Underwriters
1922 F St., NW
Washington, DC 20006
(202) 331-6000

Society of Certified Insurance Counselors
P.O. Box 27027
Austin, TX 78755
(512) 345-7932

PROFESSIONAL PUBLICATIONS:

Best's Review
Business Insurance
Independent Agent
Insurance Advocate
National Underwriter

DIRECTORIES:

Best's Directory of Recommended Insurance Adjusters (A. M. Best Co., Oldwick, NJ)
Insurance Almanac (Underwriter Publishing Co., Englewood, NJ)
Kirschner's Insurance Directory (Kirschner's Publishing Co., Santa Cruz, CA)
New York Insurance Brokers Directory (American Underwriter, Media, PA)

NEW YORK EMPLOYERS:

Aetna Insurance
2 World Trade Center
New York, NY 10048
(212) 912-3200
Director of Human Resources: Warnie Bishop
Life, property, and casualty insurance.

Alexander and Alexander of New York
1185 Avenue of the Americas
New York, NY 10036
(212) 575-8000

Allstate Life and Reinsurance
1 Allstate Drive
Farmingdale, NY 11738
(516) 451-5000
Property, casualty insurance.

American International Group - AIG
70 Pine St.
New York, NY 10270
(212) 770-7000
Property and casualty insurance.

Atlantic Mutual Companies
45 Wall St.
New York, NY 10005
(212) 943-1800
Personnel office at 195 Broadway, NY 10007.
Employment Representative: Maryann Choynow

Commercial Union Insurance Company
77 Water St.
New York, NY 10005
(212) 440-6500
Personnel: Eleanor McCaffrey
Property and casualty insurance.

Continental Insurance Companies
180 Maiden Lane

New York, NY 10038
(212) 440-3000
Personnel Director: Barbara Burkpile
Property and casualty insurance.

Crum and Forster Managers Corporation
Subsidiary of Xerox Corporation
110 William St.
New York, NY 10038
(212) 306-4985
Personnel Manager: Jack McBride
Property and casualty insurance.

Empire Blue Cross/Blue Shield of Greater New York
622 3rd Ave.
New York, NY 10017
(212) 476-1000
Non-profit health care plan serving 5 boroughs and 12 surrounding counties.

The Equitable
787 7th Ave.
New York, NY 10019
(212) 554-1234
Director of Human Resources: David Caufield
Life insurance.

Fireman's Fund Insurance Company
1 Liberty Plaza
New York, NY 10006
(212) 962-6800
Human Resources Manager: Linda Scott

General Accident Insurance Company
One Seaport Plaza
P.O. Box 2320
New York, NY 10272-2320
(212) 635-0300
Property and casualty insurance.

General Reinsurance
160 Water St.
New York, NY 10038
(212) 770-0100

Government Employees Insurance Co. (GEICO)
750 Woodbury Road
Woodbury, NY 11797
(516) 496-5000
Manager Human Resources: John Thorne

Guardian Life Insurance Company of America
201 Park Ave. S.
New York, NY 10003
(212) 598-8000
Second Vice Pres. Human Resources: Kenneth Klein

Insurance Services Offices
7 World Trade Center
New York, NY 10048
(212) 898-6000
Carries insurance for insurance companies nationwide.

Johnson and Higgins
125 Broad St.
New York, NY 10004
(212) 574-7000
Human Resources Department Manager: Debbie Yanyo

Kemper Group
2 World Trade Center
New York, NY 10048
(212) 313-4281
Human Resources Manager: Helene Schwartz

Liberty Mutual Insurance Company
10 Rockefeller Plaza
New York, NY 10020
(212) 489-8500
Director of Personnel: Georgette Pripodi
Life, property, and casualty insurance.

Loew's Corporation
667 Madison Ave.
New York, NY 10021-8087
(212) 545-2000
Insurance, financial services, entertainment, lodging services, other.

Manhattan Life Insurance Co.
111 W. 57th St.
New York, NY 10019
(212) 484-9300

Marsh and McLennan
1166 Avenue of the Americas
New York, NY 10019
(212) 345-5000
Personnel Director: Ariel Boverman
Major insurance brokerage firm.

Metropolitan Life Insurance
1 Madison Ave., Area 1 MVW

New York, NY 10010
(212) 578-2211
Life, property, and casualty insurance.

Mutual of America
666 5th Ave.
New York, NY 10103
(212) 399-1600
Life insurance.

Mutual Life Insurance Company of New York
1740 Broadway
New York, NY 10019
(212) 708-2000
Manager Human Resources: Wes Masters
Life insurance.

New York Life
51 Madison Ave.
New York, NY 10010
(212) 576-7000
Life insurance.

Rollins Hudig Hall Co.
549 Pleasantville Road
Briarcliff Manor, NY 10516
(914) 769-9200
605 3rd Ave.
New York, NY 10158
(212) 973-6200
Human Resources in Chicago:
123 N. Wacker Drive
Chicago, IL 60606
(312)701-4000

Sedgwick, James, Inc.
1285 Avenue of the Americas
New York, NY 10019
(212) 333-8900
International insurance broker.

Teacher's Insurance and Annuity Associates of America
730 3rd Ave.
New York, NY 10017
(212) 490-9000
Life insurance and insurance funds.

Transamerica Insurance Group
40 Fulton St.
New York, NY 10038
(212) 602-6400
Property and casualty insurance.

Traveler's Insurance Companies
80 John St.
New York, NY 10038
(212) 574-2000
Human Resources office in Hartford, CT, office: (203) 277-0111
Property and casualty insurance.

Wausau Insurance Companies
1177 Avenue of the Americas
New York, NY 10019
(212) 489-7500
Personnel Director: Robert Jackson
Property and casualty insurance.

Willis Corroon
Wall Street Plaza
New York, NY 10005
(212) 363-4100

CONNECTICUT EMPLOYERS:

Aetna Life and Casualty
151 Farmington
Hartford, CT 06156
(203) 273-0123

Berkey, W. R., Corporation
165 Mason St. P.O. Box 2518
Greenwich, CT 06836
(203) 629-2880

Connecticut General Life (Cigna)
900 Cottage Grove Road
Bloomfield, CT 06002
(203) 726-6000

General Reinsurance
P.O. Box 10351
Stamford, CT 06904
(203) 328-5000

General Signal
P.O. Box 10010
Stamford, CT 06904
(203) 328-5000

National Reinsurance Corporation
777 Long Ridge Road
Stamford, CT 06902
(203) 329-7700

Phoenix Mutual Life Insurance
100 Bright Meadow Blvd.
Enfield, CT 06082
(203) 253-1000

Travelers, The
1 Tower Square
Hartford, CT 06183
(203) 277-0111

NEW JERSEY EMPLOYERS:

Chubb Group
15 Mountainview Road
Warren, NJ 07060
(908) 580-2000

Home Life Insurance
268 Green Village Road
Green Village, NJ 07935
(201) 377-9135
Property and casualty insurance.

Mutual Benefit Life
520 Broad St.
Newark, NJ 07101
(201) 481-8000

Prudential of America
751 Broad St.
Newark, NJ 07102
(201) 877-6000

Law Firms

For networking in law and related fields, check out the following professional organizations listed in Chapter 5:

PROFESSIONAL ORGANIZATIONS:

National Conference of Black Lawyers
National Lawyers Guild
New York County Lawyers Association

For more information, you can contact:

American Bar Association
750 N. Lake Shore Drive
Chicago, IL 60611
(312) 988-5000

Association of Trial Lawyers of America
1050 31st St., NW
Washington, DC 20007
(202)965-3500

National Bar Association (Minority Lawyers)
1225 11th St., NW
Washington, DC 20001
(202) 842-3900

National Paralegal Association
P.O. Box 406
Solebury, PA 18963
(215) 297-8333

New York State Trial Lawyers Association
132 Nassau St.
New York, NY 10038
(212) 319-5890

PROFESSIONAL PUBLICATIONS:

ABA Journal
American Lawyer
Banking Law Journal
Criminal Law Bulletin
For the Defense
Law Enforcement Technology
The Paralegal
Trial

DIRECTORIES:

ABA Directory (American Bar Association, Chicago, IL)
Directory of Local Paralegal Clubs (National Paralegal Assoc., Solebury, PA)
Martindale-Hubbell Law Directory (Martindale-Hubbell, Summit, NJ)
1993 Employer Directory (National Association for Law Placement, Washington, DC)

NEW YORK EMPLOYERS:

Breed, Abbott & Morgan
Citicorp Center
153 E. 53rd St.
New York, NY 10022
(212) 888-0800
Recruiting Director: Francesca Runge

Brown & Wood
1 World Trade Center
New York, NY 10048
(212) 839-5300
Hiring Coordinator: Tina Ogawa

Cahill Gordon & Reindel
80 Pine St.
New York, NY 10005
(212) 701-3000
Recruiting Director: Margaret Saling

Chadbourne & Park
30 Rockefeller Plaza
New York, NY 10112
(212) 408-5100

Cleary, Gottlieb, Steen and Hamilton
1 Liberty Plaza
New York, NY 10006
(212) 225-2000
Recruiting Director: Norma Cirincione

Coudert Brothers
1114 Avenue of the Americas
New York, NY 10036-7794
(212) 626-4400
Recruiting Coordinator: Lisa Kim

Cravath, Swaine & Moore
World Wide Plaza
825 8th Ave.
New York, NY 10019

(212) 474-1000
Recruiting Director: Lorraine Winheim

Curtis, Mallet-Prevost, Colt and Mosle
101 Park Ave.
New York, NY 10178
(212) 696-6000
Recruiting Director: Bernadette Miles

Davis Polk and Wardwell
450 Lexington Ave.
New York, NY 10017
(212) 450-4000
Recruiting Director: Bonnie Hurry

Debevoise and Plimpton
875 3rd Ave.
New York, NY 10022
(212) 909-6000
Recruiting Director: Ethel Leichti

Dewey, Ballantine, Bushby, Palmer and Wood
1301 Sixth Ave.
New York, NY 10019
(212) 259-8000
Recruiting Director: Kathleen Fredrickson

Donovon Leisure Newton and Irvine
30 Rockefeller Plaza
New York, NY 10112
(212) 632-3000
Recruiting Coordinator: Patricia Galvin

Fried, Frank, Harris, Shriver and Jacobson
1 New York Plaza
New York, NY 10004
(212) 820-8000
Recruiting Director: Donna Hurry

Haight, Gardner, Poor and Havens
195 Broadway
New York, NY 10007
(212) 341-7000
Recruiting Coordinator: Elise Rippe

Kaye, Scholer, Fierman, Hays and Handler
425 Park Ave.
New York, NY 10022
(212) 836-8000

Kelley, Drye and Warren
101 Park Ave.

New York, NY 10178
(212) 808-7800
Recruiting Coordinator: Libby Black

LeBoeuf, Lamb, Lieby, McRae
125 W. 55th St.
New York, NY 10019
(212) 424-8000
Personnel Director: Jennifer Tarlow

Millbank, Tweed, Hadley and McCloy
1 Chase Manhattan Plaza
New York, NY 10005
(212) 530-5000
Recruiting: Christine Kendall

Mudge Rose Guthrie Alexander & Ferdon
180 Maiden Lane
New York, NY 10038
(212) 510-7000
Recruiting Director: Ann Brenner

Parker Chapin Flattau and Klimpl
1211 Avenue of the Americas
New York, NY 10036
(212) 704-6000
Personnel Director: Jenifer Peters

Patterson, Belknap, Webb and Tyler
30 Rockefeller Plaza
New York, NY 10112
(212) 698-2500
Recruiting Coordinator: Robin Klum

Paul, Weiss, Rifkind, Wharton and Garrison
1285 Sixth Ave.
New York, NY 10019
(212) 373-3000
Recruiting Coordinator: Robin Edwards

Proskauer Rose Goetez and Mendelsohn
1585 Broadway
New York, NY 10036
(212) 969-3000
Personnel Director: Lesley Palmer

Rogers and Wells
200 Park Ave.
New York, NY 10166
(212) 878-8000
Recruiting Coordinator: Lisa Colby

Shearman and Sterling
599 Lexington Ave.
New York, NY 10022
(212) 848-4000
Recruiting Coordinator: Holly Schargel

Simpson Thacher and Bartlett
425 Lexington Ave.
New York, NY 10017
(212) 455-2000
Recruiting Director: Dee Pifer

Skadden, Arps, Slate, Meagher and Fiom
919 3rd Ave.
New York, NY 10022
(212) 371-6000
Recruiting Director: Carol Sprague

Stroock and Stroock and Lavan
7 Hanover Square
New York, NY 10004
(212) 806-5400
Recruiting Director: Jane Rothschild

Sullivan and Cromwell
125 Broad St.
New York, NY 10004
(212) 558-4000
Recruiting Director: Marie Alkiewicz

Weil, Gotshal and Manges
767 5th Ave.
New York, NY 10153
(212) 310-8000
Recruiting Administrator: Donna Lang

White and Case
1155 Avenue of the Americas
New York, NY 10036
(212) 819-8200
Controller: Richard Piotrowicz

Wilkie Farr and Gallagher
1 Citicorp Center
53 E. 53rd St.
New York, NY 10022
(212) 935-8000
Recruiting Director: Billy A. Levine

Wilson, Else, Moskowitz, Edelman and Dicker
150 E. 42nd St.
New York, NY 10017

(212) 490-3000
Hiring Committee

CONNECTICUT EMPLOYERS

Cummings & Lockwood
Ten Stamford Forum, P.O. Box 120
Stamford, CT 06904
(203) 327-1700

Pullman & Comley
850 Main St., P.O. Box 7006
Bridgeport, CT 06601-7006
(203) 330-2000

Whitman & Ransom
2 Greenwich Plaza
Greenwich, CT 06830
(203) 869-3800

NEW JERSEY EMPLOYERS

Connell, Foley & Geiser
85 Livingston Ave.
Roseland, NJ 07068
(201) 535-0500

Hannoch Weisman
4 Becker Farm Road
Roseland, NJ 07068-3788
(201) 535-5300

Lowenstein, Sandler, Kohl, Fisher & Boylan
65 Livingston Ave.
Roseland, NJ 07068
(201) 992-8700

Management Consultants

For networking in management consulting and related fields, check out the following professional organizations listed in Chapter 5:

PROFESSIONAL ORGANIZATIONS:

American Management Association
Association of Management Consulting Firms (ACME)
Institute of Management Consultants

For more information, you can contact:

Institute of Management Consultants
230 Park Ave.
New York, NY 10169
(212) 697-8262

National Management Association
2210 Arbor Blvd.
Dayton, OH 45439
(513) 294-0421

Society of Professional Consultants
95 Sawyer Road
Waltham, MA 02154
(617) 894-2547

PROFESSIONAL PUBLICATIONS:

ACME Newsletter
Academy of Management Journal
Academy of Management Review
Administrative Management
Business Quarterly
Consultant News
Executive
Harvard Business Review
Management Accounting

DIRECTORIES:

ACME Directory (Association of Management Consultants, New York, NY)
Bradford's Directory of Management Consultants (Bradford Publications, Fairfax, VA)
Consultants and Consulting Organizations (Gale Research, Detroit, MI)

Directory of Management Consultants (Kennedy & Kennedy, Fitzwilliam, NH)
Dun's Consultants Directory (Dun and Bradstreet Corp., Parsippany, NJ)
IMC Directory (Institute of Management Consultants, New York, NY)

EMPLOYERS:

Actmedia, Inc.
301 Merritt 7, P.O. Box 5102
Norwalk, CT 06856
(203) 845-6000
Sr. Vice Pres.,Human Resources: Linden Smith

Andersen Consulting
1345 Avenue of the Americas
New York, NY 10105
(212) 708-4000
Managing Partner: George T. Shaheen

Atkins, Frederick, Inc.
1515 Broadway
New York, NY 10036
(212) 840-7000
Vice Pres., Human Resources: Patricia McNamara

Booz Allen & Hamilton
101 Park Ave.
New York, NY 10178
(212) 697-1900
Manager Human Resources: Jeffrey Hull

Carey, W.P., & Co
620 Fifth Ave.
New York, NY 10020
(212) 492-1100
Manager, Personnel: Sheila Murphy

Communispond, Inc.
485 Lexington Ave.
New York, NY 10017-2630
(212) 687-8040

Ebasco Services
Two World Trade Center
New York, NY 10048
(212) 839-1000
Vice Pres., Human Resources: James L. Lipari

Forest and Sullivan
106 Fulton St.

New York, NY 10038
(212) 233-1080

Gartner Group
56 Top Gallant Road, P.O. Box 10212
Stamford, CT 06904-2212
(203) 964-0096
Administrator, Human Resources: Eve Cartwright

Hall, Frank B., & Co.
261 Madison Ave.
New York, NY 10016
(212) 922-1300
Asst. Vice Pres., Human Resources: Jane Meyer

Johnson & Higgins
125 Broad St.
New York, NY 10004-2424
(212) 574-7000
Manager, Corporate Recruitment: Margaret Howes

McKinsey and Company
55 E. 52nd St.
New York, NY 10022
(212) 446-7000
Personnel Director: Jerome Vascellaro

Mercer Consulting Group
1166 Avenue of the Americas
New York, NY 10036-2708
(212) 345-7000
Director, Human Resources: Harold Gudenberg

Nielsen-Wurster Group
1060 Route 206
Princeton, NJ 08540-1423
(609) 497-7300

NYNEX Worldwide Services Group
4 W. Red Oaks Lane
White Plains, NY 10604-3603
(914)644-7800

Stone & Webster
One Penn Plaza
250 W. 34th St.
New York, NY 10119
(212) 290-7500
Personnel Manager: Jennie David

Towers, Perrin, Forster & Crosby
245 Park Ave.

New York, NY 10167
(212) 309-3400

Market Research Firms

For networking in market research and related fields, check out the
following professional organizations listed in Chapter 5. Also see
"Advertising Agencies" and **"Public Relations."**

PROFESSIONAL ORGANIZATIONS:

Advertising Club of New York
The Advertising Council
Advertising Women of New York
American Association of Advertising Agencies

For more information you can contact:

American Advertising Federation
1400 K St., NW
Washington, DC 20005
(202)598-0089

American Marketing Association
250 S. Wacker Drive
Chicago, IL 60606
(312)648-0536

Direct Marketing Association
11 W 42nd St.
New York, NY 10036

Marketing Research Association
2189 Silas Deane Hwy., #5
Rocky Hill, CT 06067
(203)257-4008

PROFESSIONAL PUBLICATIONS:

Direct Marketing Magazine
Industrial Marketing
Journal of Marketing Research
Marketing and Media Decisions
Marketing Times

DIRECTORIES:

Bradford's Directory of Marketing Research Agencies (Bradford Publishing Co., Fairfax, VA)
Handbook of Independent Advertising and Marketing Services (Executive Communications, Inc., New York, NY)
International Membership Directory and Marketing Services Guide (American Marketing Association, Chicago, IL)
Membership Roster (American Marketing Association, Chicago, IL)
Multinational Marketing and Employment Directory (World Trade Academy Press, Inc., New York, NY)

EMPLOYERS:

Amoroso, Michael, Inc.
276 5th Ave.
New York, NY 10001
(212) 686-1072
President: Michael Amoroso
Customized research for marketing planning and development.

BAI
580 White Plains Road
Tarrytown, NY 10591
(914) 332-5300

David & Associates
40 Dover St.
New York, NY 10038
(212) 393-9100
Vice President: Patty McGrath
Marketing, advertising, and social research.

Development Counselors International, Ltd.
220 5th Ave.
New York, NY 10001
(212) 725-0707
Personnel Director: Andrew Levine
Advertising, promotion, marketing, consulting, and public relations for states, cities, counties, communities, and transportation organizations.

Donnelly Marketing Information Services
70 Seaview Avenue
Stamford, CT 06902
(203)353-7262

Doyle, Richard L., Associates
15 Maiden Lane
New York, NY 10028
(212) 349-2828

Personnel Director: Kimberly Kruck
Communications services to the insurance industry, including direct advertising, public relations, and sales promotion.

Nielsen, A.C., Inc.
1290 Avenue of the Americas
New York, NY 10104
(212) 708-7500
Vice Pres., Personnel: William Feehan

Opatow Associates
Marketing and Research Consultants
919 3rd Ave.
New York, NY 10022
(212) 421-4837
Consulting and survey research firm providing information for marketing, communications, and design.

Packages Facts
581 Sixth Ave.
New York, NY 10011
(212) 627-3228
Personnel Director: Connie Grueber
Information/research services such as competitive advertising tearsheets, backdated newspaper and magazine clippings, colorful historical facts, and market studies.

SPAR, Inc.
555 White Plains Road
Tarrytown, NY 10591
(914) 332-4100
Director Human Resources: Jim Ross
Minneapolis Office: (612)944-6727

Yankelovich Skelly & White
13 Riverside Ave.
Westport, CT 05880
(203) 227-2700
Director Human Resources: Debbie Conway

Media, Print

For networking in the magazine and newspaper publishing business, check out the following professional organizations listed in Chapter 5. Also see **"Broadcasting," "Book Publishing,"** and for trade publications, Chapter 4.

PROFESSIONAL ORGANIZATIONS:

American Booksellers Association
Magazine Publishers Association
National Association of Media Women
New York Financial Writers' Association
Newswomen's Club of New York
Public Relations Society of America
Women in Communications–New York

For additional information, you can contact:

American Newspaper Publishers Association
P.O. Box 17407
Washington D.C. 20041
(703) 648-1000

Audit Bureau of Circulations
900 N.Meacham Road
Schaumburg, IL 60173
(708)605-0909

Magazine Publishers Association
575 Lexington Ave.
New York, NY 10022
(212) 752-0055

National Newspaper Association
1627 K St., NW
Washington D.C. 20006
(202) 466-7200

National Press Club
529 14th St. NW
Washington, DC 20045
(202)622-7500

Suburban Newspapers of America
401 N. Michigan Ave.
Chicago, IL 60611
(312)644-6610

PROFESSIONAL PUBLICATIONS:

The Columbia Journalism Review
Editor and Publisher
Folio
The Writer
Writer's Digest

DIRECTORIES:

Editor and Publisher International Yearbook (Editor and Publisher, New York, NY)
Hispanic Media and Markets Directory (Standard Rate & Data Service, Wilmette, IL)
Literary Market Place (R.R. Bowker, New York, NY)
Magazine Industry Market Place (R. R. Bowker, Inc., New York, NY)
Magazines Career Directory (Career Press, Inc., Hawthorne, NJ)
National Directory of Magazines (Oxbridge Communications, Inc., New York, NY)
Newspapers Career Directory (Career Press Inc., Hawthorne, NJ)
SNA Membership Directory (Suburban Newspapers of America, Chicago, IL)

MAGAZINES, EMPLOYERS:

Archie Comics Publishers
325 Fayette Ave.
Mamaroneck, NY 10543
(914) 381-5155

Art News
48 W. 38th St.
New York, NY 10018
(212) 398-1690
Editor: Milton Esterow

Billboard Publications
1515 Broadway
New York, NY 10036
(212) 764-7300
Personnel Manager: Deborah Kahlstrom

Bookazine Company
75 Hook Road
Bayone, New York 07002
(201) 339-7777

Bowker, R.R., Co.
121 Chanlon
New Providence, NJ 07974

357

(908) 464-6800
Publishes books, magazines, and related media such as Publishers Weekly, Literary Market Place, Books in Print, and Library Journal.

Bride's Magazine
350 Madison Ave.
New York, NY 10017
(212) 880-8800
Editor: Barbara Tober

BusinessWeek
McGraw-Hill Building
1221 Avenue of the Americas
New York, NY 10020
(212) 512-2000
Managing Editor: John Dierdorff

Changing Times
15 W. 44th St.
New York, NY 10036
(212) 398-6320
Consumer magazine.

Conde Nast Publications
360 Madison Ave.
New York, NY 10017
(212) 371-1330
Publisher: Peter Armour
Publisher of a broad range of nationally distributed magazines: Vanity Fair, Vogue, Glamour, Self, and Gentleman's Quarterly.

Consumers Union of US
Publishers of *Consumer Reports Magazine.*
101 Truman Ave.
Yonkers, NY 10703
(914) 378-2000
Administration: Josephine Lerro

Cosmopolitan
224 W. 57th St.
New York, NY 10019
(212) 649-2000
Editor: Helen Gurley Brown
Monthly magazine with features on glamour, fashion, and women's issues.

Country Living
224 W. 57th St.
New York, NY 10019
(212) 649-2000
Monthly magazine.

Davis Publications
380 Lexington Ave.,14th Floor
New York, NY 10017
(212) 557-9100
Personnel Director: Phyllis Cohen

DC Comics Group
666 5th Ave.
New York, NY 10103
(212) 484-2800
Office Manager: Linda Fields

Editor and Publisher Magazine
11 W. 19th St.
New York, NY 10011
(212) 675-4380
Managing Editor: John Consoli

Esquire
1790 Broadway
New York, NY 10019
(212) 459-7500
Monthly magazine for the sophisticated urban reader.

Essence
1500 Broadway
New York, NY 10036
(212) 642-0600
Editor: Susan Taylor
Fashion magazine for black women.

Family Circle
110 5th Ave.
New York, NY 10011
(212) 463-1000
Personnel Director: Rosalyn Courtney
Large circulation. General interest, family-oriented magazine.

Field and Stream
2 Park Ave.
New York, NY 10016
(212) 779-5000
Editor: Duncan Barnes

Forbes Magazine
60 5th Ave.
New York, NY 10011
(212) 620-2200
Editor: James Michaels

Foreign Affairs
58 E. 68th St.

New York, NY 10021
(212) 734-0400
Editor: William G. Hylund
Scholarly magazine on international relations.

Fortune
1271 Avenue of the Americas
New York, NY 10020
(212) 522-1212
Editor: Marshall Loeb

Gentlemen's Quarterly
350 Madison Ave.
New York, NY 10017
(212) 880-8800
Editor: Arthur Cooper
Men's fashion magazine.

Geyer-McCallister Publications
51 Madison Ave.
New York, NY 10010
(212) 689-4411
Personnel Director: Aileen Ryan

Glamour
350 Madison Ave.
New York, NY 10017
(212) 880-8800
Editor: Ruth Whitney

Golf Magazine
2 Park Ave.
New York, NY 10016
(212) 779-5000
Editor: George Peper

Gourmet Magazine
560 Lexington Ave.
New York, NY 10022
(212) 371-1330
Editor in Chief: Gail Zweigenthal

Harper's
666 Broadway, 11th Floor
New York, NY 10012
(212) 614-6500
Monthly literary magazine.

Harper's Bazaar
1700 Broadway
New York, NY 10019
(212) 903-5000

Editor: Elizabeth Tilberis
Fashion magazine.

Hearst Corporation
959 8th Ave.
New York, NY 10019
(212) 649-2000
Contact: Recruiting
Publisher of many general interest magazines: *House Beautiful,
Cosmopolitan, Town and Country, Science Digest.*

House Beautiful
1700 Broadway
New York, NY 10019
(212) 903-5000
Editor: Louis Oliver Gropp

Hudson Valley Magazine
297 Main Mall
Poughkeepsie, NY 12602
(914) 485-7844
Editor: Susan Agrest

Ladies Home Journal
100 Park Ave.
New York, NY 10017
(212) 953-7070
Editor: Myrna Blyth
Monthly women's magazine.

Lebhar-Friedman
425 Park Ave.
New York, NY 10022
(212) 371-9400
Personnel Administrator: Loretta Milizzo

LIFE
1271 Avenue of the Americas
New York, NY 10020
(212) 522-1212
Editor: Jim Gaines
Monthly photojournalism magazine.

Mademoiselle
350 Madison Ave.
New York, NY 10017
(212) 880-8800
Managing Editor: Gabe Doppelt

Marvel Comic Group
387 Park Ave. So.
New York, NY 10016

(212) 696-0808
Editor: Thomas DeFalco

McCall's
110 5th Ave.
New York, NY 10011
(212) 463-1000
Editor: Kate White
Monthly women's magazine.

Modern Bride
249 W. 17th St.
New York, NY 10011
(212) 337-7000
Editor: Cele Lalli

Money
1271 Avenue of the Americas
New York, NY 10020
(212) 586-1212
Editor: Frank Lalli

Ms. Magazine
230 Park Ave.
New York, NY 10169
(212) 551-9595
Personnel: Julie Felner, Asst. Editor
Monthly with a feminist viewpoint.

National Lampoon
155 Avenue of the Americas
New York, NY 10013
(212) 645-5040
Editor: Larry Solomon
Humor magazine.

New American Magazine Co.
80 5th Ave.
New York, NY 10016
(212) 727-1093
Contact: Personnel
Publisher of *Boating, Flying, Psychology Today.*

New York Magazine
755 2nd Ave.
New York, NY 10017
(212) 880-0700
Editor: Ed Kosner

New Yorker, The
20 W. 43rd St.
New York, NY 10036

(212) 840-3800
Personnel Director: Anthony Pisano
Weekly literary magazine.

Newsweek
444 Madison Ave.
New York, NY 10022
(212) 350-4000
Editor: Maynard Parker
Weekly news magazine.

Outdoor Life
2 Park Ave.
New York, NY 10016
(212) 779-5000
Editor: Vin Sparano

Parade Publications
750 3rd Ave.
New York, NY 10017
(212) 573-7000
Employment Manager: Barbara Wachtel

Parents Magazine
685 3rd Ave.
New York, NY 10017
(212) 878-8700
Editor-in-Chief: Ann Murphy
Monthly magazine on contemporary child care issues.

People
Time and Life Building
1271 Avenue of the Americas
New York, NY 10020
(212) 586-1212
Editor: Landon Jones
Weekly entertainment magazine.

Popular Mechanics
224 W. 57th St.
New York, NY 10019
(212) 262-4284
Editor: Joe Oldham
Monthly magazine for workshop enthusiasts.

Popular Photography
1633 Broadway
New York, NY 10019
(212) 767-6000
Editor: Jason Schneider

Popular Science
2 Park Ave.
New York, NY 10016
(212) 779-5000
Editor: Fred Abatemarco
Monthly that focuses on the sciences.

Psychology Today
80 5th Ave.
New York, NY 10011
(212) 242-2460
Editor: Marilyn Web

Reader's Digest
Pleasantville, NY 10570
(914) 241-5172
Human Resources: Judith Schoenfeld
Monthly mass-circulation magazine.

Redbook
224 W. 57th St.
New York, NY 10019
(212) 649-2000
Editor: Ellen Levine
Monthly women's magazine.

Rolling Stone
745 5th Ave.
New York, NY 10022
(212) 758-3800
Personnel Department: Pamela Fox
Monthly magazine about the entertainment and recording businesses.

Scholastic Magazines
730 Broadway
New York, NY 10003
(212) 505-3000
Contact: Personnel
Publishers of *Junior Scholastic, Senior Scholastic, Scholastic Search,* and other magazines used in schools.

Scientific American
415 Madison Ave.
New York, NY 10017
(212) 754-0550
Editor: Jonathan Piel
Science magazine for the serious reader.

Self
350 Madison Ave.
New York, NY 10017

(212) 880-8834
Editor: Alexandra Penney

Seventeen
850 3rd Ave.
New York, NY 10022
(212) 759-8100
Chief Editor: Midge Richardson

Sport Magazine
437 Madison Ave.
New York, NY 10022
(212) 935-9150
Contact: Personnel

Sports Illustrated
1271 Avenue of the Americas
New York, NY 10020
(212) 552-1212
Managing Editor: John Papanek

Time
Time and Life Building
1271 Avenue of the Americas
New York, NY 10020
(212) 552-1212
Managing Editor: Henry Muller
Weekly news magazine.

Town and Country
1700 Broadway
New York, NY 10019
(212) 903-5000
Managing Editor: Susan Jenett Bleecker

Travel & Leisure
1120 Avenue of the Americas
New York, NY 10036
(212) 382-5600
Editor: Ila Stanger

U S
1 Dag Hammarskjold Plaza
New York, NY 10017
(212) 836-9200
Editor: Jan S. Wenner
Entertainment weekly.

U.S. News
599 Lexington Ave.
New York, NY 10022

(212) 326-5350
Editor: Richard Thompson

Vanity Fair
Conde Nast
350 Madison Ave.
New York, NY 10017
(212) 880-8800
Editor: E. Graydon Carter
Monthly magazine focusing on literature and the arts.

Vogue
350 Madison Ave.
New York, NY 10019
(212) 880-8800
Editor: Anna Wintour

Weight Watcher's Magazine
360 Lexington Ave.
New York, NY 10017
(212) 370-0644
Editor: Lee Haiken

Woman's Day
1633 Broadway
New York, NY 10019
(212) 767-6000
Editor: Jane Chestnut
Mass circulation women's magazine.

Working Woman
230 Park Ave.
New York, NY 10169
(212) 551-9500
Editor: Judsen Culbreth
Monthly magazine that focuses on women in the work force.

Ziff Davis Publishing Company
One Park Ave.
New York, NY 10016
(212) 503-3500
Ziff-Davis publishes a variety of computer magazines including *PC Computers, PC Week,* and *Macuser.*

NEWSPAPERS, NEW YORK EMPLOYERS:

Barron's Financial Weekly
200 Liberty St.
New York,NY 10281
(212) 416-2700
New York news department.

Crain Communications
220 E. 42nd St.
New York, NY 10017
(212) 210-0100
Trade publisher and business newspaper.

El-Diario Prensa
143-155 Varick St.
New York, NY 10013
(212) 807-4600
Newspapers for the Spanish-speaking population of New York.

Gannett Westchester Newspapers
1 Gannett Drive
White Plains, NY 10604
(914) 694-9300
News Editor: Toni Davenport
Chain of suburban newspapers.

New York Daily News
220 E. 42nd St.
New York, NY 10017
(212) 210-2100
Managing Editor: Lou Colasuonno
Mass circulation newspaper that publishes Manhattan, Queens, and Long Island editions.

Getting the scoop on a newspaper career

Jeff Canning was a high school student when he began working part time for the Gannett Westchester newspaper chain. He enjoyed the work so much that he returned to Gannett Westchester after serving in the armed forces. Today, Canning serves as a senior news editor for the chain. We asked him about his career path in the news business.

"I've done everything from cub reporter to working the copy desk to serving as the chief of the metro desk," says Canning. "Now I'm a senior news editor. The important thing is that each time I made a move, I became more valuable to the company or any company that would have hired me."

Canning offers the following advice to people who want to break into the news business. "I always tell young people who express an interest in the business to do two things: get some writing samples together—even if they are only articles in a school or community newspaper—anything to show you can handle the English language. Then, try to gain some work experience. College newspapers, local weekly suburban newspapers, and local feature magazines are sometimes understaffed and willing to give newcomers a try.

"When you begin looking for a full-time job, hit every publication in the area. It's a good idea to send your resume to the news editor instead of the managing editor or editor-in-chief. The latter are certainly good choices, but if a paper has a senior news editor, he or she may not receive as much mail as other editors on staff. News editors will usually forward any resumes to the proper people, along with a personal note.

"After you've been working for at least a year, you can consider moving around. Most newspapers like to see two to three years experience in one area, and some positions require as much as five to seven years' experience. Keep that in mind if you get tired of covering a beat you really don't like. You have to pay your dues. When you are ready to move, you can check trade journals like *Editor* and *Publisher*, although they list primarily entry-level jobs. Your contacts and word of mouth will get you the jobs you really want. So make networking one of your priorities right from the beginning." ■

New York Newsday
Melville, NY 11747
(516) 454-2020
Managing Editor: Howard Schneider
Long Island's leading daily newspaper.

New York Post
210 South St.
New York, NY 10002
(212) 815-8000
Major metropolitan newspaper.

New York Times, The
229 W. 43rd St.
New York, NY 10036
(212) 556-1234
Managing Editor: Joseph Lelyveld
The most respected New York daily newspaper.

Staten Island Advance
950 Fingerboard Road
Staten Island, NY 10305
(718) 981-1234
Editor: Brian Laline
Managing Editor: William Huus
Local daily.

Village Voice
36 Cooper Square
New York, NY 10003
(212) 475-3300
Personnel Administrator: Terry West
Weekly newspaper covering the arts and local feature news.

Wall Street Journal
Dow Jones and Company
22 Cortlandt St.
New York, NY 10007
(212) 416-2000
Managing Editor: Paul Steiger
Business newspaper published Monday through Friday.

Westchester/Fairfield Business Journals
22 Saw Mill River Road
Hawthorne, NY 10532
(914) 347-5200
Managing Editor: John Jordan

NEWSPAPERS, CONNECTICUT EMPLOYERS:

Connecticut Post
410 State St.
Bridgeport, CT 06604
(203) 333-0161
General Manager: Jim Frustere

Danbury News Times
333 Main St.
Danbury, CT 06810
(203) 744-5100
Managing Editor: Paul Steinmetz

Greenwich News
36 Sherwood Place
Greenwich, CT 06830
(203) 869-1777
Managing Editor: Tim Dumas

Hour, The
346 Main Ave.
Norwalk, CT 06851
(203) 846-3281
Managing Editor: Jackson Ferry

NEWSPAPERS, NEW JERSEY EMPLOYERS:

Bergen Record
150 River St.
Hackensack, NJ 07601

(201) 646-4000
Managing Editor: Vivian Waixel

Herald and News
P.O. Box 1019
Passaic, NJ 07055
(201) 365-3000
Managing Editor: Diane Haines

Morristown Daily Record
629 Parsippamy Rd.
Parsippany, NJ 07054
(201) 428-6200
Managing Editor: Jack Bowie

Newark Star–Ledger
1 Star Ledger Plaza
Newark, NJ 07102
(201) 877-4141
Managing Editor: Chick Harrison

NEWSPAPER MAGAZINE SECTIONS, EMPLOYERS:

New York Times Magazine
229 W. 43rd St.
New York, NY 10036
(212) 556-1745
Managing Editor: Jack Rosenthal

Newsday Magazine
Melville, NY 17747
(516) 454-2020
Managing Editor: Noel Rubbenton

Parade Magazine
750 3rd Ave.
New York, NY 10017
(212) 573-7000
Managing Editor: Larry Smith

NEWS SERVICES AND FEATURE SYNDICATES, EMPLOYERS:

A. P. Newspapers
Division of the Associated Press
50 Rockefeller Plaza
New York, NY 10020
(212) 621-1821

Dow Jones & Company
World Financial Center
200 Liberty St.

New York, NY 10281
(212) 416-2000

Frontier News Service
25 E. Shore Drive
Massapequa, NY 11758
(516) 798-2688

Hearst Newspapers
959 8th Ave.
New York, NY 10019-3737
(212) 649-2000

King Features Syndicate
235 E. 45th St.
New York, NY 10017
(212) 455-4000
Personnel Manager: Audra Astion
Feature syndicate that distributes to thousands of small newspapers nationwide.

Religious News Service
P.O. Box 1015
Radio City Station
New York, NY 10101
(212) 315-0870
Executive Editor: Judy Weidman

United Media Enterprises
200 Park Ave., Suite 602
New York, NY 10166
(212) 692-3700
Personnel Director: Maryann Palesado
News feature service. Owners of Newspaper Enterprise Association and United Feature Syndicate.

VNU Business Publications
10 Holland Drive
Hasbrouck Heights, NJ 07604
(201) 393-6000
Personnel Manager: Meg Weiss
Technical trade and consumer magazines.

Museums/Art Galleries

To help you learn more about running museums and art galleries, you can contact:

PROFESSIONAL ORGANIZATIONS:

American Association of Museums
1225 I St., NW
Washington, DC 20005
(202)289-1818

American Federation of Arts
41 E. 65th St.
New York, NY 10021
(212)988-7700

Arts and Business Council
25 W 45th St.
New York, NY 10036
(212) 819-9287

National Assembly of Local Arts Agencies
1420 K St., NW, Suite 204
Washington, DC 20005
(202)371-2830

National Association of State Art Agencies
1010 Vermont Ave., NW
Washington, DC 20005
(202)347-6352

PROFESSIONAL PUBLICATIONS:

Art Forum
Art World
Avisco
Museum News
NASAA News

DIRECTORIES:

Directory for the Arts (Center for Arts Information, New York, NY)
NASAA Directory (National Assembly of State Art Agencies, Washington, DC)
Official Museum Directory (American Association of Museums, Washington, DC)

MUSEUMS, NEW YORK EMPLOYERS:

American Museum of Immigration
Liberty Island, New York Harbor
New York, NY 10004
(212) 422-2150

American Museum of Natural History
Central Park West at 79th St.
New York, NY 10024
(212) 769-5000
Director of Personnel: Geraldine Smith

For art's sake

The least expensive club you can join, if you want to network with New York's business and cultural elite, is an art museum. You'll be invited to "openings" and members' nights, where, between sips of white wine, you can introduce yourself to descendants of Rockefellers, Fricks, Whitneys, and Vanderbilts; and the members' dining rooms are lovely places to entertain your friends and colleagues with reasonably priced food and drink amidst beautiful surroundings. ■

Brooklyn Children's Museum
145 Brooklyn Ave.
Brooklyn, NY 11213
(718) 735-4400

Brooklyn Museum
200 Eastern Parkway
Brooklyn, NY 11238
(718) 638-5000
Director: Robert T. Buck

Bronx Museum of the Arts
1040 Grand Concourse
Bronx, NY 10456
(212) 681-6000
Museum Director: Grace Spanislaus

Caramoor Center for Music and the Arts
Girdle Ridge Road
Katonah, NY 10536
(914) 232-5035
Museum Coordinator: Libby Alson

Children's Museum of Manhattan
212 W. 83rd St.
New York, NY 10024
(212) 721-1223

Cloisters
Metropolitan Museum of Art
Fort Tryon Park
New York, NY 10040
(212) 923-3700
Contact: Personnel

Cooper-Hewitt Museum/Smithsonian Institution's National Museum of Design
2 E. 91 St.
New York, NY 10128
(212) 860-6868
Personnel Director: Belynda Roebuck

Frick Collection, The
1 E. 70th St.
New York, NY 10021
(212) 288-0700
Curator: Edgar Munhall

Guggenheim, Solomon R., Museum
1071 5th Ave.
New York, NY 10003
(212) 360-3500
Guggenheim Museum, SoHo
575 Broadway (at Prince St.)
New York, NY
Personnel Manager: Michele Rubin

Hayden Planetarium at the American Museum of Natural History
Central Park West at 81st St.
New York, NY 10024
(212) 769-5920
Director of Personnel: Geraldine Smith
Part of the American Museum of Natural History.

Hispanic Society of America
613 W. 155th St.
New York, NY 10032
(212) 926-2234
Curator: Priscilla E. Muller

Historic Hudson Valley
150 White Plains Road
Tarrytown, NY 10591
(914) 631-8200
Director Human Resources: Karen Sharman
Includes: Philipsburg Manor, Sunnyside, Van Cortlandt Manor

Hudson River Museum at Yonkers
511 Warburton Ave.

Yonkers, NY 10701
(914) 963-4550
Director: Philip Verve

International Center of Photography
1130 5th Ave.
New York, NY 10128
(212) 860-1777

Jewish Museum, The
1109 5th Ave.
New York, NY 10128
(212) 423-3200
Curator: Vivian Mann

Katonah Museum of Art
Route 22 and Jay St.
Katonah, NY 10536
(914) 232-9555
Director: George King

Lyndhurst
635 South Broadway
Tarrytown, NY 10591
(914) 631-0046
Director: Suzanne Pandick

Metropolitan Museum of Art
1000 5th Ave.
New York, NY 10028
(212) 879-5500

Morgan, Pierpont, Library
29 E. 36th St.
New York, NY 10016
(212) 685-0008

Museum of American Folk Art
2 Lincoln Square
New York, NY 10023
(212) 977-7170
Director: Gerard C. Wertkin

Museum of Modern Art
11 W. 53rd St.
New York, NY 10019
(212) 708-9400
Founded by Abby Aldrich Rockefeller, this museum houses one of the world's leading collections of l9th and 20th century painting and sculpture.

Museum of New York City
103rd St. at 5th Ave.
New York, NY 10029
(212) 534-1672
Personnel Director: Miesha Harris

Museum of Television and Radio
25 W. 52nd St.
New York, NY 10019
(212) 621-6600
Director: Dr. Robert Batscha

New York Hall of Science
47-01 111 St.
Corona, NY 11368
(718) 699-0005
Hands-on science museum.

New York Historical Society
170 Central Park West
New York, NY 10024
(212) 873-3400
Personnel Director: Paula Francis Campbell

Queens Museum
The New York City Building
Flushing Meadow-Corona Park
Flushing, NY 11368
(718) 592-2405
Exec. Director: Sharon Vatsky

South Street Seaport Museum
207 Front St.
New York, NY 10038
(212) 669-9400
President: Peter Neal

Whitney Museum
945 Madison Ave.
New York, NY 10021
(212) 570-3600
Personnel Administrator: Mary McGoldrich

ART GALLERIES, NEW YORK EMPLOYERS:

ACA Galleries
41 E. 57th St.
New York, NY 10022
(212) 644-8300
Director: Jeff Bergen

Castelli, Leo, Gallery
420 W. Broadway
New York, NY 10012
(212) 431-5160
Director: Susan Brundage

Christie's Fine Art Auctioneers
55 E. 59th St.
New York, NY 10022
Mail: 502 Park Ave.
New York, NY 10022
(212) 546-1000
Personnel Director: Kirby Williams

Dittenfass
50 W. 57th St.
New York, NY 10019
(212) 581-2268
Director: Terry Dittenfass

Emmerich, Andre, Gallery
41 E. 57th St.
New York, NY 10022
(212) 752-0124
Director: James Yohe

Feldman Fine Arts
31 Mercer St.
New York, NY 10013
(212) 226-3232
Directors: Ronald and Alfrayfa Feldman

Findlay, Wally, Galleries
17 E. 57th St.
New York, NY 10022
(212) 421-5390
Personnel Director: Simone Karoff

Galerie Felix Vercel
17 E. 64th St.
New York, NY 10021-7002
(212) 744-3131

Hammer Galleries
33 W. 57th St.
New York, NY 10019
(212) 644-4400
Director: Richard Lynch

Hanson Galleries
465 W. Broadway
New York, NY 10012

(212) 353-2080
Director: Mary Selton

Kennedy Galleries
40 W. 57th St.
New York, NY 10019
(212) 541-9600
Personnel: Lillian Brenwasser

Sotheby Galleries
1334 York Ave.
New York, NY 10012
(212) 606-7000
Personnel Department: Ms. Daryl Krimsky

Wildenstein and Company
19 E. 64th St.
New York, NY 10021
(212) 879-0500

MUSEUMS, CONNECTICUT EMPLOYERS:

Barnum Museum, The
820 Main St.
Bridgeport, CT 06604
(203) 331-9881

Stowe, Day Foundation
77 Forest St.
Hartford, CT 06105
(203) 522-9258

Twain, Mark, Memorial
351 Farmington Ave.
Hartford, CT 06105
(203) 247-0998

Wadsworth Atheneum
600 Main St.
Hartford, CT 06103
(203) 278-2670

MUSEUMS, NEW JERSEY EMPLOYERS;

Clinton Historical Museum Village
56 Main St.
Clinton, NJ 08809
(908) 735-4101

Montclair Art Museum
3 S. Mountain Ave.
Montclair, NJ 07042

Montclair Historical Society
108 Orange Road
Montclair, NJ 07042
(201) 744-1796

Morris Museum
6 Normandy Heights Road
Morristown, NJ 07960
(201) 538-0454

New Jersey State Museum
205 W. State St. CN530
Trenton, NJ 08625
(609) 292-6300

Oil and Gas

For networking in oil and gas and related fields, check out the following professional organizations listed in Chapter 5. Also see **"Engineering."**

PROFESSIONAL ORGANIZATIONS:

American Institute of Chemical Engineers
Association of Consulting Chemists and Chemical Engineers
Chemists' Club of New York

For more information, you can contact:

American Gas Association
1515 Wilson Blvd.
Arlington, VA 22209
(703) 841-8400

American Petroleum Institute
1201 Main St.
Dallas, TX 75202
(214) 748-3841

PROFESSIONAL PUBLICATIONS:

Drilling
Modern Plastics
National Petroleum News
Oil and Gas Digest
Oil and Gas Journal
Pipeline

DIRECTORIES:

Energy Job Finder (Mainstream Access, New York, NY)
Modern Plastics, encyclopedia issue (McGraw Hill, New York, NY)
Oil and Gas Directory (Geophysical Directory, Inc., Houston, TX)
US Oil Industry Directory (Penwell Publishing, Tulsa, OK)

EMPLOYERS:

Amax, Inc.
200 Park Ave.
New York, NY 10166
(212) 856-4200
Director Human Resources: Helen M. Feeney
Metals, oil, gas.

Amerada Hess
1185 Avenue of the Americas
New York, NY 10036
(212) 997-8500
Recruiting Director: Robert Weiss
Company headquarters.

Chevron Companies
520 Madison Ave.
New York, NY 10022
(212) 303-3800
Personnel in San Francisco Headquarters.
225 Bush St.
San Francisco, CA 94104
(415)894-7700
One of the largest refiners and manufacturers of petroleum
products in the country.

Cibro Petroleum Co.
1066 Zerega Ave.
Bronx, NY 10462
(212) 824-5000

Exxon Corp.
180 Park Ave.
Florham Park, NJ 07932
(201) 765-7000
Director of Personnel: Cheryl Thomas
The largest petroleum refiner and manufacturer of pretroleum
products in the world.

Nichimen America
1185 Avenue of the Americas
New York, NY 10036
(212) 719-1000
Director of Personnel: Gary Ferraro

Phillipp Brothers
1221 Avenue of the Americas
New York, NY 10020
(212) 575-5900
Marketer of raw petroleum materials and owner of Hill Petroleum, a refiner of petroleum products.

Texaco, Incorporated
2000 Westchester Ave.
White Plains, NY 10650
(914) 253-4000
Contact: Employee Relations
Major refiner and manufacturer of petroleum products.

Paper and Allied Products

For more information about the paper industry, you can contact:

PROFESSIONAL ORGANIZATIONS:

American Paper Institute
260 Madison Ave.
New York, NY 10016
(212)340-0600

Paper Industry Management Association
2400 E. Oakton St.
Arlington Hts., IL 60005
(708)956-0250

Technical Association of the Pulp and Paper Industry
Technology Park, Box 105113
Atlanta, GA 30348
(404)446-1400

PROFESSIONAL PUBLICATIONS:

Fibre Market News
Packaging
Paper Age
Paper Sales
PIMAPaper Industry Management Association
Pulp and Paper

DIRECTORIES:

Ameircan Papermaker—Mill and Personnel Issue (ASM Communications, Inc., Atlanta, GA)
Directory of the Forest Products Industry (Miller Freeman, San Francisco, CA)
Lockwood–Post's Directory of the Paper and Allied Trades (Miller Freeman, San Francisco, CA)
Paper Yearbook (Harcourt Brace Jovanovich, New York, NY)
Paperboard Packagings International Container Directory (Harcourt Brace Jovanovich, Cleveland, OH)
Secondary Wood Products Manufacturers Directory (Miller Freeman, New York, NY)

EMPLOYERS;

Baldwin Paper Company
Subsidiary of Alco Standard Corporation
161 Avenue of the Americas

New York, NY 10013
(212) 255-1600
Personnel Director: Donald Heller

Canover Industries
48th St. and Maspeth Ave.
Maspeth, NY 11378
(718) 456-8900
Personnel Director: Stella Sarasy
Industrial papers.

Champion International Paper
One Champion Plaza
Stamford, CT 06921
(203) 358-7000

Federal Paper Board
75 Chestnut Ridge Road
Montvalle, NJ 07645
(201) 391-1776
Director Employer Relations: Barry A. Smedstad
Major manufacturer of paper and allied products.

Gilman Paper Co.
111 W. 50th St.
New York, NY 10020
(212) 246-3300
Vice President of Human Resources: John Faiella

Imperial Paper Box Corp.
252 Newport
Brooklyn, NY 11212
(718) 346-6100

International Paper Company
2 Manhattanville Road
Purchase, NY 10577
(914) 397-1500
Paper and paper products.

Millar, George W., and Company
161 Avenue of the Americas, 2nd Floor
New York, NY 10013
(212) 645-7200

New York Envelope Corporation
29-10 Hunters Point Ave.
Long Island City, NY 11101
(718) 786-0300

New York Woven Label Company
10 W. 33rd St.

New York, NY 10001
(212) 244-4395

Paper Corporation of U.S.
100 5th Ave.
New York, NY 10011
(212) 645-5900
Personnel: Rosa Gardner
Paper and paper products.

Reproducta Company
11 E. 26th St.
New York, NY 10010
(212) 685-0751
Personnel Director: Robert Rudolf
Greeting card designer and manufacturer.

Royal Paper Corporation
185 Madison Ave.
New York, NY 10016
(212) 684-1200

Westvaco Corporation
299 Park Ave.
New York, NY 10171
(212) 688-5000
Employment Manager: Donald Taylor
Paper manufacturer.

Printing

For networking in printing and related fields, check out the following professional organizations listed in Chapter 5:

PROFESSIONAL ORGANIZATIONS:

Club of Printing Women of New York
Type Directors Club
Typographers Association of New York
Women in Production

For more information, you can contact:

National Association of Printers and Lithographers
780 Palisade Ave.
Teaneck, NJ 07666
(201) 342-0700

Printing Industries of America
100 Daningerfield Road
Alexandria, VA 22314
(703) 519-8100

Technical Association of the Graphic Arts
P.O. Box 9887
Rochester, NY 14614-0887
(716) 272-0557

PROFESSIONAL PUBLICATIONS:

American Printer
Graphic Arts Monthly
Printing News

DIRECTORIES:

Directory of Typographic Services (National Composition Association, Arlington, VA)
Graphic Arts Green Book (A.F. Lewis & Co., Hinsdale, IL)
Printing Trades Blue Book (A.F. Lewis & Co., New York, NY)

EMPLOYERS:

American Bank Note
345 Hudson St.
New York, NY 10004
(212) 425-5100
Major securities printer.

American Standard
1114 Avenue of the Americas
New York, NY 10036
(212) 703-5100
Personnel Director: Mr. Adrienne Deshotel
Executive offices.

Arcata Graphics Group
1185 Avenue of the Americas
New York, NY 10036
(212) 827-2700

Beacon Printing Co.
121 Varick St.
New York, NY 10013
(212) 924-1000
Lithographic printing.

Bowne and Company
345 Hudson St.
New York, NY 10014
(212) 741-6600
Corporate, legal, and financial.

Charles Communications
1290 Avenue of the Americas
New York, NY 10104
(212) 924-7551
Commercial offset printer.

Donnelly, R.R., and Sons
75 Park Place
New York, NY 10007
(212) 233-9600
Books, magazines, catalogs, and tabloids.

Empire Color Lithography
200 Varick St.
New York, NY 10014
(212) 924-7866

Georgian Press
175 Varick St.
New York, NY 10014
(212) 924-4820
President: Jonathan Lehman
Commercial offset printer.

Goldman, M.L., & Son
62 White St.
New York, NY 10013

(212) 431-5000
Legal printers.

International Banknote
345 Hudson St.
New York, NY 10014
(212) 741-8500
Personnel Director: Serge Droujinsky
Securities, currency, and tickets.

Merrill Corporation
200 Hudson St.
New York, NY 10014
(212) 219-3290

Sailsman Graphics
137 Varick St.
New York, NY 10014
(212) 463-7245

Shorewood Packaging
55 Engineers Lane
Farmingdale, NY 11635
(516) 694-2900
Personnel Director: Ron Botticchio
Offset and gravure.

U.S. Bank Note Corporation
345 Hudson St.
New York, NY 10014
(212) 741-8500
Personnel Director: Serge Droujinsky
Bonds, stocks, government securities, and traveler's checks.

World Color Press
101 Park Ave., 19th Floor
New York, NY 10178
(212) 986-2440
Director, Human Resources: Mr. Chris Feagans
Offset, gravure, and letterpress.

Public Relations

For networking in public relations and related fields, check out the following professional organizations listed in Chapter 5. Also see **"Advertising Agencies"** and **"Market Research Firms."**

PROFESSIONAL ORGANIZATIONS:

Public Relations Society of America
Publishers Publicity Association
Women in Communications—New York
Women Executives in Public Relations
Women's Media Group

For more information, you can contact:

International Association of Business Communicators
1 Hall Plaza
San Francisco, CA 94102
(415)433-3400

Public Relations Society of America
33 Irving Place
New York, NY 10003
(212)995-2230

Women Executives in Public Relations
P.O. Box 609
Westport, CT 06881
(203)226-4947

PROFESSIONAL PUBLICATIONS:

O'Dwyer's Newsletter
PR News
PR Reporter
Public Relations Journal
Publicist

DIRECTORIES:

Bacon's Publicity Checker (Bacon's Publishing Company, Chicago, IL)
New York Publicity Outlets (Public Relations Plus, Washington Depot, CT)
O'Dwyer's Directory of Corporate Communications and *O'Dwyer's Directory of Public Relations Firms* (J.R. O'Dwyer Co., New York, NY)

Public Relations Journal—Directory Issue (Public Relations
   Society of America, New York, NY)
Who's Who in P.R. (P.R. Publishing Co., Exeter, NH)

NEW YORK EMPLOYERS:

Abernathy/MacGregor Group
501 Madison Ave.
New York, NY 10022
(212) 371-5999

Andersen, Gavin, & Co.
11 W. 42nd St.
New York, NY 10036
(212) 921-1060

Ayer Public Relations
Worldwide Plaza, 825 8th Ave.
New York, NY 10019
(212) 474-5000

Bozell Public Relations
75 Rockefeller Plaza
New York, NY 10019
(212) 484-7400

Burson-Marsteller
230 Park Ave. S.
New York, NY 10003-1566
(212) 614-4000

Creamer Dickson Basford
1633 Broadway
New York, NY 10019
(212) 887-8010
Personnel Director: Kim Couzzens

De Vries Public Relations
30 E. 60th St., Suite 1408
New York, NY 10022
(212) 891-0400

Doremus and Company
200 Varick St.
New York, NY 10014
(212) 366-3000
Personnel Director: Patricia Cremin

Dorf/Stanton
111 5th Ave.
New York, NY 10003
(212) 420-8100

Edelman, Daniel J.
1500 Broadway, 25th Floor
New York, NY 10036
(212) 768-0550

Factor, Mallory, Inc.
275 7th Ave., 19th Floor
New York, NY 10001
(212) 242-0000

Financial Relations Board
675 3rd Ave.
New York, NY 10017
(212) 661-8030

GCI Group
777 3rd Ave.
New York, NY 10017
(212) 546-2200

Gibbons & Soell
126 E. 38th St.
New York, NY 10016
(212) 481-4488

Hill and Knowlton
420 Lexington Ave.
New York, NY 10017
(212) 697-5600

Kanan, Corbin, Schupak, and Aronow
820 2nd Ave.
New York, NY 10017-4504
(212) 682-6300
Managing Partner: Joseph Manci

Ketchum Public Relations
1133 Avenue of the Americas
New York, NY 10036
(212) 536-8700
Personnel Director: Mitzi Needham

Manning, Selvage and Lee
79 Madison Ave.
New York, NY 10016
(212) 213-0909
Personnel Manager: Mirian Coleman

Morgan-Walke Associates
420 Lexington Ave.
New York, NY 10170
(212) 986-5900

Ogilvy Adams and Reinhart
708 3rd Ave.
New York, NY 10017
(212) 557-0100
Sr. Managing Director: Elena Sanfalone

Rogers and Cowan
122 E. 42nd St., Suite 210
New York, NY 10168
(212) 490-8200

Rowland Worldwide
1675 Broadway
New York, NY 10019
(212) 527-8800
Office Manager: Helen Schenker

Rubenstein, Howard J., Associates
1345 Avenue of the Americas
New York, NY 10105
(212) 489-6900

Ruder Finn
301 E. 57th St.
New York, NY 10022
(212) 593-6400

Schwartz, G.S., & Co.
One Madison Ave.
New York, NY 10010
(212) 696-4744

CONNECTICUT EMPLOYERS:

Amen, Robert, & Associates
Melrose Square, Melrose Ave.
Greenwich, CT 06830
(203) 629-2244

CDHM/Ramer Public Relations
750 E. Main St.
Stamford, CT 06902
(203) 967-7200

Donahue Public Relations
227 Lawrence St.
Hartford, CT 06106
(203) 527-1400
President: Jim Donahue

Dorf and Stanton Communications
201 Sumner St.

Stamford, CT 06901
(203) 327-3555

Heinemann, R.E., and Co.
111 Charter Oaks Ave.
Hartford, CT 06106
(203) 722-1703
President: Robert E. Heinemann

Marquardt and Roche
600 Summer St.
Stamford, CT 06901
(203) 327-0890
Executive Vice President: Edwin Roche

Martin, Peter, Associates
1200 High Ridge Road
Stamford, CT 06905
(203) 322-4700
Personnel: Jan

O'Neal and Prelle
95 Elm St.
Hartford, CT 06101
(203) 527-3233

NEW JERSEY EMPLOYERS:

Allen Associates
111 Northfield Ave.
West Orange, NJ 07052
(201) 325-0303

Andover Communications
One Bridge Plaza, Suite 110
Fort Lee, NJ 07024
(201) 947-4133

Coleman & Pellet
2700 Route 22 East
P.O. Box 3789
Union, NJ 07083
(908) 687-7767

Freeman, Gerald, Public Relations
855 Valley Road
Clifton, NJ 07013
(201) 470-0400

Hall Decker McKibbin
2100 Route 208 S.
Fairlawn, NJ 07410

(201) 794-6100
President: Frank Hoffman

Holt and Ross
2035 Lincoln Highway
Edison, NJ 08817
(908) 287-0045

Infocus, Inc.
707 State Road, Suite 102
Princeton, NJ 08540
(609) 683-9055
Exec. Vice President: Tony Casale

Issues Management
104 Campus Drive
Princeton, NJ 08540
(609) 452-9191
Managing Director: Michael Faigen

Real Estate Developers and Brokers

To learn more about the real estate industry, you can contact:

PROFESSIONAL ORGANIZATIONS:

American Association of Certified Appraisers
800 Compton Road
Cincinnati, OH 45231
(531) 729-1400

American Society of Appraisers
535 Herndon Pkwy., #150
Herndon, Va 22070
(703) 478-2228

Building Owners & Managers Association of Greater New York
350 5th Ave.
New York, NY 10118
(212) 239-3632

International Real Estate Institute
8383 E. Evans Road
Scottsdale, AZ 85260
(602)998-8267

National Association of Realtors
430 N. Michigan Ave.
Chicago, IL 60611
(312) 329-8200

National Network of Commercial Real Estate Women
808 17th St., NW, #3200
Washington, DC 20006
(202) 223-9669

PROFESSIONAL PUBLICATIONS:

Appraiser News
Commercial Investment Real Estate Journal
National Real Estate Investor
Real Estate Insider Newsletter
Real Estate News
Realty and Building

DIRECTORIES:

American Real Estate Guide (LL&IL Publishing, Marhasset, NY)
American Society of Real Estate Counselors Directory (ASREC, Chicago, IL)
Directory of Certified Residential Brokers (Retail National Marketing Institute, Chicago, IL)
National Roster of Realtors (Stanats Communications, Cedar Rapids, IA)
Who's Who in Creative Real Estate (Who's Who in Creative Real Estate Inc., Ventura, CA)

EMPLOYERS:

Abrams, Benisch Riker
733 3rd Ave.
New York, NY 10017
(212) 682-4900
Sr. Partner: Robert Abrams
Commercial management, leasing, and sales.

Adams and Company Real Estate
411 5th Ave.
New York, NY 10016
(212) 679-5500
Commercial management, leasing, appraisals, consulting, and sales.

Century 21 of the Northeast
1 World Trade Center
New York, NY 10048
(212) 775-0021
Personnel Director: Carolyn Debevoise
Commercial and residential real estate brokers.

Location, location, location

Bob Billingsley is a partner in a firm that leases office space in Midtown Manhattan. We talked with him recently about getting started in commercial real estate. "Leasing commercial real estate in New York is a very tough business," says Billingsley. "You don't make any money during your first year or two in the business. There's a very high attrition rate.

"But if you stick with it, you can make more money than your peers in other fields ever dreamed of. Six-figure incomes are not uncommon among people who have been in the business only five years.

"At our firm, we don't hire people right out of school; we look for people with some experience in the business world and in real estate. But many of the larger firms will hire recent grads and train them. In fact, some large firms have formal training programs.

"If you're a young person just starting out, I'd suggest getting a job with a bigger firm. Then be like a blotter—soak up everything they can teach you. After a few years, reevaluate your position with the company. The problem with the bigger firms is that they sometimes tend to ignore you once they've trained you. In a smaller firm, the senior people see more of a relationship between your success and the overall success of the company. Also, there's a lot of competition within a large firm. It's easy to get lost in the shuffle."

We asked Billingsley what qualifications are needed to succeed in commercial real estate. "You have to be tough because you'll face a certain amount of rejection. You have to be hungry because this is an extremely competitive business. A college degree is helpful, but it isn't required. This business is basically sales— getting out and seeing people, convincing them that your skills and knowledge are up to snuff. When you're just starting out, it's also very important to have a mentor in the company— someone to help you and look out for you." ∎

Chase Manhattan Bank
Commerical Real Estate Division
101 Park Ave.
New York, NY 10178
(212) 907-6000

Citibank
Real Estate Division
399 Park Ave.
New York, NY 10043
(212) 559-1000

Coldwell, Banker Commercial Real Estate Services
433 Hackensack Ave.
Hackensack, NJ 07601
(212) 534-2191
Nationwide diversified real estate service company.

Continental Insurance Companies
Real Estate Division
180 Maiden Lane
New York, NY 10038
(212) 440-3000

Cushman and Wakefield
1166 Avenue of the Americas
New York, NY 10036
(212) 841-7500
Employment Supervisor: Grace Ben Ezra

Elliman, Douglas
575 Madison Ave.
New York, NY 10022
(212) 832-4100
Director, Human Resources: Joyce Sponholz
Sales and leasing of residential and commercial properties. Along with management, insurance, appraisals, and consulting.

Greenthal, Charles H., and Company
4 Park Ave.
New York, NY 10016
(212) 340-9300
Personnel Director: Judy Berstein
Real estate management, sales, and brokerage. Conversion specialists.

Greiner-Maltz Company
42-12 28th St.
Long Island City, NY 11101
(718) 786-5050
Personnel Director: Lisa Marino
Commercial properties, including factories, warehouses, offices, sites, and stores.

Grubb and Ellis Company
55 E. 59th St.
New York, NY 10022
(212) 838-2000
Commercial and residential properties and brokerage.

Hekemian and Co.
505 Main St.
Hackensack, NJ 07601
(201) 487-1500

Helmsley-Spear
60 E. 42nd St.
New York, NY 10165
(212) 687-6400
Commercial leasing, mortgages, appraisals, consulting, sales, and insurance.

Houlihan, Lawrence
244 Westchester Ave.
White Plains, NY 10604
(914) 946-6724

Mason, Alice F., Ltd.
635 Madison Ave.
New York, NY 10022
(212) 832-8870
Office Manager: Dominic Richard
Cooperatives, luxury rentals, town houses, and furnished sublets.

May, William B., Inc.
555 Madison Ave.
New York, NY 10022
(212) 688-8700
Commercial management, sales and leasing, appraisals, conversion, rentals, and residential management.

Metropolitan Life Insurance Co.
Real Estate Division
1 Madison Ave.
New York, NY 10010
(212) 578-2211
Personnel Director: Judith Gaecher

Newmark and Co.
477 Madison Ave.
New York, NY 18022
(212) 836-9300

Noyes, Charles F.
22 Courtland St.
New York, NY 10007
(212) 693-4400

Sopher, J.I., and Company
425 E. 61st St.
New York, NY 10021
(212) 486-7000
Luxury apartment rental and sales agency.

Sulzberger-Rolte
575 Madison Ave.
New York, NY 10022
(212) 891-7600

Summit Realty Corporation
6 Frontage St.
Elmsford, NY
(914) 592-5000
Industrial, office, and commercial realtors.

Sylvan Lawrence and Company
100 William St.
New York, NY 10038

(212) 344-0044
Consulting, brokerage, and management of commercial space.

Trump Group
765 5th Ave.
New York, NY 10022
(212) 832-2000

Walters and Samuel
419 Park Ave. S.
New York, NY 10016
(212) 685-6200

White, William A., Grubb and Ellis
55 E. 59th St.
New York, NY 10022
(212) 759-9700

Williams and Company
530 5th Ave.
New York, NY 10036
(212) 704-3500
Managing agents of more than 200 commercial buildings.

Retailers/Wholesalers

For networking in retailing and wholesaling, check out the following professional organizations listed in Chapter 5:

PROFESSIONAL ORGANIZATIONS:

Apparel Guild
National Retail Federation

For more information, you can contact:

General Merchandise Distributors Council
1275 Lake Plaza Drive
Colorado Springs, CO 80906
(719) 576-4260

Manufacturers' Agents National Association
23016 Mill Creek Road
Laguna Hills, CA 92654
(714) 859-4040

National Association of Convenience Stores
1605 King St.
Alexandria, VA 22314
(703) 684-3600

National Association of Wholesale Distributors
1725 K St., NW
Washington, DC 20006
(202) 872-0885

National Retail Merchants Federation
100 W. 31st St.
New York, NY 10036
(212) 244-8780

Warehouse Distributors Association for Leisure and Mobile Products
600 S. Federal St.
Chicago, IL 60605
(312) 922-6222

PROFESSIONAL PUBLICATIONS:

Chain Store Age
College Store Executive
Fabricnews
Fashion Newsletter

Merchandising
New York Apparel News
Store Planning
Stores
Women's Wear Daily

DIRECTORIES:

Fairchild's Financial Manual of Retail Stores (Fairchild Books,
    New York, NY)
Nationwide Directory—Mass Market Merchandisers (Salesman's
    Guide, Inc., New York, NY)
Shelton's Retail Directory of the U.S. and Canada (PS & H, Inc.,
    New York, NY)

EMPLOYERS:

Abraham and Strauss
Division of Federated Department Stores
422 Fulton St.
Brooklyn, NY 11201
(718) 802-7500

Amcena Corporation
1114 Avenue of the Americas
New York, NY 10036
(212) 391-4141
Corporate headquarters of this nationwide retailer.

Ann Taylor, Inc.
Corporate Offices
142 W. 57th St.
New York, NY 10022
(212) 541-3200
Women's clothing chain.

Arden, Elizabeth, Inc.
691 5th Ave.
New York, NY 10022
(212) 546-0200
Women's specialty retail store chain.

Associated Merchandising Corp.
1440 Broadway
New York, NY 10001
(212) 536-4000

Barnes and Noble Bookstores
105 5th Ave.
New York, NY 10003

(212) 633-3300
V.P. Human Resources: Gail Gittleson

Barney's of NY
106 7th Ave.
New York, NY 10011
(212) 929-9000
Women's and men's specialty retail store chain.

Bendel, Henri
712 5th Ave.
New York, NY 10019
(212) 247-1100
Manager, Human Resources: Kathleen Fitzgerald
Women's apparel retailer.

Bergdorf Goodman and Company
754 5th Ave.
New York, NY 10019
(212) 753-7300
Sr.V.P., Human Resources: Marita Odea
Apparel store that caters to upper-income customers.

Blass, Bill, Ltd.
550 7th Ave.
New York, NY 10018
(212) 221-6660
Women's apparel wholesaler.

Bloomingdale's
Division of Federated Department Stores
Lexington Ave. at 59th St.
New York, NY 10022
(212) 705-2000
Personnel Services: Margaret Offbeck
Major department store chain.

Bolton's
47-36 36th St.
Long Island City, NY 11101
(718) 786-7777
Personnel: Susan Polotti
Women's retailer.

Brittania Sportswear
1411 Broadway
New York, NY 10018
(212) 921-0060
Personnel Director: Dave Koons
Apparel manufacturer and wholesaler.

Brooks Brothers
346 Madison Ave.
New York, NY 10017
(212) 682-8800
Vice President, Human Resources: Eileen Irving
Men's and women's apparel retailer known for its conservative,
upper-income clientele.

Burlington Coat Factory
263 W. 38th St.
New York, NY 10018
(212) 221-0010
Women's apparel retailer.

Cartier, Inc.
653 5th Ave.
New York, NY 10022
(212) 753-0111
Personnel Director: Ms. Teri Schaffer
Retailer of jewelry, silverware, crystal, watches and clocks,
stationery, gifts, and china.

Charivari Ltd.
2315 Broadway
New York, NY 10024
(212) 873-1424
Women's and men's specialty stores.

Cluett Peabody & Co.
530 5th Ave.
New York, NY 10036
(212) 930-1900
Personnel Director: Charles Fergusen
Men's apparel wholesaler.

Constable, Arnold, Corporation
250 W. 39th St.
New York, NY 10016
(212) 997-0085
Personnel: Marianne Digliano
Women's and men's specialty retail store chain.

Fortunoff
1300 Old Country Road
Westbury, NY 11590
(516) 832-1520
Executive Recruiter: Robyn Ornstein

G and G Shops
Division of Petrie Stores
520 8th Ave.
New York, NY 10018

(212) 279-4961
Personnel Director: Kevin Collins
Women's specialty store. Operates a total of 85 stores.

Garan, Inc.
350 5th Ave.
New York, NY 10118
(212) 563-2000
Personnel Director: Dana Therese
Apparel wholesaler.

Grand Union Co.
201 Willowbrook Blvd.
Wayne, NJ 07470
(201) 890-6000
Corp. Vice President Executive Development and Training:
Robert Ferla
Large supermarket chain.

Great Atlantic and Pacific Tea Co.
2 Paragon Drive
Montvale, NJ 07645
(201) 930-4416
Manager Personnel Employment: Corinne Blake
Major food retail chain.

Herman's World of Sporting Goods
2 Germak Drive
Carteret, NJ 07008
(201) 541-1550

Kinney Shoe Corporation
233 Broadway
New York, NY 10279
(212) 720-3700
V.P.Human Resources: John Kozlowski
Women's specialty store chain that operates 283 junior apparel
stores throughout the United States.

Lerner Stores Corporation
460 W. 33rd St.
New York, NY 10001
(212) 736-1222
Director of Recruitment: Joan Witterhott
Women's and children's apparel retailer. Operates 792 stores
nationwide.

Limited, The
1450 Broadway, 4th Floor
New York, NY 10018
(212) 221-0030

Logan, Jonathan
A division of United Merchants and Manufacturers Corp.
980 Avenue of the Americas
New York, NY 10018
(212) 465-3900
Major women's apparel wholesaler.

Lord and Taylor
424 5th Ave.
New York, NY 10018
(212) 382-7800
Personnel Director: Rosemary Russell
Major department store chain.

Macy, R.H., and Company
151 W. 34th St.
New York, NY 10001
(212) 695-4400
Corporate headquarters for the Macy's chain, which operates 17
stores in several states.

May Company
1120 Avenue of the Americas
New York, NY 10036
(212) 704-2764
Department store chain operating 168 stores, including Caldor's
and Loehmann's.

McGregor Corp.
135 W. 50th St.
New York, NY 10020
(212) 307-8100
Personnel Director: Mercedes Cologne
Men's apparel wholesaler.

Modell's
3424 Vernon Blvd.
Long Island City, NY 11106
(718) 956-8600
Personnel Director: Phylis Fietel
Discount sportswear. Operates 18 retail outlets.

Neiman Marcus
Maple and Paulding
White Plains, NY 10601
(914) 428-2000

Nichols, S.E., Inc.
275 7th Ave.
New York, NY 10001
(212) 206-9400
Personnel Director: Joseph Keller, Jr.

Discount department store chain. Operates 41 stores in several states.

Saks Fifth Ave.
Division of Batus Retail
611 5th Ave.
New York, NY 10022
(212) 753-4000
Director Personnel: Deborah McRae, Beverly Cassidy
Exclusive apparel retailer known for its showcase window displays on 5th Avenue.

Schwartz, FAO
767 5th Ave.
New York, NY 10153
(212) 644-9400
Toy retailer that operates 38 stores.

Sperry-Hutchinson Company
315 Park Ave. S.
New York, NY 10010
(212) 598-3100
Personnel Director: Vicki Reid
Manufacturer and distributor of S & H Green Stamps.

Swank, Inc.
90 Park Ave.
New York, NY 10016
(212) 867-2600
Director: Jeffrey Lesinger
Retailer of jewelry for men, leather goods, gifts, men's accessories, toiletries, and perfume.

Tiffany and Company
727 5th Ave.
New York, NY 10022
(212) 755-8000
Director Staffing: Katheryn Murphy

Toys R Us
461 From Road
Paramus, NJ 07652
(201) 262-7800
V.P. Human Resources: Jeffrey Wells, Elizabeth Jordan

Ventura Luggage
32-33 47th Ave.
Long Island City, NY 11101
(718) 392-6200
Personnel Director: Thomas Dunn
Luggage and business cases.

Waldbaum Inc.
Hemlock St.
Central Islip, NY 11722
(516) 582-9300
Director Human Resources: Ruth Collins
Grocery chain.

WaldenBooks
201 High Ridge Road
P.O. Box 10218
Stamford, CT 06904
(203) 352-2000
National chain of retail booksellers.

Winston, Harry, Inc.
718 5th Ave.
New York, NY 10019
(212) 245-2000
Precious jewels.

Woolworth, F.W., Company
233 Broadway
New York, NY 10279
(212) 553-2000
Company headquarters. Operates 36 J. Brannam Apparel Discount Stores and 1,254 Woolworth stores.

Stock Brokers/Financial Services/ Investment Banking

For networking in finance and related fields, check out the following professional organizations listed in Chapter 5. Also see **"Banks: Commercial and Savings."**

PROFESSIONAL ORGANIZATIONS:

American Finance Association
American Management Association
Association of Investment Brokers
Financial Analysts Federation
Financial Women's Association of New York
Investment Council Association of America
New York Society of Security Analysts
Securities Industry Association
Security Traders Association

For more information, you can contact:

International Association of Financial Planning
2 Concourse Pkwy.
Atlanta, GA 30328
(404)395-1605

National Association of Personal Financial Advisors
1130 Lake Cook Road, Suite 105
Buffalo Grove, IL 60089
(708) 537-7722

National Association of Securities Dealers
1735 K St., NW
Washington, DC 20006
(202)728-8000

National Venture Capital Association
1655 N. Fort Myer Drive., #700
Arlingtion, VA 22209
(703)528-4370

PROFESSIONAL PUBLICATIONS:

Barron's National Business and Financial Weekly
D & B Reports
Commodity Journal
Corporate Finance
Credit and Financial Management
Financial Executive

Financial World
Financier
Institutional Investor
Investment Dealer's Digest
Securities Week
Stock Market Magazine
Wall Street Transcript

DIRECTORIES:

Corporate Finance Sourcebook (National Register, Wilmette, IL)
CUSIP Master Directory (Standard & Poor's, New York, NY)
Directory of Registered Investment Advisors (Money Market
    Directories, Charlottesville, VA)
Money Market Directory (Money Market Directories, Inc.,
    Charlottesville, VA)
Nelson's Directory of Investment Research (W.R. Nelson, Port
    Chester, NY)
Security Dealers of North America (Standard and Poor's, New
    York, NY)
Who's Who in the Securities Industry (Economist Publishing Co.,
    New York, NY)

EMPLOYERS:

Alexander and Alexander Services
1211 Avenue of the Americas
New York, NY 10036
(212) 840-8500
Assistant Personnel Manager: Geraldine Kraemer
Brokerage firm, risk management and financial services.

American Express
3 World Financial Center
New York, NY 10285
(212) 640-2000
Travel-related insurance, investment, and international banking
services.

American Stock Exchange
86 Trinity Place
New York, NY 10006
(212) 306-1000
Stock exchange market for stocks and bonds of mid-range growth
companies. Nation's second largest stock exchange.

Bear Stearns and Company
245 Park Ave.
New York, NY 10167
(212) 952-5000

Personnel Director: Anne Corwin
Worldwide securities trading and financial services partnership.

Blair, D.H., and Company
44 Wall St.
New York, NY 10005
(212) 495-4000
Assistant Director of Personnel: Ruth Robles
One of New York's biggest investment firms.

Brown Brothers Harriman and Company
59 Wall St.
New York, NY 10005
(212) 483-1818
Asst.Personnel Manager: Jim DeLorenzo
Commercial banking, investment advisory, brokerage, and
custody services.

Commodity Exchange
4 World Trade Center
New York, NY 10285
(212) 938-2000

Dean Witter Reynolds
2 World Trade Center
New York, NY 10048
(212) 392-2222

**Bullish on
Wall Street**

Lisa Marini, an options trader with a major New York firm, gave us this rundown on New York's trading scene. "New York is the equities market capital of the world. On the trading floor, what you see is the most naked form of supply and demand in action. It's an outcry market. Floor traders literally shout out their bids on stocks, options, commodities, metals, whatever.

"There are two classes of people in the market—the traders and everybody else. You start out as a runner, running orders to the floor traders, who are the only ones who can actually bid. Next you become a phone clerk; they're the people who answer the phones and give the orders to the runners. From phone clerk you move up to crowd assistant or market-maker clerk. A crowd assistant helps the broker or trader execute the orders. A market maker clerk monitors a trader's position and risk in the market.

"Many phone clerks earn upward of $75,000 a year. I know one market maker clerk who made $140,000 last year. If you are very successful you may be able to buy equity into the firm and become a market maker (floor trader)." ∎

Dillon Read and Company
535 Madison Ave.
New York, NY 10022
(212) 906-7000
Personnel Director: Laurie Hinchmon
Investment banking firm.

Donaldson, Lufkin and Jenrette
140 Broadway
New York, NY 10005
(212) 504-3000
Director of Human Resources: Gerald Rigg
International banking and securities firm.

Dreyfus
200 Park Ave.
New York, NY 10166
(212) 922-6000

Dun & Bradstreet Corporation
299 Park Ave.
New York, NY 10177
(212) 593-6800
Financial information services.

First Boston Corporation
Park Avenue Plaza
55 E. 52nd St.
New York, NY 10055
(212) 909-2000
Personnel Director: David O'Leary, Tower 49, 12 E.49th St.
International banking firm.

First Investors Corporation
95 Wall St.
New York, NY 10260
(212) 858-8000

Franklin Funds
500 5th Ave.
New York, NY 10036
(212) 869-1776

Goldman Sachs and Company
85 Broad St.
New York, NY 10004
(212) 902-1000

Personnel Director: Jim Morrison
Investment banking firm.

Gruntal
14 Wall St.
New York, NY 10005
(212) 858-6000
Personnel Department: Gary Moss
Securities brokerage firm.

Janney Montgomery Scott
26 Broadway
New York, NY 10004
(212) 510-0600
Personnel Department: Philadelphia office
(215) 665-6000
Investment banking firm.

Josephthal, Lyon & Ross
45 Broadway
New York, NY 10006
(212) 483-1800
Full service securities brokerage firm.

Kemper Securities Group
1 World Trade Center
New York, NY 10006
(212) 938-7000

Kidder Peabody and Company
10 Hanover Square
New York, NY 10005
(212) 510-3000
Personnel Department: 60 Broad St., 4th Floor, New York,
NY 10004
International investment banking firm.

Lazard Freres and Company
1 Rockefeller Plaza
New York, NY 10020
(212) 489-6600
V.P.,Director of Personnel: Deborah A. Senkier
Investment banking firm.

Lehman Brothers
3 World Financial Center, 12th Floor
New York, NY 10285
(212) 464-2477
Commission work in stocks, bonds, and commodities.

MasterCard International
888 Seventh Ave.

New York, NY 10106
(212) 649-4600
Director Staffing: Gerald McGrath
Financial services.

Merrill Lynch and Company
World Financial Center
New York, NY 10281
(212) 449-1000
One of the nation's largest investment banking and securities
brokerage firms.

Morgan, J. P., and Company
60 Wall St.
New York, NY 10260
(212) 483-2323

Morgan Stanley
1251 Avenue of the Americas
New York, NY 10020
(212) 703-4000
Personnel Director: William Higgins
Investment banking firm.

NASDAQ
33 Whitehall St.
New York, NY 10004
(212) 858-4409
Over-the-counter exchange.

Neuberger & Berman Management
605 3rd Ave.
New York, NY 10017
(212) 476-9000

New York Stock Exchange
11 Wall St.
New York, NY 10005
(212) 656-3000
Principal marketplace for trading securities, stocks, and bonds in
the United States.

Nuveen Jonaco
140 Broadway
New York, NY 10005
(212) 208-2300
Municipal bonds specialist.

Oppenheimer and Company
One World Financial Center
New York, NY 10281
(212) 667-7000

Director of Personnel: Madelyn Devine
Real estate brokerage operations and other financial services.

Oppenheimer Fund Management
2 World Trade Center
New York, NY 10048
(212) 323-0200

Paine Webber Group
1285 Avenue of the Americas
New York, NY 10019
(212) 713-2000
Contact: Human Resources/Employment Division
One of the world's largest investment firms.

Primerica Financial Services
65 E. 55th St.
New York, NY 10022
(212) 891-8900

Prudential Securities
100 Gold St.
New York, NY 10292
(212) 776-1000
Asst. Manager Corporate Staffing: Stephanie Stabile
International securities brokerage and investment banking firm.

Salomon Brothers
7 World Trade Center
New York, NY 10048
(212) 747-7000
International investment banking and research firm.

Scudder Family of Funds
345 Park Ave.
New York, NY 10021
(212) 326-6300

Smith Barney, Harris Upham and Company
1345 Avenue of the Americas
New York, NY 10105
(212) 399-6000
Major international investment banking firm.

Spear Leeds and Kellogg
115 Broadway
New York, NY 10006
(212) 587-8900
Securities brokerage firm.

Tucker, Anthony, & R.L. Day
1 World Financial Center

200 Liberty St.
New York, NY 10281
(212) 225-8000
Personnel Officer: Marge Fedowitz
Money management, corporate finance, and venture capital.

Value Line
711 3rd Ave.
New York, NY 10017
(212) 687-3965
Personnel Coordinator: Ann Darnan
Asset management investment advising and financial materials
publisher.

Travel/Shipping/Transportation

To learn more about travel and transportation, you can contact:

PROFESSIONAL ORGANIZATIONS:

Airline Employees Association, International
5600 S. Central Ave.
Chicago, IL 60638
(312) 767-3333

Air Line Pilots Association
1625 Massachusetts Ave., NW
Washington, DC 20036
(202) 689-2270

American Society of Travel Agents
1101 King St., #200
Alexandria, VA 22314
(703) 739-2782

American Trucking Association
200 Mill Rd.
Alexandria, VA 22314
(703) 838-0230

Association of American Railroads
50 F St., NW
Washington, DC 20001
(202) 639-2100

Aviation Distributors & Manufacturers Association
1900 Arch St.
Philadelphia, PA 19103
(215) 564-3484

Institute of Transportation Engineers
525 School St., SW
Washington, DC 20024
(202) 554-8050

National Air Transportation Association
4226 King St.
Alexandria, VA 22302
(703) 845-9000

Travel Industry Association of America
1133 21st St., SW
Washington, DC 20024
(202) 293-1433

United States Tour Operators Association
211 E. 51st St., Suite 128
New York, NY 10022
(212) 944-5727

PROFESSIONAL PUBLICATIONS:

Air Travel Journal
ASTA Travel News
Aviation Week and Space Technology
Business and Commercial Aviation
Commercial Carrier Journal
Motor Age
Tours and Resorts
Traffic Management
Transportation & Distribution
Travel Agent

DIRECTORIES:

Aviation Directory (E.A. Brennan Co., Garden Grove, CA)
Membership Directory (Aviation Distributors & Manufacturers
    Association, Philadelphia, PA)
Moody's Transportation Manual (Moody's Travel Service, New
    York, NY)
Travel Industry Personnel Directory (Travel Agent Magazine,
    New York, NY)
World Aviation Directory (Mcraw-Hill, New York, NY)

EMPLOYERS:

Air India
345 Park Ave.
New York, NY 10154
(212) 407-1300

Personnel Manager: Nicholas Metz
U.S. headquarters location.

Alitalia Airlines
666 5th Ave.
New York, NY 10103
(212) 903-3300
Contact: Selection and Training Department

American Airlines
Personnel Department
1 American Plaza
Hartford, CT 06103
(800) 433-7300
One of the largest U.S. airlines, serving 101 airports in 32 states.

American Express Travel Related Services
3 World Financial Center
200 Vesey St.
New York, NY 10285-3400
(212) 640-2000
International travel coordinator.

Amtrak
390 7th Ave.
New York, NY 10001
(212) 630-7100
Nation's only long-distance passenger railroad.

Avis, Inc.
900 Old Country Road
Garden City, NY 11530
(516) 222-3000
Contact: Director of Executive Recruitment
Rental and leasing of vehicles worldwide.

British Airways
75-20 Astoria Blvd.
Jackson Heights, NY 11370
(800) 247-9297
One of the largest air carriers in the world; wholly owned by the
British government.

Camp Baumann Buses
107 Lawson Blvd.
Oceanside, NY 11572
(516) 766-6740
Personnel Director: Helen Allocco
Transportation management firm, providing bus service to local
school districts.

Cook, Thomas, Travel Services
2 Penn Plaza, 18th Floor
New York, NY 10121
(212) 967-4390
Contact: John Harvey
One of the world's largest travel agencies.

CTI Contain Transport
445 Hamilton Ave.
White Plains, NY 10601
(914) 933-2688
Personnel Manager: Helen Ginsberg
Major international lessor of marine containers.

EL AL Israel Airlines
850 3rd Ave.
New York, NY 10022
(212) 486-2600

Emery Worldwide Air Freight Corporation
184-54 149th Ave.
Springfield Gardens, NY 11413
(800) 443-6379
One of the world's largest air cargo carriers.

Farrell Lines
1 Whitehall St.
New York, NY 10004
(212) 440-4200
General Manager, Human Resources: Daniel Cappozalo
Major steamship service.

Federal Express
560 W. 42nd St.
New York, NY 10036
(212) 777-6500
Contact: Personnel
Headquarters location in Memphis, TN:
2005 Corporate Ave
P.O Box 727
Memphis, TN 38132
(901) 369-3600
"Overnight, door-to-door" transportation of packages and documents through a fleet of more than 60 aircraft and numerous trucks and vans.

Green Bus Lines
165-25 147th Ave.
Jamaica, NY 11434
(718) 995-4700
Office Manager: Doris Drantch
Major bus transportation line servicing Queens and Manhattan.

Greyhound Corporation
625 8th Ave.
New York, NY 10018
(212) 971-6321
Contact: Personnel
Holding company, operating several subsidiaries, including
Greyhound Bus Lines, Greyhound Manufacturing Group, and
Armour and Company.

Hertz Corporation
225 Brae Blvd.
Park Ridge, NJ 07656
(201) 307-2000
Worldwide company that rents and leases automobiles and
trucks.

Liberty Lines
P.O. Box 624
Yonkers, NY 10703
(914) 969-6900
Commuter bus operation, servicing Yonkers and Westchester
area.

Liberty Travel
1430 3rd Ave.
New York, NY 10028
(212) 772-3808
Personnel office for Manhattan locations. Send resumes, attn:
Victor Fernandez

Long Island Railroad
Jamaica Station
Jamaica, NY 11435
(718) 990-7400
One of the busiest passenger railroad operations in the United
States.

McCallister Brothers
17 Battery Place
New York, NY 10004
(212) 269-3200
Personnel Director: Jean Brown
Major U.S. marine services firm. Operates the largest fleet of tugs
and barges on the East Coast and in the Caribbean.

Metro North Commuter Railroad
347 Madison Ave.
New York, NY 10017
(212) 340-2143
Personnel Director: Celia Ussak

Metropolitan Suburban Bus Authority
700 Commercial Ave.
Garden City, NY 11530
(516) 542-0100
Bus company that operates as part of the Metropolitan Transportation Authority.

Metropolitan Transportation Authority
347 Madison Ave.
New York, NY 10017
(212) 878-7407
Manager Staffing and Employee Relations: Sheldon Dixon
A public benefit transportation corporation whose subsidiaries include the New York City Transit Authority, Manhattan and Bronx Surface Transit Operations Authority, the Staten Island Rapid Transit Operating Authority, Metropolitan Suburban Bus Authority, the Long Island Railroad, Metro North Commuter Rails, and the Triborough Bridge and Tunnel Authority.

Perillo Tours
577 Chestnut Ridge Road
Woodcliff Lake, NJ 07675
(800) 431-1515
International tour service.

Port Authority of New York and New Jersey
1 World Trade Center
New York, NY 10048
(212) 466-8159
Agency responsible for operation, maintenance, and development of public transportation facilities in New York and New Jersey metropolitan area. Also operates Kennedy, La Guardia, and Newark airports; the Lincoln and Holland tunnels; the George Washington Bridge; Marine Terminals; Port Authority Bus Terminal; World Trade Center; and PATH Rapid Transit.

Swissair
John F. Kennedy International Airport
Jamaica, NY 11430
(718) 481-4500
U.S. headquarters

Trans America Leasing
711 Westchester Ave.
White Plains, NY 10604
(914) 682-3300
Vice President Human Resources: Geri Theodore

Trans World Airlines
100 S. Bedford Road
Mt. Kisco, NY 10549
(914) 242-3000

Triboro Coach Corporation
85-01 24th Ave.
Jackson Heights, NY 11369
(718) 335-1000
Local area bus service.

United Parcel Service
643 W.43rd St.
New York, NY 10036
(212) 695-7500
Human Resources Representative: Eileen Breen
650 Winters Ave.
Paramus, NJ 07652
(201) 599-3191
Parcel pick-up and delivery service, with nationwide operations.

Universal Maritime Service Corporation
10 Exchange Place, Suite 1600
Jersey City, NJ 07302
Personnel in Madison, NJ:
C/O Maersk
Madison Ave.
P.O. Box 880
Madism, NJ 07940
(201) 514-5000
Major marine cargo handler.

We Transport
42 E. Carl St.
Hicksvile, NY 11801
(516) 822-5800
Personnel and other offices in Brentwood, NY.
Emjay Blvd.
Brentwood, NY 11717
(516) 436-5051
Contact: Pat Zilko

Yellow Freight Systems
149 Leroy St.
New York, NY 10014
(212) 691-8203
Personnel Administrator: Jerry Cannata
Nationwide common carrier trucking firm.

Utilities

For more information about the utilities industry, you can contact:

PROFESSIONAL ORGANIZATIONS:

American Public Gas Association
Box 1426
Vienna, VA 22183
(703) 281-2910

American Public Power Association
2301 M St., NW
Washington, DC 20037
(202) 467-2900

Institute of Public Utilities
113 Olds Hall
Michigan State University
East Lansing, MI 48824
(517) 355-1876

North American Telecommunications Association
2000 M St., NW
Washington, DC 20036
(202)296-9800

United States Telephone Association
900 19th St., NW
Washington, DC 20006
(202)835-3100

Utilities Telecommunications Council
1140 Connecticut Ave., NW
Washington, DC 20036
(202) 872-0030

PROFESSIONAL PUBLICATIONS:

Communications Daily
Electric Light and Power
Electrical World
Public Utilities
Telephone Engineering and Management
Telephony

DIRECTORIES:

APGA Directory of Municipal Gas Systems (American Public Gas Assoc., Vienna, VA)

Brown's Directories of North American Gas Companies (Edgel Communications, Cleveland, OH)

Directory of Communications Management (Applied Computer Research, Phoenix, AZ)

Electrical World Directory of Electrical Utilities (McGraw-Hill, New York, NY)

Moody's Public Utility Manual (Moody's Investor Service, New York, NY)

EMPLOYERS:

Brooklyn Union Gas
1 Metro Tech Center
Brooklyn, NY 11201
(718) 408-5092
Personnel Director: A. Fraticelli
Natural gas company servicing Brooklyn and Long Island.

Consolidated Edison Company
4 Irving Place
New York, NY 10003
(212) 460-2014
Manager, Professional Recruitment: Kevin Morgan
Electric power and gas supplier to most of New York City and Westchester County.

Jamaica Water Properties
410 Lakeville Road
Lake Success, NY 11042
(516) 488-4600
Personnel Director: Janice Varley
Holding company that supplies water to Long Island and Queens.

Long Island Lighting Company
175 E. Old Country Road
Hicksville, NY 11801
(516) 933-4590
Major electric and gas supplier to Long Island.

Long Island Water Corporation
733 Sunrise Highway
Lynbrook, NY 11563
(516) 593-1000
Personnel Director: Anne Simmons
Water supplier to Long Island residents.

New York Power Authority
123 Main St.

White Plains, NY 10601
(914) 681-6200
Employment Administrator: Ann Tivenan
The nation's largest nonfederal public power organization, providing more than one-third of the electricity for New York State.

New York Telephone
1095 Avenue of the Americas
New York, NY 10036
(212) 395-2552
Personnel Director: Roy Dollard
Executive offices of New York's telephone service.

Orange and Rockland Utilities
One Blue Hill Plaza
Pearl River, NY 10965
(914) 577-2765

Public Service Electric & Gas Co.
80 Park Plaza
Newark, NJ 07101
(201) 430-7000
Director Human Resources: Gregory Thompson
Third largest combined gas and electric company in the United States.

Employers Index

I

J

General Index

A

Accounting/Auditing: selected firms; professional groups, professional magazines, and directories, 155-161

Advertising: selected agencies; professional groups, professional magazines, and directories, 162-166

Aerospace: selected firms; professional groups, publications, and directories, 167-170

Aid, charitable, 133-134

Aid, government, 131-132

Apparel/Textiles: selected firms; professional groups, professional magazines, and directories, 170-180

Architecture: selected firms; professional groups, professional magazines, and directories, 181-185

Associations: see Information Resources for listing of local Network Groups

Auto/Truck/Transportation Equipment: selected manufacturers; trade groups, trade magazines and directories, 186-188

B

Banking: selected institutions; professional groups, professional magazines, and directories, 189-196

Beverage Industry: see Food/Beverage

Book Publishers/Literary Agents: selected publishers and agents; professional groups, professional magazines, and directories, 197-208

Books: see Resource Books

Broadcasting: selected TV and radio stations; professional groups, trade magazines, and directories, 209-217

C

Career Analysis: see Vocational Analysis and Testing

Career Consultants, 13-16, 105

Career Transition Issues, 136, 145

Chambers of Commerce, 4

Charitable Organizations, 133-134

Chemical Industry: selected companies; trade groups, trade magazines, and directories, 218-224

Colleges, list of local: see Educational Institutions

Computer Industry: selected hardware and software companies; trade groups, trade magazines, and directories, 225-230 (hardware); 230-233 (programming and software)

Construction: selected firms; professional groups, professional magazines, directories, 234-237

Consultants, Career: see Career Consultants

Consumer Protection Agencies, 14, 96

Cosmetics/Perfume/Toiletries: selected firms; professional groups, professional magazines, and directories, 238-242

Counseling, Psychological: as support during job search, 138 local resources, 139-142

Cover Letter: see also Resume preparation of, 27, 35 sample formats, 32-34

Crisis Centers, 139-142

D

Data Processing: see Computer Industry

Department Stores: see Retailers/Wholesalers

Directories, 39-47 (see also under specific employment categories)

Disabled Workers: see Handicapped Workers

Drugs/Pharmaceuticals: selected manufacturers; trade groups, trade magazines,and directories, 243-248

E

Educational Institutions: selected school districts, universities, colleges; professional groups, professional magazines, and directories, 248-258

Electronics/Telecommunications: selected firms; trade groups, trade magazines, and directories, 259-269

Restaurants: see Hospitality
Resume: See Chapter 3; see also
  Cover Letter
  distribution of, 27
  function of, 19-20
  preparation of, 20-21, 27-28
  professional resume preparers,
    22-25
  resource books on, 21
  sample formats, 29-31
  screening done by employer, 69
Retailers/Wholesalers: selected
  retailers and wholesalers;
  professional groups, professional
  magazines, and directories, 400-
  407

S

Salary Strategy, 146
  resource books on, 146
SCORE (Service Corps of Retired
  Executives), 17
Small Businesses, 17-18
Small Business Administration
  assistance, 17
Social Service Agencies, 106-110
Sports: see Entertainment/ Recre-
  ation
Stock Brokers/Financial Services/
  Investment Banking: selected
  firms; professional groups,
  publications, and directories, 408-
  415

T

Tax Deductible Expenses, 61
Telecommunications: see Electronics/
  Telecommunications; see also
  Computer Industry
Telemarketing, 130
Television: see Broadcasting
Temporary Employment: see Part-
  Time Employment

Testing, Vocational, 13-17
Trade Magazines, 52-57
Trade Organizations, 70-93, see also
  under employment categories
Transportation: see Auto/Truck/
  Transportation Equipment and
  Travel/Shipping/Transportation.
  For getting around in the New
  York area, 4-6
Travel/Shipping/Transportation:
  selected companies; professional
  groups, professional magazines,
  and directories, 415-421

U,V

Unemployment Benefits, 132-133
Universities: see Educational
  Institutions
Utilities: major companies; trade
  groups, trade magazines, and
  directories, 422-424
Veterans Services, 106, 108, 111, 132
Vocational Analysis and Testing,
  13-17
  types of assessment tests, 13
  where offered, 15-17
Vocational Consultants: see Career
  Consultants
Vocational Objective:
  how to develop, see Chapter 2
  self-appraisal exercise, 8-9
Volunteer Work, possiblity of leading
  to employment, 76, 149

W

Wall Street, 153, 410
Want-ads, 47-48, 49, 69
Wholesalers: see Retailers/
  Wholesalers
Women:
  career resources, 47, 83, 92, 102,
    106, 108, 112, 139
  resource books for, 12-13, 83